Scrip
Middle East
Leaders

Scripting
Middle East
Leaders

The Impact of Leadership Perceptions
on US and UK Foreign Policy

EDITED BY

LAWRENCE FREEDMAN

AND

JEFFREY H. MICHAELS

BLOOMSBURY
NEW YORK · LONDON · NEW DELHI · SYDNEY

Bloomsbury Academic
An imprint of Bloomsbury Publishing Plc

175 Fifth Avenue
New York
NY 10010
USA

50 Bedford Square
London
WC1B 3DP
UK

www.bloomsbury.com

First published 2013

Library of Congress Cataloging-in-Publication Data
Scripting Middle East leaders : the impact of leadership perceptions on US and UK foreign policy / edited by Lawrence Freedman and Jeffrey H. Michaels.
p. cm.
Includes bibliographical references and index.
ISBN 978-1-4411-9165-6 (hardcover : alk. paper)– ISBN 978-1-4411-0841-8 (pbk. : alk. paper) 1. Middle East–Foreign relations–United States. 2. United States–Foreign relations--Middle East. 3. Middle East–Foreign relations–Great Britain. 4. Great Britain–Foreign relations–Middle East. 5. Middle East–Kings and rulers. 6. Middle East–Politics and government–1945-1979. 7. Middle East–Politics and government–1979- 8. Leadership–Middle East. I. Freedman, Lawrence. II. Michaels, Jeffrey H.
DS63.2.U5S314 2012
327.56073–dc23
2012021555

ISBN: HB: 978-1-4411-9165-6
PB: 978-1-4411-0841-8

Typeset by Fakenham Prepress Solutions, Fakenham, Norfolk NR21 8NN
Printed and bound in the United States of America

CONTENTS

LIST OF CONTRIBUTORS

Christopher Andrew is Professor of Modern and Contemporary History, Former Chair of the History Faculty at Cambridge University, Official Historian of the Security Service (MI5), Honorary Air Commodore of 7006 Squadron (Intelligence) in the Royal Auxiliary Air Force, Chair of the British Intelligence Study Group, and former Visiting Professor at Harvard, Toronto and Canberra. His main research interests include twentieth-century political history and international relations with particular reference to the role and influence of intelligence agencies.

Nigel Ashton is Professor of International History at the LSE. His main fields of interest are contemporary Anglo–American relations and the modern history of the Middle East. These interests came together in his first book, *Eisenhower, Macmillan and the Problem of Nasser: Anglo–American Relations and Arab Nationalism, 1955–59* (Macmillan, 1996), which looked at the strategies adopted by Britain and the United States to deal with the Arab nationalist challenge during the 1950s. His second book, *Kennedy, Macmillan and the Cold War: the Irony of Interdependence* (Palgrave, 2002), broadened the frame of reference to look at Anglo-American relations over a whole range of international issues during the Kennedy Presidency. This book was awarded the Cambridge Donner Book Prize for 2003. In 2008 his most recent book, *King Hussein of Jordan: A Political Life*, was published by Yale University Press.

Toby Dodge is a Reader in the International Relations Department at the LSE and a Senior Consulting Fellow for the Middle East, International Institute for Strategic Studies, London. From September 2004 until September 2011 Dr Dodge taught international relations and the comparative politics of the Middle East in the School of Politics and International Relations, Queen Mary, University of London. His research concentrates on the evolution of the post-colonial state in the international system. The main focus of this work on the developing world is the state in the Middle East, specifically Iraq.

Sir Lawrence Freedman has been Professor of War Studies at King's College London since 1982, and Vice-Principal since 2003. Elected a Fellow of the British Academy in 1995 and awarded the CBE in 1996, he was appointed Official Historian of the Falklands Campaign in 1997. He was awarded the KCMG in 2003. In June 2009 he was appointed to serve as a member of the official inquiry into Britain and the 2003 Iraq War. Professor Freedman has written extensively on nuclear strategy and the Cold War, as well as commentating regularly on contemporary security issues. His most recent book, *A Choice of Enemies: America Confronts the Middle East* (Doubleday Canada, 2008), won the 2009 Lionel Gelber Prize and Duke of Westminster Medal for Military Literature.

Rosemary Hollis is Professor of Middle East Policy Studies and Director of the Olive Tree Scholarship Programme at City University London. Her writing, teaching and research focuses on international political and security issues in the Middle East, particularly UK, European and US relations with the region and the international dimensions of regional conflicts. Professor Hollis was formerly Director of Research at Chatham House, with overall responsibility for the research and publications output of the institute, including the formulation, funding, quality and delivery of projects. From 1995 to 2005 she was Head of the Middle East Programme at Chatham House, having spent five years in a similar post at the Royal United Services Institute for Defence Studies. During the 1980s she was a lecturer in Political Science and International Politics at George Washington University in Washington, DC, where she gained her PhD in Political Science, focusing on Britain and the Middle East.

David Houghton is an Associate Professor of Political Science at the University of Central Florida. His most recent books are *U.S. Foreign Policy and the Iran Hostage Crisis* (Cambridge University Press, 2001), *Controversies in American Politics and Society* (Blackwell, 2002, co-authored with David McKay and Andrew Wroe) and *Political Psychology: Situations, Individuals, and Cases* (Routledge, 2008). His area of expertise is decision-making in international relations, with a particular focus on American foreign policy and foreign policy analysis. He has also taught at the Universities of Pittsburgh and Essex, and has been a Visiting Scholar at the Mershon Center for International Security Studies at the Ohio State University.

David Lesch is Professor of Middle East History in the Department of History and Coordinator of the Middle East Concentration in the International Studies Program at Trinity University in San Antonio. He received his MA and PhD (1991) in History and Middle Eastern Studies from Harvard University. Among his publications are the following books: *The New Lion of Damascus: Bashar al-Asad and Modern Syria* (Yale University Press, 2005); *Syria and the United States: Eisenhower's Cold War in the Middle East* (Westview Press, 1992); *The Middle East and the United States: A Historical and Political Reassessment* (editor, Westview Press, 1996, 1999, 2003, 4th edn, 2006); *1979: The Year that Shaped the Modern Middle East* (Westview Press, 2001); the two-volume edited work, *History in Dispute: The Middle East Since 1945, Volumes 14 and 15* (St James Press, 2003); and *The Arab–Israeli Conflict: A History With Documents* (Oxford University Press, 2006).

Scott Lucas is Professor of American Studies at the University of Birmingham. A specialist in US and British foreign policy, he has written and edited seven books, including *Divided We Stand: Britain, the US and the Suez Crisis* (Hodder & Stoughton, 1991); *Freedom's War: The US Crusade Against the Soviet Union, 1945–56* (Manchester University Press, 1999); *George Orwell: Life and Times* (Haus, 2003); and *The Betrayal of Dissent: Beyond Orwell, Hitchens and the New American Century* (Pluto, 2004), and published more than 30 major articles. Professor Lucas is Editor of the *Journal of American Studies* and the founder and editor of EA WorldView, one of the leading news and analysis sites on US foreign policy and international affairs, especially in the Middle East and Turkey, Iran, Afghanistan, and Pakistan. He wrote and presented *Suez: The Missing Dimension* for BBC Radio 4 and co-directed the 2007 film *Laban!* on the 'People's Power' rising of 1986 in the Philippines.

Jeffrey Michaels is Research Associate in the Department of War Studies, King's College London, coordinating an ESRC-sponsored project entitled 'Strategic Scripts for the 21st Century', which is headed by Professor Sir Lawrence Freedman. He concurrently works as a Teaching Fellow at the UK Defence Academy. Prior to this, he served as a Lecturer with the Air Power Studies Division of the Defence Studies Department. Earlier experience has included serving as an intelligence officer attached to the US European Command and the Pentagon's Joint Staff, consulting for the Office of Net Assessment, Office of the Secretary of Defense, working as a research assistant and an occasional lecturer on the staff of the NATO School (SHAPE) in Oberammergau, Germany, and interning with the Office of the Special Advisor for Central and Eastern European Affairs, Private Office of the Secretary General of NATO in Brussels. He completed his PhD in War Studies at King's in 2009, focusing on contemporary US political-military discourse.

Peter Neumann is Professor of Security Studies at the War Studies Department, King's College London and serves as Director of the International Centre for the Study of Radicalisation, which he founded in early 2008. He has authored or co-authored five books, including *Old and New Terrorism*, published by Polity Press in 2009; and *The Strategy of Terrorism* (with M.L.R. Smith), published by Routledge in 2008. He is the author of numerous peer-reviewed articles, dealing with different aspects of terrorism and radicalization, especially 'homegrown' radicalization in Western countries.

William Quandt is Edward R. Stettinius Professor of Politics at the University of Virginia, having formerly served as Vice Provost for International Affairs at the University. He teaches courses on the Middle East and American Foreign Policy. Prior to this, he was a Senior Fellow in the Foreign Policy Studies Program at the Brookings Institution, where he conducted research on the Middle East, American policy towards the Arab-Israeli conflict, and energy policy. Professor

Quandt served as a staff member on the National Security Council (1972–74, 1977–79) and was actively involved in the negotiations that led to the Camp David Accords and the Egyptian-Israeli Peace Treaty. He was also an Associate Professor of Political Science at the University of Pennsylvania, worked at the Rand Corporation in the Department of Social Science, and he taught at UCLA and MIT. He has written numerous books, and his articles have appeared in a wide variety of publications.

Dina Rezk is a final-year PhD candidate at the University of Cambridge researching Anglo-American perceptions of Egypt and the Middle East in the post-Suez era. She uses recently declassified political and intelligence assessments to expose both the spoken and unspoken assumptions underlying Anglo-American assessments of the region, including controversial 'Orientalist' depictions of 'the Other'. In an attempt to bridge the historiographical divide between Arab and Western narratives of this period she has also relied on interviews with prominent surviving Egyptians of the era including Hassanein Heikal, Hoda abdel Nasser and Abdel Magid Farid. She contributes to the LSE IDEAS Middle East blog and teaches undergraduates at the University of Cambridge. She has presented research papers to the Cambridge Intelligence Seminar, the International Research Group at the University of Aberystwyth and the Global Futures Forum.

Janice Gross Stein is Belzberg Professor of Conflict Management in the Department of Political Science and Director of the Munk School of Global Affairs at the University of Toronto. She is a Fellow of the Royal Society of Canada and a member of the Order of Canada and the Order of Ontario. Her most recent publications include *Networks of Knowledge: Innovation in International Learning* (University of Toronto Press, 2001); *The Cult of Efficiency* (House of Anansi Press, 2001); and *Street Protests and Fantasy Parks* (UBC Press, 2002). She is a contributor to *Canada by Picasso* (Conference Board of Canada, 2006) and co-author of *The Unexpected War: Canada in Kandahar* (Viking Canada, 2007). She was the Massey Lecturer in 2001 and a Trudeau Fellow. She was awarded the Molson Prize by the Canada Council for an outstanding contribution by a social scientist to public debate. She is an Honorary Foreign Member of the American Academy of Arts and Sciences. She has been awarded Honorary Doctorate of Laws by the University of Alberta, the University of Cape Breton and McMaster University.

Fernande van Tets graduated with distinction from King's College London with an MA in War Studies. She previously completed degrees in both Political Science and Arabic at the University of Amsterdam, where she wrote a thesis on the ideological shift and de-radicalization of the Egyptian Gama'a al-Islamiyya. During her studies, she was a researcher at the International Centre for the Study of Radicalisation and Political Violence (ICSR) in London, and subsequently worked for the Baladna English newspaper in Syria and the

Dutch Embassy in Beirut. Currently, she is working as a freelance journalist and commentator based in Beirut. She is a correspondent for the Dutch current affairs magazine *de Groene Amsterdammer* as well as writing for various local and international (online) publications.

ACKNOWLEDGEMENTS

This book derives from papers delivered at a conference held at King's College London in June 2011 entitled 'Making it Personal: Anglo-American Perceptions of Middle East Adversaries'. The conference was convened as part of the *Strategic Scripts for the 21st Century* project, which is sponsored by the Research Councils UK Global Uncertainties Programme and Economic and Social Research Council. We are grateful to all the participants who were kind enough to allow their papers to be published. Even though they were unable to attend the conference, both Janice Gross Stein and David Lesch graciously agreed to contribute chapters to this volume as well. Special thanks must also be given to Sarah Chukwudebe for her outstanding assistance in making the conference, and hence this book, a reality.

Lawrence Freedman
Jeffrey H. Michaels

CHAPTER ONE

Introduction: Strategies, stories and scripts

Lawrence Freedman

There is a famous law of the internet, attributed to lawyer Mike Godwin. It states that 'As an online discussion grows longer, the probability of a comparison involving Nazis or Hitler approaches'.[1] For students of international affairs this should come as no surprise. Ever since the end of the Second World War it has become an almost reflex action in the United States and the United Kingdom to compare actual or putative enemies with Hitler. One to acquire this status was Gamal Abdel Nasser, who posed a persistent and perplexing challenge to Britain's position in the Middle East from the Suez Crisis of 1956 until his death in 1970. As late as 1963 Harold Macmillan was writing on a dispatch from the British Embassy in Cairo: 'For Nasser read Hitler and it's all very familiar.'[2] The Egyptian president was presented as being the latest representative of a radical dictatorial type, of which Hitler was the most notorious, who combined an affront to civilized values with hostility to British interests. Such men were portrayed as ruthless demagogues, stirring up unhealthy nationalist sentiments in order to undermine the established order, and so must be confronted vigorously before they had a chance to cause too much trouble. There is no reason to suppose that such comparisons were made for purely rhetorical effect to help convince a sceptical public that the country must deal with a truly bad man. Macmillan's comment was found in his official papers. Yet what Macmillan actually meant is still open to conjecture. Did he really mean that a study of Hitler would yield clues to Nasser's character? Or was it more that, whatever their differences, both men posed an extreme, comparable set of problems? If we are uncomfortable with the comparison is it because of an inappropriate analogy or because of a category mistake?

The same comparison was made by President George H.W. Bush, this time with Saddam Hussein. The Iraqi leader had ordered both the occupation and then the plundering of Kuwait in August 1990. These actions could be 'morally condemned', observed Bush after the event, 'and lead one to the proper conclusion that it was a matter of good versus evil'.[3] If the comparison was supposed to lead to policy guidance then it was problematic. Up until August 1990 as Vice President under President Reagan and now as President himself, Bush might be accused of exactly the sort of appeasing policy with regard to Saddam that was widely supposed to have been so catastrophic with Hitler by offering trade credits, providing covert help in the war with Iran, and playing down lingering links with terrorism and the use of chemical weapons. The occupation of Kuwait might have crossed a new line but this was hardly the first offence. Saddam had ordered the invasion of Iran a decade previously. A couple of years earlier he had used chemical weapons against Kurds, so it was not as if this side of his character had previously been kept well hidden. Though Saddam's past misdemeanours were well known, during this period the policy had been to establish constructive and profitable relations with Iraq. This could all be justified by the 'realist' tendency in American foreign policy, which Bush ably represented, which kept questions of power and interest to the fore and did not allow itself to get too distracted by moral considerations. Past optimism about Saddam's presumed pragmatism, and in particular his apparent regard for American interests, may have turned out to be optimistic, but they argued for presenting the response to the invasion of Kuwait in terms of the demands of international order. Bush would not have been the first 'realist', when faced with truly awful behaviour, to be genuinely outraged. In making the Hitler comparison he may have had in mind the difficulties of mobilizing public opinion in order to promote order rather than to reverse an outrage.

Once Saddam was cast as the epitome of evil, however, so long as he survived in office it was difficult to see how there could be peace and security. Unfortunately the United States was acting in response to an offence against international order rather than to deal with a Hitler and that was reflected in the mandate under which the coalition of 1990 to 1991 was put together. The actual policy remained realist: the Bush Administration was unwilling to take responsibility for a volatile state. The result was that Bush set Saddam up as a problem that he was unwilling or unable to solve and so concluded a successful war with a sense of unfinished business.

If Bush really had been trying to find an appropriate model he was looking in the wrong direction. While there was no evidence that Saddam saw Hitler as a role model, that was not the case within Josef Stalin. Said Aburish, who had observed Saddam at close quarters, described Stalin as

Saddam's 'hero'. He saw similarities: both came from a humble background, were brought up by their mothers, and relied on their security service more than the army. Aburish reported that Saddam had a 'full library of books about Stalin'.[4] He certainly shared Stalin's attention to organization and his advanced paranoia, leading to pre-emptive ruthlessness when dealing with potential rivals. As a comparator Stalin has never attracted much interest, despite his cruelty and the trouble he caused the Western democracies. One reason is that the policy legacy of the Stalin years is much more ambiguous. He had at one point – in the Second World War – been an ally. Moreover, there was no simple morality tale with Stalin. He presided over civil war, collectivization, purges, the German invasion and the subjugation of Eastern Europe, and then died of natural causes, an apparently successful and still feared dictator, without ever having been called to account for his crimes against humanity.

Hitler's fate, a desperate suicide in a battered bunker, is altogether more satisfactory. The policy legacy is also enduring, since the Hitler analogy leads naturally to the Munich analogy. The point was not whether Nasser in 1956 or Saddam in 1990 were replicating Hitler's policies, but that those responding, forewarned by history, were alive to the danger of not replicating the appeasing policies of British Prime Minister Neville Chamberlain. They had led, notably at the Munich summit of 1938, not to peace but to an even worse conflagration than might have resulted from taking a robust stance from the start. Even when not facing opponents that could be characterized as 'Hitlers', Western political leaders were constantly influenced by Munich. For instance, the Munich analogy had a major influence on Lyndon Johnson as he considered his options in Vietnam.[5] Politicians who felt it wise to talk to adversaries were aware that they risked accusations of appeasement. In the summer of 1979, when meeting Soviet leader Leonid Brezhnev to sign the SALT II Treaty, President Jimmy Carter would rather be rained upon than carry anything reminiscent of Chamberlain's trade-mark umbrella.[6] Justifying the 1986 bombing of Libya, Ronald Reagan observed: 'Europeans who remember their history understand better than most that there is no security, no safety, in the appeasement of evil.'[7] Despite over 70 years' experience of diplomacy and various forms of conflict resolution, so that Munich stands in relation to the present day as, say, the Crimean War did to Munich itself, a reference is still considered an eloquent way of making a damning political point, for example, with regard to the dangers of negotiations with Iran over its nuclear programme.[8]

Before Munich, the set of events shaping responses to crises was likely to be those leading up to the 1914 to 1918 Great War, which pointed to political failures of a quite different sort. The view that the statesmen of the day had allowed an exaggerated patriotism, fears of adversary ambitions, and an imprudent military logic to cloud their judgement and propel them into a calamitous war helps explain their later caution. John Kennedy, who invoked Munich during the Cuban Missile Crisis,[9] was also aware of the lessons of 1914. He had been reading Barbara Tuchman's *The Guns of August* (as George Bush had been reading Martin Gilbert's history of the *Second World War* in 1990). Kennedy was fearful of presiding over an even greater calamity, this time with nuclear weapons, as a result of a terrible misunderstanding with the Soviet Union. Already when he had met with Nikita Khrushchev in Vienna in June 1961 he sought a dialogue on the dangers of 'miscalculation', much to the irritation of the Soviet leader, who could not agree that Soviet leaders could be prone to such an unscientific fault ('You ought to take that word and bury it in cold storage'). Kennedy had to remind himself not to raise the issue again.[10] That did not stop him fretting about whether Khrushchev had as much trouble with his generals as he did with his Joint Chiefs of Staff. During the Berlin and Cuban crises he was constantly asking about the likely Soviet response to whatever move he was contemplating, and was fearful of the potential for escalation in the most carefully crafted moves. One of his innovations, after Cuba, was to push for a 'hot-line' direct from Washington to Moscow so that direct communication could replace anxious speculation at times of crisis.

The contrasting stories of 1914 and 1939, of miscalculation or appeasement, exercised powerful holds on Western consciousness. Both of course were problematic, neglecting the many other factors that led to war. They picked up on certain aspects of their respective situations to the neglect of others, and simplified choices that appeared complicated and uncertain to those who actually faced them. Their historical accuracy, however, has long since ceased to matter. When references are made to the 'railway timetables of Europe' or to 'Munich' these are now shorthands that help make a political point, without getting into elaborate arguments about how military timetables can pre-empt political decisions or the consequences of buying off tyrants with concessions. It is much easier to play on familiar images of hapless young men stuck in the trenches or a familiar story about a well-meaning but spineless democrat taken for a fool by a cynical but strategically shrewd dictator. The combination of simple lessons and cataclysmic events has allowed these images and stories to become so ingrained in our collective consciousness that it is hard to see how they will be readily replaced. This does not mean that they drive policy. It may well be that it is not so much that politicians think appeasement and then worry about negotiating, but that they worry about negotiating and then rationalize using appeasement. If they want to negotiate with someone previously considered bad the shorthand might be 'Northern Ireland'.

There are other such shorthands. Although less common now, a reference to 'Suez' in Britain was once considered by some as sufficient warning of not allowing a conviction that another Hitler was being faced to lead to an act of diplomatic and military recklessness. The same reference could also be taken to warn that at moments when another aggressor might need to be faced the Americans would let you down. Both meanings were prominent during the Falklands conflict of 1982. When US Secretary of State Alexander Haig began his shuttle diplomacy between London and Buenos Aires he promised Sir Nico Henderson, the British Ambassador to Washington, that this would not be 'another Suez', aware that the apparently neutral stance of the United States was already being judged in London in precisely those terms.[11] During the 1990 to 1991 Gulf Crisis, references to Korea provided both an indication that it was possible to keep a war limited without seeking the total defeat of the enemy, and also a warning that it was unwise to try, lest it lead to an equivalent response to that of the Chinese who were provoked into a massive counter-offensive as American forces approached the North Korean-China border on the Yalu in 1950. This made the 'realist' point that unrestrained objectives can lead to trouble and then stalemate. A reference to Korea was an argument to stay focused on liberating Kuwait rather than overthrowing Saddam. Perhaps future generations will use '9/11', or 'Afghanistan' or 'Iraq' as shorthand for their own lessons about the reliability of intelligence or the hazards of certain types of overseas interventions. No doubt if they do academics will warn that these cases were more complex than the popular versions of the stories implied and challenge the validity of their strict relevance for contemporary circumstances.

Stories such as these, whether about Hitler and Stalin or about appeasement and arms races, are not important in international affairs as reliable guides to events but as influences on policy-makers. As intelligible cultural references they come to mind almost intuitively in the face of certain categories of events. As moments of crisis and war are not so regular there is not a large stock of such references upon which to draw, which is why the same ones are so regularly repeated. They have become part of the 'script' in the sense that the term has come to be used by psychologists, as a framework for interpreting events and behaviour.[12] They reflect our expectations at the start of a series of events, about how they are likely to unfold, and will shape our actions as we seek to shape these events, but will then need to be adapted as our understanding of the particular situation expands, and challenges the original script.

This concept of scripts draws upon aspects of the way we think that have long been understood, and have been reinforced rather than challenged by recent advances in cognitive science. We rely on prior interpretive frameworks to make sense of incoming information. They occur in the literature as operational codes, mind-sets, belief systems, paradigms, biases, assumptions, images, constructs, framing mechanisms, schemas, and so on. They may not all mean quite the same thing but all accept that as human beings try to make sense of their circumstances they are never able to fully reconstruct reality and must always draw on a pre-existing mélange of acquired knowledge, cultural references and conceptual frameworks. Cognitive processes are now divided into the intuitive System 1 and the deliberative System 2.[13] The System 1 processes are largely unconscious, implicit, coming in quickly and automatically when needed and managing cognitive tasks of great complexity. They make possible evaluations of situations and options before they reach consciousness, reflecting the extraordinary computational and storage power of the brain, and the ways that have been found to draw on past learning and experiences. They pick up on and interpret cues and signals from the environment, suggesting appropriate and effective behaviour, enabling individuals to cope with the circumstances in which they might find themselves without having to consider every move. Here can be found a grasp of how individuals operate, what has been internalized about societies and a variety of situations, bringing it all together in ways far faster and more focused than would be possible by more explicit and deliberate means. The outcomes are feelings, including strong senses of like and dislike, signals and patterns, with scripts for action which may be difficult to articulate but are still followed. We know what to do without quite knowing why we know it. Then come the slower System 2 processes. These are conscious, explicit, analytical and deliberative, more intellectual, and inherently sequential. We can think of System 2 as what we might expect from strategic reasoning.

In many circumstances System 1 processes serve us extraordinarily well, and they become even better as more knowledge and experience is internalized. Nonetheless, when it comes to situations when the stakes are high we tend to prefer our leaders to rely a bit more on the conscious and explicit System 2, weighing risks and opportunities, costs and benefits, with some deliberation and care. In this regard we can think of a 'strategic script' as one that has moved from System 1 to System 2, from an intuitive set of expectations that lead to almost instinctive actions, to a more carefully constructed set of expectations that result in courses of action that have been more carefully and explicitly chosen. An example of the difference might be President Kennedy's instinctive response to news of Soviet missiles being based in Cuba, which was of air strikes, to the more considered response, after days of consultation and deliberation, of a limited blockade. The first point about a strategic script therefore is that it forces to the surface the subconscious assumptions that might shape the first responses to a new situation and subjects them to scrutiny, leading to elaboration and amendment.

These issues did not really begin to grip the international relations community until the 1970s. There was a precursor (which reflected the presumption that the United States did not have as much of a problem comprehending reality as the Soviet Union) in Leites' path-breaking work on operational codes that asked about the impact of ideology on Soviet behaviour.[14] His approach was later picked up by Alexander George, who pointed out its more general relevance.[15] It was unwise to assume that the misperceptions were only on the other side. This thought grew as analysts tried to understand the sources of miscalculation in Vietnam during the 1960s.[16] The landmark book was Robert Jervis' *Perception and Misperception in International Politics*. For our purposes it was especially important because he went beyond demonstrating that misperceptions were rife to considering hypotheses that would suggest when a distorted view of reality was most likely to develop and what might be done to correct for it. Too much attention, he suggested, had been placed on emotional factors when accounting for cognitive faults rather than accepting that calm and apparently rational people were also susceptible, or that their origins could be found in conflicts of interest that led to genuine differences in how situations were viewed.[17] Political leaders did have incentives to get their perceptions right. There was often a lot at stake. He avoided condescension: the real issue was about serious adults facing difficult choices with uncertain information, trying to get it right and still getting it wrong.

'Actors must remember', Jervis urged, 'that both they and others are influenced by their expectations and fit incoming information into pre-existing images'. His advice was to be more explicit about beliefs, so that there could be proper debates about broad views rather than over interpretations of particular incidents. Those lacking in self-consciousness about the structures of their own beliefs take far too much for granted, and then stick with conclusions that are perfectly reasonable when first formulated but become more doubtful with the passing of time and changing circumstances. Instead of seeking new answers to old questions they might wonder instead whether the questions needed updating. It was unwise to become too wedded to a particular point of view, as they might then be slow to change their minds in the face of new information or too quick to discard alternative explanations. Nor should they overestimate the ease with which they could influence the perceptions of others. He also warned against the assumption that the other side is highly centralized and carefully plans its moves, and also the accompanying belief that 'favourable actions by the other are a response to the actor's behaviour but that unfriendly acts spring from unprovoked hostility'.[18]

The approach to these questions of prior beliefs and their persistence has been influenced by another development, which is the focus on narratives. As stories came to be recognized as essential to thought processes and social communication the meaning of the word was expanded. Narratives were once rather special stories. As a result of what has been called a 'narrative turn', in many fields of human enquiry they are now seen as one of the basic units of thought, encouraging the view that this is the only way we can experience and interpret the world.[19] This approach reflects an uncertain confidence about what we actually know, fascination with the variety of interpretations that can be attached to the same event, and awareness of the choices we make when constructing our own identity and those of others. They highlight the importance of human imagination and empathy while challenging the idea that we can have perfect knowledge of an external reality.

The focus on narrative has encouraged the idea that part of our better understanding of the way in which thought processes develop might make it possible to find ways of manipulating those of others so that they are encouraged to see the world differently. While those of the most committed enemies might be considered to be beyond influence in the context of battles for 'hearts and minds' in counterinsurgency campaigns there is at least a case for trying to encourage positive views of one's own side and negative views of the other. Practitioners of the arts of political 'spin' have made a good living out of this possibility for some time and have a number of examples to prove how a perceptual shift can turn a close election. On the other hand, in these cases they are also operating within a culture they understand and know how to send out messages that have a chance of being accepted as credible and intelligible. The more unfamiliar the cultural operating environment the more difficult it is to get the messages right.

This suggests a way that the idea of a strategic script can be taken a step further. It allows us to move beyond the question of original perceptions into the series of moves that will follow. In doing so it provides an alternative to the conventional consideration of strategies as plans, relating available means to desired ends through a series of steps which if followed carefully and in sequence produce the desired outcome. While a plan suggests a predictable world, with cause and effect known in advance, a script warns of a more uncertain environment, and recognizes the need to anticipate the interaction of a number of players over an extended period of time, pulled together by some sense of how a plot could and should develop. Strategies are scripts, however, which must leave considerable scope for improvisation. There is only one set of actions that can be anticipated with any degree of certainty, and that is of the one central player for whom the strategy has been devised. Whether the plot will unfold as intended will then depend on not only the acuity of the starting assumptions but also whether other players follow the script or deviate significantly from it, possibly because they are following some different script of their own. Or else something quite unexpected will turn up, independently of any of the actions of the scripted players, which will challenge the plot and require yet more improvisation and adjustment.

In this respect a strategy is a story about the future. It is a story because it exists only in the imagination until an attempt is made to turn it into reality. The story will be in the future tense, describing an unfolding narrative as moves by key players. Though their independence is accepted the possibility that their moves might be changed by those of others and the way they are presented is at the heart of any strategy. The challenge is to identify patterns of actions that will require other players to follow your script out of the logic of the developing situation. The opening bid in negotiations, a feint on a battlefield, a bellicose statement at a time of crisis, may well all assume a likely response by the other side. If that is not forthcoming then the improvisation will start early or some anticipation will have been made of an alternative response, for which a counter had already been prepared.

In his essay 'The Trouble with Stories', Charles Tilly worried about the persistent human tendency, often by working backwards from actual outcomes, to seek explanations in the form of stories. These stories were normally about individuals (although they could be about institutions such as churches or categories such as classes) acting deliberately and consciously to achieve definite goals – and also being successful. However vivid and compelling they might be in the telling, stories unfortunately tended to offer generally poor explanations. In practice the most significant cause–effect relations were 'indirect, incremental, interactive, unintended, collective, or mediated by the nonhuman environment rather than being direct, willed consequences of individual action'. The demand for stories encourages us to look for actors making deliberate choices from among well-defined alternatives, when actual decision-making was likely to be far less calculating and deliberate, more improvised, often quite wobbly, even when it comes to elements assumed to be fixed, because in practice so much is in flux.

This was of course as likely to be as true of the future as of the past, but while it is possible as a historian to acknowledge a range of factors that contributed to an eventual outcome it is much harder for the strategist to anticipate all of these things. This is why the strategic plot has to change and adapt with circumstances, but it is also why it is difficult to find a better starting point than what is believed about the interests, motives, characters and conditions of other relevant parties. Even when it came to explaining the past, and though urging social scientists to find something better, Tilly was not optimistic, suspecting that we were just too hard-wired when it came to telling stories. In which case, he asked, at least make sure that they are superior stories, doing justice to the impersonal and collective forces at work as well as the human, and making the appropriate connections with time, places, actors and actions outside its purview. Better still, we should tell stories about stories, giving them context and considering how they are generated.[20]

It is in this spirit that this book has been put together. The chapters confirm the importance of how policy-makers see the world and the impact of cognition. Even when they are trying they find it hard to overcome the weight of culture and tradition, are stuck with limited information and first impressions, and, for want of anything better, draw on inappropriate analogies and metaphors. Yet this is also a more knowing age, and there is widespread awareness of the problems and ubiquity of cognitive bias.

There is a subset of social scientists who still find it helpful to pretend that the world is full of rational actors but, other than when they are able to approximate from many cases (as with some problems in economics), their work now diverges even more than ever from what is known about cognition and behaviour, and therefore unsurprisingly tends to findings that veer between the banal and the trivial. It is therefore no longer good enough to demonstrate that rational actor theory is an inadequate basis for theorizing. Given that people cannot be cognitively unbiased because interpreting the world around us is a constant challenge and without some embedded constructs to guide us we could not cope, the task is to work out what we now do with this basic insight into the human condition.

The first step is to encourage more awareness of the dangers, so that we are less likely to be caught out by preconceptions and prejudice. The next steps are more difficult, as they involve difficult questions about the relationship between apparently ill-founded beliefs and social action. In this respect cognitive psychologists may find themselves in the same dilemma long faced by reflexive philosophers. How can seekers of cognitive bias in others be sure that they are not victims of their own? Are they apt to see evidence of unfortunate misunderstandings where others just see the inexorable logic of conflicts of interests? Consider, for example, an article by two scholars who have done much to develop a sophisticated approach to the influence of psychological factors on international affairs. Dominic Johnson and Dominic Tierney have written on how a move from a 'deliberative' to an 'implemental' mind-set triggers 'a number of psychological biases, most notably overconfidence'.[21] The problems come when this move to the implemental mind-set is triggered not so much by deliberations concluding but by a sense of the imminence of war. This can then become a self-fulfilling prophecy, as actions that are more hawkish and provocative than might otherwise have been the case are adopted. Using examples from the run-up to both World Wars they provide evidence of how, once conflicts were perceived to be likely, political leaders became more convinced that they would prevail. Only when still worrying about what to do were they likely to appraise potential outcomes realistically. A commitment to a decision encouraged confidence that it would turn out to be correct.

The authors seem to expect their readers to find this alarming and disappointing, but arguably the alternative would also be worrisome. The key thing is to be realistic when making a decision. Thereafter a political leader that carried on dithering, offering an 'uncertain trumpet', would not be much of a war leader. After a certain point an open mind becomes dysfunctional in a politician because even in issues far away from war, policy might well then just become vacillating and confusing so that nothing can be implemented. A more accurate perception may still miss out a crucial factor, while an exaggerated confidence in dubious beliefs may make possible a bold move that turns out to be effective. None of this is to suggest that overconfidence cannot lead to trouble, especially if it leads to discounting evidence that earlier assumptions were wrong. But it does argue for avoiding psychological reductionism and taking care to consider the issue of cognitive processes within their broader context. Otherwise we could end up with a shorthand explanation for the start of the First World War that merely substitutes 'mind-sets' for 'railroads'.

This book considers the strategic scripts of the Middle East, focusing in particular on the assumptions about 'significant others', and in particular opponents, that influence policy-making. We have concentrated on the Middle East for two reasons. First, this region has seen a number of conflicts involving a range of players since the end of the Second World War and this provides a comparative perspective. Second, in the Middle East durable 'strong men' have been common. They have made it their business to concentrate power in their hands, and have managed to keep their positions for extended periods. In addition, because of their apparent grip over their internal politics their country's policies are assumed, not always correctly, to be reflections of their own preferences, prejudices and predilections. It has therefore been reasonable to pay attention to their attitudes and behaviour when it comes to making sense of conflicts and how they might develop in the future. In many cases, relations with these key personalities and their policies have gone through a number of stages, from pariahs to possible partners and back to pariahs again (in the case of Gaddafi) or from a man we can do business with to a man who must be removed as a matter of urgency (in the case of Saddam).

Some of the most important misreadings have not been in the direction of exaggerated threat but in simply missing the importance of a new figure on the stage. For example, with the Ayatollah Khomeini assessments suffered as a result of the lack of precedent, no 'role model' for an elderly cleric acting so shrewdly and with such single-mindedness of purpose. The idea that he might be a 'Gandhi-like' figure seems preposterous in retrospect but that demonstrates just how much people can invest their hopes and fears in a new figure, especially when Khomeini was determined to encourage people to see him as non-threatening. It was not as if there were no clues in his past pronouncements and activities. There was no reason to suppose that he had moderated with age, but he knew enough about the West to know the right things to say about his aspirations to encourage complacency. He also misled the other political groupings in Iran. Another example was Anwar el Sadat, before Nasser's death known only as his loyal servant. His tenure was expected to be an interlude before the harder line, more pro-Soviet faction took power. The issue was not only whether he was prepared to depart from Nasser's policies but also whether he had the political clout to pull it off. In both cases Western policy-makers took a while to shake off first impressions.

In some cases the difficulty lies in coming to terms with individuals who may have very human frailties but who represent something larger than themselves. One of the differences between the various personalities considered in this volume is whether or not they enjoyed a link with something much bigger. Nasser represented a new type of socialist, nationalist, anti-Zionist, anti-colonialist leader, who could speak for wider third world aspirations. Arafat followed in the same tradition, except that he came to embody the Palestinian cause and every bit of notice he achieved was a blow on behalf of his people. The Palestinian state was an aspiration, denied by a succession of Israeli leaders and not taken seriously by many Westerners, but he kept it alive. While his methods and his manner may have turned people off, his dogged pursuit of the cause, including direct negotiations with Israel, gave him credibility. Bin Laden aspired to such a position, and for a while he certainly symbolized a singular threat based on a particular interpretation of Islam. But his authority depended on being able to instigate spectacular acts of violence, and as he failed to do so he declined as a potential leader of Muslim opinion and as a real challenge to the West. Saddam, Gaddafi and Asad had the weight of their states behind them but their ideological message was confused, and they gradually came to stand for little more than their tribes and families. They might have come to power with a vision for their countries, but eventually became totally preoccupied with their personal position, with real or assumed rivals, and securing their dynasties.

The script writers for Western policy therefore need to be aware not only of the personalities of the key figures for whom they have assigned roles, but also their broader role in their political systems. They need to recall the importance of Tilly's list of causal factors as being 'indirect, incremental, interactive, unintended, collective, or mediated by the nonhuman environment rather than being direct, willed consequences of individual action' and to keep a sense of the wider economic, social and political forces that are reshaping and often subverting the environment in which the leaders apparently dominate. The fixation on the 'strong men' has led to missing out on what was stirring around and beneath them, which is why Western intelligence agencies can be as surprised as the men themselves when all of a sudden their regimes looked vulnerable.

If the scripts are going to work as guides for policies then they certainly need to guard against cognitive distortions and cultural baggage (for instance, the issue of 'orientalism' may need to be addressed). To counter these tendencies, policy-makers can draw on regional specialists and obtain psychological profiles. It may be, however, that the script has another purpose. It might still rely on exaggerated representations of the enemy because that will best serve the policy purpose of rallying support. A lot of the discussion of cognitive bias focuses on the mind-set of the key decision-makers and possibly the group around them (as with 'groupthink'). It therefore assumes that the problem is imperfect cognition so that if only more information was collected and thinking raised to a higher level mistakes could be avoided. But some representations suit the policy-makers. When foreign policy becomes a matter of intense public debate, so that the persuasive effort goes beyond elite circles, there will be more use of rhetorical shorthands. At best, the rhetoric will simply emphasize those factors which were found most convincing when the initial decision was made. At worst, often when the policy debate gets so intense that the leader dare not budge from an initial position, statements may bear little relationship to what has come to be known in the bureaucracy. Once policy-makers start propagating caricature versions of an issue for public consumption this is rarely accompanied by more rounded views for internal deliberations.

When contemplating the way in which the Bush Administration dealt with irritating facts that contradicted its core message, for example, on the Iraq War, the American satirist Stephen Colbert introduced the concept of 'truthiness'. This was something that was not exactly the truth but felt like the truth, something you knew with your heart even if your head could not find the evidence to support it. His target was the claim that emotion and 'gut feeling' were the best guides in political discourse. In 2006 the American Dialect Society chose 'truthiness' as the word of the year and gave it a formal definition: 'the quality of preferring concepts or facts one wishes to be true, rather than concepts or facts known to be true.'[22] As this book demonstrates, truth can be a problematic concept, but best efforts at identifying something approximating to truth remain preferable to wishful thinking.

Notes

1 Tom Chivers, 'Internet Rules and Laws: The Top 10, from Godwin to Poe', *Daily Telegraph*, 23 October 2009.

2 See Nigel Ashton, Chapter 4, this volume.

3 George Bush and Brent Scowcroft, *A World Transformed* (New York: Alfred A. Knopf, 1998), p. 375. Steven Hurst, 'The Rhetorical Strategy of George H. W. Bush during the Persian Gulf Crisis 1990–91: How to Help Lose a War You Won', *Political Studies*, Vol. 52, No. 2, 2004, pp. 376–92.

4 See interview with Aburish at: http://www.pbs.org/wgbh/pages/frontline/shows/saddam/interviews/aburish.html.

5 Yuen Foong Khong, *Analogies at War: Korea, Munich, Dien Bien Phu, and the Vietnam Decisions of 1965* (Princeton, NJ: Princeton University Press, 1992).

6 In a later interview he could not recall this but did not deny the story. See: http://openvault.wgbh.org/catalog/wpna-49777d-interview-with-jimmy-carter-1987-part-2-of-2.

7   Ronald Reagan, 'Address to the Nation: United States Air Strike Against Libya', *Weekly Compilation of Presidential Documents*, Vol. 22, No. 16, 21 April 1986, p. 491. Cited in Robert J. Beck, 'Munich's Lessons Reconsidered', *International Security*, Vol. 14, No. 2, 1989, pp. 161–91.

8   Jeffrey Record, 'Retiring Hitler and "Appeasement" from the National Security Debate', *Parameters*, Vol. 38, No. 2, summer 2008, pp. 91–101.

9   He invoked the 'clear lesson' of the 1930s: 'Aggressive conduct, if allowed to go unchecked, ultimately leads to war.' Quoted in Theodore C. Sorensen, *Kennedy* (New York: Harper & Row, 1965), p. 703.

10 Lawrence Freedman, *Kennedy's Wars: Berlin, Cuba, Laos and Vietnam* (New York: Oxford University Press, 2000), p. 56.

11 Lawrence Freedman, *The Official History of the Falklands Campaign, Vol. II, War & Diplomacy* (London: Taylor & Francis, 2005), p. 129.

12 Robert C. Schank and Robert P. Abelson, *Scripts, Plans, Goals and Understanding: An Inquiry into Human Knowledge Structures* (Hillsdale, NJ: Lawrence Erlbaum Associates, 1977).

13 Daniel Kahneman, *Thinking Fast and Slow* (London: Allen Lane, 2011).

14 Nathan Leites, *The Operational Code of the Politburo* (New York: McGraw Hill, 1951).

15 Alexander L. George, 'The "Operational Code": A Neglected Approach to the Study of Political Leaders and Decision-Making', *International Studies Quarterly*, Vol. 13, No. 2, (1969), pp. 190–222.

16 For an early example considering John Foster Dulles see Ole Holsti, 'Cognitive Dynamics and Images of the Enemy', in David J. Finlay, Ole R. Holsti and Richard R. Fagen (eds) *Enemies in Politics* (Chicago, IL: Rand McNally, 1967).

17 See Janice Gross Stein, Chapter 2, this volume, for an argument that emotion and cognition are mutually supportive.

18 Robert Jervis, *Perception and Misperception in International Politics* (Princeton, NJ: Princeton University Press, 1976), p. 424.

19 W.T.J. Mitchell (ed.), *On Narrative* (Chicago, IL: University of Chicago Press, 1981).

20 Charles Tilly, 'The Trouble with Stories', in *Stories, Identities, and Social Change* (New York: Rowman & Littlefield, 2002), pp. 25–42.

21 Dominic D.P. Johnson and Dominic Tierney, 'The Rubicon Theory of War: How the Path to Conflict Reaches the Point of No Return', *International Security*, Vol. 36, No. 1, (2011), pp. 7–40. The importance of the transition from 'contemplating to enacting actions' is drawn from Heinz Heckhausen and Peter M. Golwitzer, 'Thought Contents and Cognitive Functioning in Motivational versus Volitional States of Mind', *Motivation and Emotion*, Vol. 11, No. 2, (1987), pp. 101–120.

22 http://www.merriam-webster.com/info/06words.htm.

CHAPTER TWO

Emotions and threat perception: New frontiers of research

Janice Gross Stein

Introduction

The colonial powers left in their wake a modern Middle East punctuated by war, civil war and foreign invasion. Some of the wars were intentional, deliberately planned and executed, while others were badly miscalculated and led to unanticipated and undesired consequences. Scholars in international relations consider war a logical mistake. If the parties to the conflict knew the outcome of fighting before they went to war, war would never happen, at least in theory. The loser would refrain from fighting and the victor would therefore find it unnecessary to go to war. Not all scholars agree with this elegant logic. At the centre of the controversies among scholars is the understanding of how threats are perceived and assessed. Thucydides wrote the foundational text on threat assessment and the need to balance against or ally with a threatening power. Yet at the core of theories of balance of power, of alliances and of war was a largely unexamined concept of threat perception. Threat was conveniently equated to power, largely to military power, and scholars moved easily from 'objective' measures of power to threat assessment, assuming equivalence between the two.

Only in the past several decades have scholars begun to look seriously at intention as a source of threat that is independent of military capabilities and to build models that focused explicitly on intention in their explanations of the causes of war.[1] This strand of scholarship produced what is generally considered 'rationalist' models of deterrence and of war where signalling and credibility are the core analytic puzzles.[2] At almost the same time, scholars in international relations schooled in political psychology began to explore threat 'perception' and 'misperception', paying careful attention to the variance between what leaders perceive as threatening and what the evidence of intentions and military capabilities suggests.[3]

'Threat' and 'perception'

I begin with working definitions of 'threat' and 'perception', the two central concepts in this argument. Threats can be verbal and physical. Verbal threats are conditional statements designed to signal the capacity and intention to inflict harm if desired results are not forthcoming. Verbal threats usually take the form of if-then statements: if you do not do as I ask, I will inflict the following harm on you. Deterrent threats require the target to refrain from committing acts that the threatener does not like and compellent threats require the target to engage in actions that they do not wish to do. Leaders do not always threaten verbally; they may also use non-verbal signals to communicate the seriousness of their intent to punish undesirable behaviour. They may withdraw their ambassadors, put their forces on alert, or move forces to contested borders. Finally, in international politics, the accumulation of economic and military power may be perceived as threatening, even if that is not its principal purpose.

Threats do not unambiguously speak for themselves. The meaning of threats, both verbal and physical, is mediated by the perception of the target. Perception is the process of apprehending by means of the senses and recognizing and interpreting what is processed. Psychologists think of perception as a single unified awareness derived from sensory processes when a stimulus is present. Perception is the basis for understanding, learning and knowing, and the motivation for action. Especially important in processes of individual perception are emotional states, information processing, and patterns of inference and attribution. At the collective level, processes of perception are more difficult to identify. Understandings are shared and communicated as are emotions to create a collective mood. In this sense, threats are constructed within and among private and public conversations of experts, political leaders and publics.[4]

Central to many rationalist accounts of threat perception is the argument that leaders perceive threat and go to war because they do not have complete information. Privately held information creates uncertainty and in this context, states at times have an incentive to misrepresent information about their capabilities and their intentions.[5] This deliberate misrepresentation and the consequent difficulty in establishing the credibility of signals is an important part of the story of crisis escalation, deterrence failure and war. If both parties accurately and completely represented their privately held information, rationalists expect that states could determine the outcome of a hypothetical confrontation and the 'loser' would forgo engagement. This logic sees war as a result of inaccurate threat perception that flows from deliberate misrepresentation and signals that are not credible.

The emphasis of these rationalist accounts is largely on the dilemmas that the 'sender' of the signals confronts in formulating credible commitments rather than on the perceptual dynamics of the perceiver. Implicit in these accounts, nevertheless, is the argument that if the sender's commitments are not credible to the receiver, the receiver may not perceive their meaning and consequently choose an inappropriate course of action. The silent, largely unexamined variable in rationalist accounts is the dynamics of threat perception by those who are the target of the signal.

When is this kind of misrepresentation and deceptive signalling most likely to occur? When, in other words, is the credibility of threats, a concern primarily of the sender rather than the perceiver, especially difficult to establish? Rationalists argue that leaders have strong incentives to bluff or deceive, to exaggerate their capabilities and to conceal their weaknesses, especially when they fear attack. Evidence now suggests that Saddam Hussein, with his eye on his historic enemy – Iran – deliberately did not reveal that that he had ended his nuclear, chemical and biological weapons programmes. He could not credibly commit to the United States that he had ended his programmes to develop weapons of mass destruction without undermining his deterrent capability with Iran. That inability to make a credible commitment pushed up the perception of threat among those in the Bush White House who were already inclined to see Saddam as a threat to US interests.[6] Generically, the difficulty of making credible commitments complicates signalling for the sender, but it simultaneously complicates threat perception for the receiver.

Signalling and threat perception also become more difficult when intentions are difficult to read because of the workings of the security dilemma.[7] A security dilemma arises between two states who are both 'security seekers'. When one takes defensive action to protect itself, but that defensive action can also be read as offensive, the other misperceives intention. This process begins a mutual misperception of each other's defensive intentions as threatening that can culminate in a spiral into war. When sovereignty is contested, for example, the consolidation and defence of the territorial status quo may be viewed as aggressive, especially when it entrenches a disadvantage for one side. As a result, both sides may see their own actions as defensive and the others as threatening, resulting in spirals of hostility as each seeks to bolster its control of contested territory.

Here the culprit is not directly in the way leaders process information, but in the inherent ambiguity of the information they get and the poor diagnostics available to distinguish defensive from offensive intent. The security dilemma, which is most acute when offence is indistinguishable from defence, complicates signalling and threat perception and makes escalation likely because of the difficulty of reading intentions and the tendency to prepare for the worst case.[8] None of these explanations, however, explicitly builds in psychological explanations which help explain what appear to be anomalous patterns of threat perception at the individual level, nor do they deal with the difficult problem of how psychological moods which shape threat perception become collective and shared.

Cognitive explanations of threat perception

A recent study of the 2003 Iraq War concludes that rationalist explanations of war are incomplete and need to be complemented by psychological explanations of threat perception and decision-making. Lake sets the rationalist model of privately held information and deliberately deceptive signals against a psychological model of cognitive biases that impaired threat perception and decision-making. Although the key players were intentionalist, or minimally rational, he argues,

> the key information failures were rooted in cognitive biases in decision-making, not intentional misrepresentations by the opponent. Both the United States and Iraq engaged in self-delusions, biased decision-making, and failures to update prior beliefs that are inconsistent with the assumption that actors will seek out and use all available information.[9]

This is a strong indictment of purely rational models of incomplete information and signalling as a sufficient explanation, an indictment that is rooted in evidence of exaggerated threat perceptions by the Bush Administration and Saddam's underestimation of the threat posed by the Bush Administration to the survival of his regime. Nevertheless, judgements of the accuracy and the adequacy of threat perception are both conceptually and empirically difficult to make, in part because the term is used to describe both an outcome and a process.[10]

When misperception describes an outcome, it is the difference between perceptions *ex ante* and the reality *ex post*. It is only possible, however, to make these judgements of accuracy or inaccuracy *ex post*; *ex ante* judgements are always uncertain. When misperception is used as process, it generally refers to the deviation from some standard model of rational information processing. Again what the standard is and how elastic the boundaries are is open to question: what, for example, constitutes a rational or optimal search for information? How much information is enough? When does additional search provide diminishing marginal returns? These are extraordinary difficult questions to answer empirically and scholars themselves are vulnerable to the 'hindsight bias' when answering the question after the fact; they know where the needle is in the haystack.[11]

Arguments of 'misperception' and 'miscalculation' are built on the assumption that accurate perception and calculation are possible, that there is some standard, some boundary, which separates inaccuracy from accuracy. Yet this boundary is extraordinarily difficult to establish, even after the fact. Historians writing years later with full access to documentary evidence argue about intentions. There are multiple, at times overlapping explanations of why leaders would deliberately distort the signals they send about their capabilities and intentions.

As we have seen, leaders may send distorted signals because they are attempting to cover up weakness. A second, quite different explanation emphasizes interests and the constraints imposed by multiple constituencies in 'two-level' games.[12] Leaders may be speaking to multiple constituencies simultaneously and therefore have an incentive to distort either their intentions or their capabilities or both. Saddam Hussein did so when, constrained by his ongoing concern about Iran, he refused to acknowledge publicly that he had ended his unconventional weapons programme. He therefore faced enormous difficulty in making his commitments credible to the United States. These difficulties have led scholars to set aside the question of accuracy, to abandon the systematic study of misperception, and to focus rather on patterns of perception under different circumstances.[13] Are certain kinds of actors, situations or crises associated with particular patterns of threat perception?

Forty years ago, psychologists started a 'cognitive revolution' as they rejected simple behaviourist models and looked again at the way people made inferences and judgements. They brought the 'mind' back into psychology. Although this was not at all its purpose, the cognitive revolution is now widely understood largely as a commentary on the limits to rationality; some psychologists explicitly developed models that demonstrated the 'deviations' from rationality. At the time, rationality was formulated in a very precise way as the capacity to maximize subjective expected utility; a micro-economic model became the foundation of rationality. To put the argument differently, the capacity for human reason was translated as rationality defined in micro-economic terms. 'Misperception' and 'miscalculation' were consequently defined against this narrow template of rationality.

How is this 'cognitive revolution' relevant to the study of international politics? Political psychologists drew on the cognitive revolution to inform their study of inference, judgement and decision-making by political leaders engaged in interactive bargaining with others even as they negotiated domestically with important constituencies in a context in which war was an option. Situated at the apex of these complex strategic and multi-layered games, political leaders, like everyone else, are limited in their capacity to process information. Their rationality is bounded.[14] Because their rationality is bounded, people use a number of cognitive short cuts and heuristics to simplify complexity and manage uncertainty, handle information, make inferences and generate threat perceptions. Analysis of these cognitive short cuts explains the threat perceptions that individual leaders make.

Research has now cumulated to show that people rarely conform to the expectations of the abstract rational model.[15] Cognitive psychology has demonstrated important differences between the expectations of rational decision models and the processes of attribution and estimation that people frequently use. It explains these differences by the need for simple rules of information processing and judgement that are necessary to make sense of environments that are both uncertain and complex. People have a preference for simplicity, they are averse to ambiguity and dissonance, and they misunderstand fundamentally the essence of probability.[16] We are not intuitively good at estimating probabilities. Together, these attributes compromise the capacity for rational inference.

Political leaders trying to assess a threat need to make a very complex world somewhat simpler. To do so, they unconsciously strip the nuance, the context, the subtleties out of the problems they face in order to build simple frames. Stripping out the context when assessing threat can lead to very oversimplified judgements. President George H. W. Bush famously said when Iraq invaded Kuwait in 1990 that Saddam Hussein was 'another Hitler'. Whatever Saddam was, it is difficult to argue that he was comparable to Hitler either in his intentions or his capabilities: the scope of his ambition or the numbers that he had killed did not compare to Hitler; nor did his relative military capabilities. That kind of simplified reasoning by analogy to develop a threat assessment is not uncommon.

Cognitive psychology has identified a number of heuristics and biases people use in environments of risk and uncertainty that can impair processes of judgement.[17] Heuristics are convenient short cuts or rules of thumb for processing information. One of the most powerful is *anchoring*. In 1973, Israel's decision-makers, although deeply aware of Egypt's determination to regain the Sinai, were nevertheless convinced that President Sadat would not attack until the Egyptian Air Force could attack deep behind Israel's lines. They systematically discounted evidence that was inconsistent with this core belief until they received information of an impending attack directly from one of their own agents who had penetrated the highest levels of decision-making in Cairo.[18] Similarly, in the United States, although very senior officials warned of the intention of Al Qaida to strike the United States, officials failed to update their estimates as they received disconnected pieces of information before 11 September. Pre-existing beliefs anchored their judgements.

Cognitive processes of attribution also shape threat perception. One of the most pervasive biases is the fundamental attribution error, where people exaggerate the importance of dispositional over situational factors in explaining the behaviour of others. They tend to place heavier emphasis on personality attributes rather than on the constraints that the other faces.[19] Closely related is the actor-observer bias, in which people tend to overemphasize the role of a situation in their behaviours and underemphasize the role of their own personalities.

These biases can work together to increase threat perception. First, people tend to consider their own behaviour differently from the behaviour of others. They use a double standard. When the government of Iran makes a threatening statement about its intention to close the Straits of Hormuz, should the US further tighten sanctions, leaders in Washington see that threat as a function of the kind of regime that Teheran is, but explain their response as evidence of the situation they confront. The double standard in reasoning is clear and can lead to significant and reciprocal overestimation of threat in strategic interactions that take place against a background of enmity. The fundamental attribution error and the actor-observer bias, working together, can explain reciprocal patterns of escalating threat perception and the dynamics of the spiral model which occur when the security dilemma is acute. The two can reinforce each other to enable exaggerated threat perception, reciprocal escalatory steps and a spiral of hostility. They can also explain the embedding of conflict over time so that it becomes protracted and resistant to resolution.

The need for simplicity and consistency and the impediments to probabilistic thinking are often treated as 'deviations' from rational models. Yet, the robustness of psychological models is now supported by a generation of research which establishes these patterns as the norm rather than the exception. Beliefs, schemas and cognitive scripts are the fundamental screens through which leaders perceive threat. New research in neuroscience has added to the complexity by bringing emotion back into reason.

Emotion and threat perception

Two decades of research in neuroscience have reshaped our understanding of the relationship between emotion, perception and cognition. Two results stand out. First, information processing seems not to be the result only of a deliberative thought process, but largely of preconscious neurological processes. The brain can absorb about 11 million pieces of information a second but can only process 40 consciously. The unconscious brain manages the rest. Second, emotion is primary and plays a dominant role in perception and thought. Research on emotion is having a significant impact upon the analysis of a wide range of global issues: theories of deterrence,[20] reputation and signalling,[21] nuclear proliferation,[22] the war on terror,[23] and revenge, anger and humiliation as responses to threat and motives for war.[24]

What is emotion? There is widespread theoretical dispute about the conceptualization of emotion. According to McDermott, 'Emotion is a large set of differentiated, biologically-based complex[es] that are constituted, at the very least, by mutually transformative interactions among biological systems (e.g. cognition, physiology, psychology) and physical and sociocultural ones.'[25] There is a growing consensus that emotion is 'first', because it is automatic and fast, and operating below the threshold of conscious awareness, it plays a dominant role in shaping perception and behaviour.[26] We generally feel before we think and, what is even more surprising, often we act before we think. There is widespread consensus that the brain implements 'automatic processes' which are faster than conscious deliberations with little or no awareness or feeling of effort.[27] Not surprisingly, the conscious brain then interprets behaviour that emerges from automatic and affective processes as the outcome of perception and deliberation.

Kahneman calls the first, emotion-based system of processing 'intuitive' and 'associative' and the second system 'reasoned' and 'rule-governed'.[28] The first system is preconscious, automatic, fast, effortless, associative, unreflective, usually with strong emotional bonds, and slow to change. The second system is conscious, slow, effortful, reflective, rule-governed and flexible. The vast majority of processing occurs through the first system which draws heavily on emotions and, in a competition between the two, always trumps the rule-governed, reasoned system. It is extraordinarily difficult, Kahneman concludes, for the second system to educate the first.

How does emotion influence threat perception and strategic scripts? Evolutionary psychologists see emotions as adaptive programmes of action that have evolved over time to ensure survival and then reproduction.[29] Emotions are the superordinate programmes that gather information from the environment and organize the raw data of experience prior to the conscious processes of thought. Emotions serve as switches, turning on and off depending on the environmental demands of the moment.[30] It is individuals' emotional states that constitute a primary influence in automatic threat detection and the bias is in favour of over-detection rather than underestimation.[31]

Political and social psychologists see evolutionary arguments as necessary but not complete. What, they ask, governs these switches, beyond the imperative of physical survival? It is social context which makes emotions meaningful.[32] It is only with a shared sense of what constitutes appropriate social behaviour that a person, a people or a government feels humiliated or threatened. When the flag of one nation is burned by another, the humiliation and anger that follow flow from a shared understanding that the burning of a flag is a deliberately insulting and threatening act. It is in this sense that emotions need to be conceived not only as an individual but also as a social process.[33]

Fear and threat perception

Among the emotions generally considered to be basic, the impact of fear is the most widely studied. Fear has been central to the study of foreign policy and international politics. From Thucydides, the great student of the Peloponnesian Wars, to Hobbes, who wrote about the state of anarchy that induced fear, to Morgenthau, the twentieth-century classical realist, who started his analysis of international politics with a Hobbesian analysis of international anarchy that generated fear and an unending search for power, realists have premised their analyses of international politics on the ubiquity of fear. In these realist and rationalist accounts, however, fear remains an assumption, unexplored, rather than a dynamic process that is experienced.

Neuropsychologists and behavioural economists treat fear very differently. Fear is conditioned in part by our evolutionary makeup and is frequently evoked by crude or subliminal cues. Fear is, of course, highly adaptive; fear heightens attention and vigilance, and prepares people to respond to what they perceive as imminent danger. Neuroscientists have now demonstrated that fear conditioning, however, may be permanent, or at least far longer lasting than other kinds of learning. 'To the extent that these differences exist between the calculus of objective risk and the determinants of fear, and to the extent that fear does play an important part in risk-related behaviors', argues Loewenstein and his colleagues, 'behavior in the face of risk is unlikely to be well-described by traditional consequentialist models'. Fear, in other words, lasts longer than the threat and can become a learned response that is embedded over time.

It is not surprising then that a decade after 9/11, leaders and publics in the United States still identify the threat of a terrorist attack as one of their primary concerns. Threat perception remains high and shapes foreign and domestic policy, even though no major attack has succeeded in the decade that followed. That several attacks have been aborted is undoubtedly a part of the continuing public and political focus on terrorism. But fear conditioning is also part of the explanation. Through repeated practice and institutionalization, a self-sustaining climate of fear was created in the United States by the Bush Administration.[34] Once a threat is perceived and institutionalized it becomes self-perpetuating, and it consequently becomes far more difficult to wind down the well-established embedded threat perceptions that drive conflict.

Emotion and the credibility of deterrent threats

Cognitive models have long informed the study of deterrence but building emotions into the explanation is shedding new light on old problems.[35] The credibility of threats, an essential component in theories of deterrence, compellence and bargaining, is not only a property of the sender, as some formal models of signalling suggest, but is also a function of the beliefs of the receiver. These beliefs are not only cognitive but emotional as well. The emotional cues that signals evoke – fear, anger – matter insofar as these emotions then prompt beliefs and action in turn. Research demonstrates that fear prompts uncertainty and risk-averse action while anger prompts certainty and risk-acceptance.

Research also demonstrates that credibility, a fundamental component to theories of action in international politics, is emotional as well as cognitive. Credibility is not simply a function of either the cost of the signal or past behaviour. It is an emotional belief that is held by its intended receiver; the belief that another's commitment is credible depends on the selection and interpretation of evidence and on the assessment of risk, both of which rely on emotion.[36]

Because Israel's leaders believe that what Hamas' leaders think of them matters, their emotional beliefs about what Hamas' leaders think about Israel matter. Israel's leaders beliefs may be – and have been in the past – significantly at variance from what Hamas' leaders actually believe about Israel's resolve. Israel's leaders nevertheless became locked into a conversation with themselves about their fragile or deteriorating reputation for resolve and have gone to war to preserve that reputation, even though they do not and cannot control how Hamas' leaders perceive Israel's threat to go to war should Hamas launch rockets across the border.

Building in emotion as a driver of threat perception changes the analysis of reputation based solely on past behaviour or costly signals. Past behaviour rarely speaks for itself but is felt and understood in multiple ways by others. What the deterrer feels and thinks of as a 'costly' signal may not necessarily be felt as costly by a would-be challenger. Cost, as we know from our own experience, is subjective.

Emotion is an assimilation mechanism that influences the selection and interpretation of evidence in threat perception. In 2009, Israeli and American leaders had access to almost all the same data and evidence on Iran's nuclear programme; there is extensive intelligence sharing among the two countries. Yet American officials estimated a much longer time horizon – five years – for the development of a nuclear weapon by Iran than did Israel's officials who estimated a year or two at most. The difference in threat perception is not explainable by the evidence but by the higher emotional loading of the likelihood of an Iranian bomb for Israel's leaders that shaped threat perception.

Building emotions – fear, anger and humiliation – into the analysis illuminates the complexity of designing threat-based strategies that are subtle and calibrated to likely emotional responses. Threat-based strategies that rely exclusively on rational calculation by an adversary and ignore the interaction among cognitive heuristics and emotional states, as well as the political and institutional context, are likely to misfire badly.[37]

Conclusion

There has been significant progress in the analysis of the close interconnections between cognition and emotion. Emotion and cognition are no longer conceived as alternative explanations, as they were as recently as a decade ago, but rather as complementary. What people feel influences what they perceive and the way they think.

This understanding of the interconnectedness of emotion and perception opens an important research agenda for scholars of international politics. First, scholars will have to consider the impact of fear, anger and humiliation upon threat perception at the individual level of leaders. As policy analysts grapple with the escalating tension between Iran and Israel, and between Iran and the United States, they should be alert to the strong likelihood that different kinds of emotions produce differences in threat perceptions which in turn produce different strategic scripts. Emotions refer not only to the intense flashes of the moment, but to the affective moods that persist over time. The troubled relationship between Iran and the United States and the inflammatory rhetoric that explodes episodically on Iran's part towards Israel set the 'hot' context for threat perception and for development of strategic scripts.

Sceptics may well ask: how important is the psychology of emotion and cognition in comparison to other explanations of threat perception? To ask this question is to ask a larger question: how important is agency in the explanation of these kinds of international outcomes? Once we move away from exclusively structural explanations and acknowledge a role for human agency, then any explanation of threat perception encompasses the analysis of feeling and information processing as essentials, as the core constitutive elements. The interesting question then becomes: what kinds of emotions have what kinds of impact upon information processing and perception, under what kinds of political conditions? When, for example, does fear-driven threat perception lead to risky behaviour, and when does it lead to risk-averse behaviour? When does humiliation-driven threat perception provoke anger and revenge, and when does it lead to retreat and passivity? Answers to these kinds of questions are critical to theories of all threat-based strategies. Scholars need to specify how emotion would modify existing theories as well as the range and types of emotions that matter.

More challenging will be integrating psychological theories into broader theories of international relations. This chapter began with an analysis of the inability of models of strategic interaction and bargaining theories to explain why the threat perception of Saddam Hussein escalated so dramatically and why the confrontation led to war. Rationalist accounts of strategic interaction cannot explain why American leaders perceived Iraq as so much more threatening in 2003 than in 1998.[38] These accounts privilege capabilities and intentions to explain changes in threat perception, but Iraq's capabilities did not grow significantly and the same leader remained in power. Rationalist theories do not give much weight to the difference in the beliefs of the Clinton and Bush administrations, yet the difference in beliefs between the senior leaders in the two administrations mattered enormously in the way they perceived the threat emanating from Saddam. Misrepresentation by the other side was far less important than self-delusion. The United States systematically discounted its own costs of fighting and Saddam ignored obvious signals of the Bush Administration's resolve. What matters is that these biases were motivated: 'Neither side wanted to know about itself or the other information that would have challenged its prior beliefs or slowed the march to war.'[39]

Lake's analysis of the patterns of threat perception and the road to war in 2003 leads him to call for a 'behavioral theory of war', a suggestion very like the recommendation that psychological theories be integrated with models of strategic interaction.[40] Much of what is important in international relations – war and peace, deterrence and collaboration – is the result of strategic interaction. A focus on the emotional cognition of threat perception allows researchers to identify those psychological processes that are especially relevant to the development of leaders' strategic scripts.

Notes

1 Stephen Walt, 'Alliance formation and the balance of world power', *International Security*, Vol. 9, No. 4, (1985), pp. 3–43.

2 James D. Fearon, 'Rationalist explanations for war', *International Organization*, Vol. 49, No. 3, (1995), pp. 379–414; Thomas C. Schelling, *The Strategy of Conflict* (Cambridge, MA: Harvard University Press, 1960); Thomas C. Schelling, *Arms and Influence* (New Haven, CT: Yale University Press, 1966).

3 Robert Jervis, *Perception and Misperception in International Politics* (Princeton, NJ: Princeton University Press, 1976); Arthur A. Stein, 'When misperception matters', *World Politics*, Vol. 34, No. 4, (1982), 505–526.

4   Christoph O. Meyer, 'International terrorism as a force of homogenization? A constructivist approach to understanding cross-national threat perceptions and response', *Cambridge Review of International Affairs*, Vol. 22, No. 4, (2009), pp. 647–66.

5   Fearon (1995); Robert Powell, 'War as a commitment problem', *International Organization*, Vol. 60, (2006), pp. 169–203.

6   David A. Lake, 'Two cheers for bargaining theory: Assessing rationalist explanations of the Iraq War', *International Security*, Vol. 35, No. 3, (2011), pp. 7–52.

7   Robert Jervis, 'Cooperation under the security dilemma', *World Politics*, Vol. 30, No. 2, (1978), pp. 167–214; Charles L. Glaser, 'The security dilemma revisited', *World Politics*, Vol. 50, No. 1, 1997, pp. 171–201; Charles L. Glaser, 'Political consequences of military strategy: Expanding and refining the spiral and deterrence models', *World Politics*, Vol. 44, No. 4, (1992), pp. 497–538; Charles L. Glaser, *Rational Theory of International Politics* (Princeton, NJ: Princeton University Press, 2010); Andrew Kydd, 'Game theory and the spiral model', *World Politics*, Vol. 49, No. 3, (1997), pp. 371–400; Andrew Kydd, 'Sheep in sheep's clothing: Why security seekers do not fight each other', *Security Studies*, Vol. 7, No. 1, (1997), pp. 114–155; Andrew Kydd, *Trust and Mistrust in International Relations* (Princeton, NJ: Princeton University Press, 2005); Ken Booth and Nicholas J. Wheeler, *The Security Dilemma: Fear, cooperation and trust in world politics* (New York: Palgrave Macmillan, 2008); Shiping Tang, 'The security dilemma: A conceptual analysis', *Security Studies*, Vol. 18, No. 3, (2009), pp. 587–623; James D. Fearon, 'Two states, two types, two actions', *Security Studies*, Vol. 20, No. 3, (2011), pp. 431–40.

8   Charles L. Glaser and Chaim Kaufman, 'What is the offense–defense balance and can we measure it?', *International Security*, Vol. 22, No. 4, (1988), pp. 44–82; Jervis (1978).

9   Lake (2011).

10   Jervis (1976).

11   Barcuh Fischoff, 'Hindsight does not equal foresight: The effect of outcome knowledge on judgment under uncertainty', *Journal of Experimental Psychology: Human Perception and Performance*, Vol. 1, (1975), pp. 288–99.

12   Peter Evans, Harold Jacobsen and Robert Putnam (eds), *Double-edged Diplomacy: International Bargaining and Domestic Politics* (Berkeley: University of California Press, 1993).

13   Jervis (1976); Jack S. Levy, 'Political psychology and foreign policy', in David O. Sears, Leonie Huddy and Robert Jervis (eds) *Oxford Handbook of Political Psychology* (New York: Oxford University Press, 2003), p. 262.

14   Levy (2003), p. 262.

15   Daniel Kahneman, *Thinking, Fast and Slow* (New York: Farrar, Strauss & Giroux, 2011); Daniel Kahneman, Paul Slovic and Amos Tversky (eds), *Judgement under Uncertainty: Heuristics and Biases* (Cambridge: Cambridge University Press, 1982); Robin Hogarth and William M. Goldstein (eds),

Judgment and Decision Making: An interdisciplinary reader (Cambridge: Cambridge University Press, 1996); Robyn Dawes, 'Judgment and choice', in Daniel Gilbert, Susan Fiske and Gardner Lindzey (eds), *Handbook of Social Psychology* (New York: McGraw Hill, 1998); Reid Hastie and Robyn M. Dawes, *Rational Choice in an Uncertain World: The psychology of judgment and decision making* (Thousand Oaks, CA: Sage, 2001); Thomas Gilovich, Dale Griffin and Daniel Kahneman (eds), *Heuristics and Biases: The psychology of intuitive judgment* (Cambridge: Cambridge University Press, 2002).

16　Dawes (1998); Philip E. Tetlock, *Expert Political Judgment: How good is it? How can we know?* (Princeton, NJ: Princeton University Press, 2005).

17　Amos Tversky and Daniel Kahneman, 'Availability: A heuristic for judging frequency and probability', *Cognitive Psychology*, Vol. 5, No. 2, (1973), pp. 207–32; Richard E. Nisbett and Lee Ross, *Human Inference: Strategies and shortcomings of social judgment* (Englewood Cliffs, NJ: Prentice-Hall, 1980); Susan T. Fiske and Shelley E. Taylor, *Social Cognition* (Reading, MA: Addison Wesley, 1984); Robert Jervis, 'Representativeness in foreign policy judgments', *Political Psychology*, Vol. 7, No. 3, (1986), pp. 483–505; Detlof Von Winterfeldt and Ward Edwards, *Decision Analysis and Behavioral Research* (New York: Cambridge University Press, 1986).

18　Janet G. Stein, 'Calculation, miscalculation, and conventional deterrence, II: The view from Jerusalem', in Robert Jervis, Richard N. Lebow and Janet G. Stein (eds) *Psychology and Deterrence* (Baltimore, MD: Johns Hopkins University Press, 1985), pp. 60–88.

19　Nisbett and Ross (1980).

20　Jonathan Mercer, 'Emotional beliefs', *International Organization*, Vol. 64, No. 1, 2010, pp. 1–31; Jonathan Mercer, 'Rationality and psychology in international politics', *International Organization*, Vol. 59, No. 1, (2005), pp. 77–106.

21　Jonathan Mercer, *Reputation and International Politics* (Ithaca, NY: Cornell University Press, 1996); Mercer (2010).

22　Jacques E.C. Hymans, *The Psychology of Nuclear Proliferation: Identity, emotions, and foreign policy* (Cambridge: Cambridge University Press, 2006).

23　William J. Bennett, *Why We Fight: Moral clarity and the war on terrorism* (New York: Doubleday, 2002); Paul Saurette, 'You dissin me? Humiliation and post-9/11 global politics', *Review of International Studies*, Vol. 32, No. 3, (2006), pp. 495–522; Roland Blieker and Emma Hutchinson, 'Fear no more: Emotions and world politics', *Review of International Studies*, Vol. 34, Supplement 1, 2008, pp. 115–35; Neta C. Crawford, 'Human nature and world politics', *International Relations*, Vol. 23, No. 2, (2009), 271–88.

24　Peter H. Gries, *China's New Nationalism* (Berkeley, CA: University of California Press, 2004); Saurette (2006); Oded Löwenheim and Gadi Heimann, 'Revenge in international politics', *Security Studies*, Vol. 17, No. 4, (2008), pp. 685–724; Richard Ned Lebow, *Why Nations Fight: Past and future motives for war* (Cambridge: Cambridge University Press, 2010).

25 Rose McDermott, 'The feeling of rationality: The meaning of neuroscientific advances for political science', *Perspectives on Politics,* Vol. 2, No. 4, (2004), p. 692.

26 Joseph LeDoux, *The Emotional Brain: The mysterious underpinnings of emotional life* (New York: Simon & Schuster, 1996); Piotr Winkielman and Kent C. Berridge, 'Unconscious emotion', *Current Directions in Psychological Science,* Vol. 13, No. 3, (2004), pp. 120–23.

27 John A. Bargh, Shelly Chaiken, Paula Raymond and Charles Hymes, 'The automatic evaluation effect: Unconditional automatic attitude activation with a pronunciation task', *Journal of Experimental Social Psychology,* Vol. 32, (1996), pp. 104–28; John A. Bargh and Tanya L. Chartrand, 'The unbearable automacity of being', *American Psychologist,* Vol. 54, No. 7, (1999), pp. 462–79.

28 Kahneman (2011).

29 Nico H. Frijda, 'The laws of emotion'. *American Psychologist,* Vol. 43, No. 5, (1988), pp. 349–58; Leonard Berkowitz, 'Anger', in Tim Dalgleish and Michael J. Power (eds) *Handbook of Cognition and Emotion* (New York: Wiley, 1999), pp. 411–28.

30 John Tooby and Leda Cosmides, 'The evolutionary psychology of the emotions and their relationship to internal regulatory variables', in Michael Lewis, Jeanette M. Haviland-Jones and Lisa Feldman Barret (eds) *The Handbook of Emotions,* 3rd edn (New York: Guilford Press, 2003), pp. 114–37.

31 Jolie Baumann and David DeSteno, 'Emotion guided threat detection: Expecting guns where there are none', *Journal of Personality and Social Psychology,* Vol. 99, No. 4, (2010), pp. 595–610.

32 Saurette (2006), pp. 507–8.

33 Andrew Ross, 'Coming in from the cold: Constructivism and emotions', *European Journal of International Relations,* Vol. 12, No. 2, (June 2006), pp. 197–222.

34 Crawford (2009); Christoph O. Meyer and Alister Miskimmon, 'Perceptions and response to threats: Introduction', *Cambridge Review of International Affairs,* Vol. 22, No. 4, (2009), pp. 625–28.

35 Jervis *et al.* (1985); Richard N. Lebow and Janet G. Stein, *We All Lost the Cold War* (Princeton, NJ: Princeton University Press, 1994).

36 Mercer (2010).

37 Janet G. Stein, 'Building politics into psychology: The misperception of threat', *Political Psychology,* Vol. 9, No. 2, (1988), pp. 245–71.

38 Lake (2011), p. 28.

39 Ibid., p. 45.

40 Ibid., pp. 45–7; Levy (2003), pp. 272–3; Robert Jervis, 'Signaling and perception: Drawing inferences and projecting images', in K.R. Monroe (ed.) *Political Psychology* (Mahwah, NJ: Erlbaum, 2002), pp. 293–312.

CHAPTER THREE

Leadership scripts and policy-making

Jeffrey H. Michaels

Introduction

American and British policies towards the Middle East since the end of the Second World War have been motivated by material, geopolitical, ideological, psychological, and any number of other motives, often overlapping and thus reinforcing one another. Attributing monocausal explanations for these policies, most notably that they are all about securing oil supplies, has the inevitable consequence of providing a simplistic and misleading meta-narrative that eliminates the role of agency, not to mention rides roughshod over a rich historical record of policy-makers engaging in highly charged internal debates and performing a complex set of calculations in which numerous issues and interests are taken into consideration. But even if one were to assume, for instance, that the oil motive is the principal reason why the US and UK have been highly activist in a region that would otherwise receive considerably less interest without the presence of such a valuable commodity, the fact remains that there would still be no easy explanations for the highly diverse range of policies that have been pursued in order to secure access to that commodity, either during the Cold War or in the post-Cold War. There is no standard template for policy-makers in Washington and London to determine which countries in the Middle East are 'friends', which are 'enemies', those that can be dealt with by diplomacy versus others that are to be at the receiving end of economic sanctions, covert action, military coercion, or potentially regime change.

While these determinations are based in part on structural factors, such as domestic and international political constraints, availability of military forces and so forth, to say nothing of the policies of the individual countries themselves, there can be little doubt that they are also based on perceptions of the leaderships of these countries.

Perceptions of foreign leaders generally, and Middle East leaders specifically, are highly variable, with the same leader being viewed very differently over time even if their behaviour is relatively uniform. Depending on which American president or British prime minister is in power, certain leaders might be viewed as pariahs to be toppled, others as pariahs to be tolerated, engaged and that one can 'do business with', or even pariahs that can be converted into friends and fully rehabilitated. Alternatively, pariahs that were once friends to be maintained in power can be abandoned, particularly if perceptions of their utility change. Given the less than pluralistic nature of most Middle Eastern governments, it has often been the practice of American and British policy-makers to personalize their relationships with them. Policy-makers will hold particular views of the leaders of these countries, and these views can inform the policies crafted to deal with them. In some cases, the views of American and British leaders may be consistent with those of their political advisers and civil servants, and may also reflect the dominant views held by their country's political elites and population. In other cases, a leader's view may diverge from those held by their subordinates yet remain the dominant view driving policy if it is strongly held.

From a political psychology perspective, leadership perceptions not only help construct policy-makers' worldviews, they can also prescribe political behaviour, thus acting as 'scripts' in the making of policy. This chapter will begin by setting out some general propositions about the value of 'scripts' as an explanatory variable in policy decisions. It will then proceed to discuss both the theory and practice of why leaders and leadership perceptions matter. Finally, it will examine several sources of policy-makers' perceptions in order to enunciate the distinction between the expertise to which leaders have access (e.g. intelligence assessments, first-hand diplomatic reports, etc.), and the actual awareness, understanding and acceptance of this expertise by policy-makers when they make judgements about foreign leaders.

Scripts and international relations

Given that policy-makers rarely have either the time or the inclination to become well versed in the intricacies of foreign affairs, they tend to fall back on cognitive constructs or schemas that help them make sense of complex issues. Thus, when confronted with new objects or situations, policy-makers will reach back into their memories for the schema that is most relevant and then use this as a basis for understanding. As such, schemas provide a structure, imposing a cast of characters and their relationship to each other. Following from this, scripts provide a guide for handling particular types of situations, acting as a trigger for a series of actions.[1] In relation to foreign policy, depending on the script employed, certain expectations can be generated about the effects one's actions will have upon another actor, and the way they would likely respond. If such a script results in a positive outcome, policy-makers may choose to adopt it as their guide, whereas scripts that result in negative outcomes may induce caution. The effects of scripts on decision-making can be profound, as has been shown with the use of analogies and metaphors in relation to the American decision to escalate the war in Vietnam. Interestingly, even leaders who were consciously aware of the dangers of reasoning by analogy and metaphor remained unconsciously trapped in these mental constructs.[2]

The existence of schemas and scripts does not cause foreign policy behaviour. It merely predisposes individual policy-makers in certain directions and away from other directions.[3] This is relevant for understanding many foreign policy decisions; not just the road taken, but also the road not taken. In situations where a great deal of 'trust' is called for (e.g. peace agreements, arms control), having a belief that the adversary is untrustworthy and unreliable may rule out or complicate negotiations. Furthermore, if one truly believes in the duplicity of one's adversary, then any conciliatory gesture on their part may be interpreted as a trick, therefore to be dismissed, or may be viewed as a sign of weakness. On the other hand, policy-makers may feel that only a coercive strategy is viable if they believe their adversaries will think that any attempt at inducement represented weakness. In the aftermath of the Second World War, both British and American policy-makers have repeatedly invoked the 'Munich analogy' in both their public rhetoric and internal deliberations to justify taking a hard line against an adversary, because the logic of the analogy dictates that 'appeasing' an unscrupulous adversary will only make matters worse rather than better. Although it is well known that the 'Munich analogy' is often misused or misunderstood, it remains prominent in policy-makers' discourse, but the very fact that it is invoked at all is the result of attitudes about the adversary leadership's character, which may be valid or invalid. Consequently, states can fail to cooperate, even when they have compatible preferences, because policy-makers make incorrect inferences about their motives and intentions.[4] While accurate perceptions of an adversary would seem to be fundamental to successful deterrence and coercion, inaccurate perceptions can result in the use of inappropriate policy tools that undermine attempts to deter or coerce.[5]

To give one historical example of the importance of scripts in US decision-making, it is worth briefly reflecting on several American views of North Vietnamese leader Ho Chi Minh and their implications for US strategy in the mid-1960s. In early 1965, President Lyndon B. Johnson analogized Ho Chi Minh to George Meany, head of the American Federation of Labor-Congress of Industrial Organizations (AFL-CIO), in relation to a plan for a massive investment in the Mekong Delta that was somewhat akin to the Tennessee Valley Authority in the 1930s. According to one account, Johnson was convinced that Ho Chi Minh would act like Meany and accept this carrot, thereby forestalling the perceived need to increase American bombing of the North.[6] Even so, while the 'charitable' Meany analogy may have been uppermost in the president's mind at that moment in time, Johnson also regularly used less savoury language and analogies with which to describe Ho Chi Minh. Another view, held by Walt Rostow, advocated the idea that bombing the North would lead to 'success'. This was based on the belief that 'Ho [Chi Minh] has an industrial complex to protect: he is no longer a guerrilla fighter with nothing to lose'.[7] Other influential advocates of bombing, such as Thomas Schelling, do not appear to have had any detailed knowledge of the North Vietnamese leadership, preferring instead to employ a universal template of bargaining and signalling behaviour which presupposed that those leaders would act in a 'rational' way.[8] At a more fundamental level were the American beliefs about Ho Chi Minh's relationship with the Soviet Union and China, and the extent to which he was a pawn of 'international communism' rather than 'independent'. Former US Defense Secretary Robert S. McNamara reflected in a 1996 interview that

> today I believe that Ho Chi Minh was more of a nationalist, more of a Tito, than a servant or a follower of Khrushchev. But at that time, we looked upon him as a vassal of the Soviets. ... There's a real possibility that if we had understood him better we could have avoided this war, or, after it started, we could have terminated it.[9]

McNamara also noted that 'we equated Ho Chi Minh not with Marshal Tito but with Fidel Castro'.[10] Had the Tito analogy dominated the mainstream view held by policy-makers, the American approach to the Vietnam conflict may have proceeded along very different lines.

As these examples from Vietnam highlight, policy-makers made important decisions on the war while holding many different ideas about the adversary leader: what his political views were, how firm they were held, and how he would respond to threats versus inducements. For some policy-makers, the adversary leader was not referred to in personal terms, but was instead discussed as an abstract concept. In other words, a personal description was sometimes employed, thus referring to Ho Chi Minh specifically, whereas at other times impersonal references were made to a generic North Vietnamese leadership. This raises the question of the degree to which American policy-makers chose to understand their adversaries as human beings, as opposed to rational actors derived from a political science script. Regardless, even in instances when they were dealing with an abstract adversary, policy-makers would still employ schemas and scripts, and these would serve to inform policy prescriptions.

Why leadership perceptions matter

In their analysis of President George W. Bush's decision to launch the 2003 Iraq War, psychologists have arrived at a number of conclusions as to his motivation. Among the more prominent of the conclusions reached was that, from an 'Oedipal perspective on adult phallic narcissism', Bush was trying to demonstrate his superiority over his father, George H.W. Bush, who had fought Saddam Hussein in 1991, but failed to slay him. It has also been noted that George W. Bush 'hated' Saddam, not for the least of reasons that he perceived him as the would-be assassin of his father.[11] While this psychological account of an American president's motives is not sufficient in itself to explain the decision to invade Iraq, it does nevertheless highlight that because of the psychological factors that were unique to Bush, he was more likely to take a belligerent approach to dealing with Saddam than some other US president would have done under similar circumstances. Indeed, it has often been remarked that had Al Gore rather than Bush won the US presidential election in 2000, the Iraq War would never have taken place. On a related point, it is worth observing that some American presidents have developed 'obsessions' with foreign leaders that bear no relation to the views of the political and bureaucratic establishment. Examples of this phenomenon have included Kennedy's perception of the threat posed by Fidel Castro, and Nixon's views on Salvador Allende.

Attempting to understand international relations through the prisms of leadership and psychology has traditionally not sat well with mainstream IR theorists who have preferred to focus on the structure of the international system, and to a lesser extent on bureaucratic processes, but have avoided looking at individuals, much less the psychology of individuals, as part of their explanatory equation. For example, realists tend to emphasize the rationality of the state as an idealized unitary actor in pursuit of security in the anarchic international system. Moreover, they argue that factors such as domestic politics and other institutional and bureaucratic constraints make the role of a leader's personality largely irrelevant.

Among the limitations of this approach to international relations is that it does not take into account the presence of a powerful leader who is able to translate their own 'impulsive, personality driven behavior into official acts of the state'.[12] For instance, during the Cold War, many Sovietologists explained Soviet behaviour in terms of a monolithic, bureaucratic and purposely driven state based on an ideology. This theoretical approach included the idea that Soviet leaders were guided in their approach to foreign affairs by an 'operational code', or rules they believed 'necessary for effective political conduct'.[13] According to this line of argument, Soviet leaders conformed to some criterion of rationality. Yet, such an explanation cannot account for, to take one prominent example, the psychological issues that were particular to Joseph Stalin's leadership of the Soviet state.[14] Similar debates have also occurred in relation to other 'supreme' leaders, such as Adolf Hitler, with some arguing that he was a rational German statesman, while others discuss his 'unique' personality that differentiated him from other German leaders.[15]

It could be argued that the importance of a leader's psychology to the foreign policy of a country only applies to particular types of political systems, such as dictatorships or monarchies, but not to democracies. In this view, regime type is the dominant consideration. However, this approach presupposes that leaders of democracies are unexceptional, or to put it another way, that any American leader, and not just Richard Nixon, could have 'gone to China'. In a British context, it would be difficult to make the case that Churchill, Eden and Thatcher were irrelevant to the making of British foreign policy towards Germany, Egypt and Argentina respectively. But even this claim differentiates between 'exceptional' leaders and more 'weak' or 'run of the mill' leaders who are less charismatic or who do not have any strong views on international affairs. However, the 'unexceptional' leaders should not be discounted as unimportant. On the contrary, if it is assumed that if strong and bellicose leaders not only affect the actions of their own states but also shape the reactions of other nations, which must respond to that leader's aggressiveness, then could not the reverse of this same principle hold true in relation to 'weak' leaders or 'nonentities'? Therefore, regardless of whether leaders are, or are at least perceived to be, 'exceptional' or 'unexceptional', they are still relevant to explaining state behaviour, and this should apply to all leaders regardless of regime type.

There is though an alternative interpretation in which leadership perceptions do not seem to matter. By this interpretation, leadership perceptions are a function of time and circumstance, and thus leaders who are perceived to be 'evil' at one moment in time can later become more palatable, or vice versa, when national interests dictate this to be the case. Just as this was true for American and British perceptions of 'Uncle Joe' Stalin during the Second World War, it has also been the case for many Middle East leaders, such as with Saddam Hussein in the 1980s. However, such an interpretation should not negate the value of leaders, or perceptions of them. Even if one takes into consideration the realist motives which dictate that a former enemy has become a friend, such as fighting against some other adversary, there will likely remain problems of intra-Alliance trust and bargaining that ensure leadership perceptions remain highly relevant as an explanatory factor. Furthermore, absent a common enemy, cooperation can break down, especially if the leaders feel they still cannot trust one another to act in a mutually beneficial manner.

Personalities and foreign policy practice

An important distinction should now be made between the role of personalities in the study of international relations compared to their role in the practice of foreign policy. As Henry Kissinger remarked, 'As a professor, I tended to think of history as run by impersonal forces. But when you see it in practice, you see the difference personalities make.'[16] Several examples serve to highlight this point.

First, it is almost inevitable that leaders personalize in their understanding of foreign governments. For reasons of protocol alone, when leaders visit foreign countries, attend international summits, negotiate agreements and so forth, their primary interlocutors are other foreign leaders. Put another way, leaders have greater interaction with the 'powerful' than the 'powerless'. Just as one puts a name to a face, leaders represent the official face of the countries they head. In the two major conflicts of the past decade, namely Iraq and Afghanistan, dealing with the leadership in Baghdad and Kabul has been a major preoccupation, albeit an extremely contentious one, of both the US and UK governments. American presidents and British prime ministers will have dealt with Nouri al-Maliki and Hamid Karzai, but have had much less interaction or knowledge of the Iraqi or Afghan political systems they represent. Conversely, with the change-over from the Bush to Obama administrations, both Maliki and Karzai had to adapt to a new president who had a different style and political views than his predecessor.[17]

Second, governments care a great deal about maintaining the stability and continuity of 'friendly' governments and either altering the leadership of governments deemed to be 'unfriendly', or seeking to change their views. In each case, the issue of political succession is of great concern. In both the US and UK, this interest in promoting or maintaining friendly leaderships has been seen as a generational problem and institutionalized in programmes that provide educational and networking opportunities to future leaders of foreign countries.[18] In their efforts to promote friendly leaders, policy-makers will take a number of factors into consideration. In terms of the views held by new leaders, particularly those in the Middle East, American and British policy-makers will be interested in knowing whether they are 'nationalists', 'radicals', 'reformers', 'anti-American', 'anti-British', 'anti-Israel', 'anti-Western', etc. The problem of determining whether these leaders will play an active role in policy-making, or whether they are simply figureheads, is also an important factor. In some countries, for instance, a civilian government may be technically in charge, but the real power rests in the hands of the military, in which case dealing with the military leadership will take precedence. Likewise, new leaders who are perceived to be politically weak, or have health problems, may occupy a limited time in power, thereby increasing the risk of a looming succession crisis, and triggering the requirement to identify and develop good relations with the next leader.

Third, supporting reliable leaders tends to trump the promotion of a preferred political system, especially in countries with important geopolitical and economic significance. During the course of the Cold War, and beyond, US policy in many parts of the world supported friendly but authoritarian regimes as this was deemed a better option than risking the emergence of an alternative form of government, to include democracy, that would have less friendly relations with the US.[19] Again, however, regime type can be irrelevant. In cases where there is a democratic regime with free elections, an outside power may prefer one candidate and provide support (e.g. overt legitimatization and advice, covert funding, etc.) while attempting to undermine the other candidate (e.g. delegitimatization).

Finally, leaders matter when friends are removed from power and adversaries come into power. These situations are often referred to as 'foreign policy crises'. This was most certainly the case with the overthrow of the Shah of Iran and the rise of the Ayatollah Khomeini. For many years the Shah served as one of America's most important 'clients' in the Middle East.[20] One of the key problems in this relationship was that the US relied on the Shah to such a degree that as the decades passed they became complacent about the prospects of his removal from power. The inability to predict the Shah's fall is still regarded as one of the CIA's most important intelligence failures. Among the reasons why CIA analysts misread the severity of the political situation in Iran was that the Shah had not followed the 'script' of cracking down on the opposition that was sparking unrest at the time and therefore the situation was believed to be relatively under control. They also believed he was a strong and decisive leader, a view that sharply contrasted with analyses of the Shah from earlier decades.[21] In 2011, the popular uprisings in Egypt that aimed to overthrow Hosni Mubarak, who represented a similar 'island of stability' for US strategy in the Middle East, sparked another crisis for American foreign policy-makers. During the course of the Egyptian crisis, the analogy of the fall of the Shah was repeatedly invoked. The looming question for American policy-makers was whether to support the friendly authoritarian leader in power, or to support the protesters seeking his ouster, thereby risking an unfriendly leader coming to power.[22] Five years earlier, American officials had to deal with a similar dilemma following the victory of Hamas in the 2006 Palestinian elections, even though Washington had openly backed Mahmoud Abbas. This dilemma was one that not only negatively reflected on the Bush Administration's policies in the Middle East, but also raised a more fundamental question about its willingness to support democracies given its outspoken rhetoric on the subject.[23] Each of these cases highlights not only America's traditional emphasis on supporting individual leaders, but also the foreign policy crises that result when these leaders are seriously challenged or overthrown. Indeed, as has been demonstrated by US reactions to the 'Arab Spring', the philosophical dilemma of whether to support 'Arab leaders' versus the 'Arab street' continues to bedevil policy-makers.

The Sources of leadership perceptions and their impact

Although the examples referred to here highlight some of the many ways personalities are deemed important in the practice of foreign policy-making, it remains to be demonstrated where the sources of leaders' perceptions of their counterparts originate, and to show the negative effects on foreign policy when these perceptions prove misleading or inaccurate. However, before doing so, it is important to note that just as 'accurate' perceptions of a foreign leader do not by themselves constitute the only, much less the most important reason behind foreign policy success, nor are 'inaccurate' perceptions similarly responsible for foreign policy failure. At a minimum, it is probably fair to say that 'inaccurate' perceptions may lead to less optimal outcomes than having 'accurate' perceptions, but this will be determined by the specific nature of the situation, and the players, issues and stakes involved.

An extreme example of the importance of having an 'accurate' perception of one's adversary may be found in the relationship between John F. Kennedy and Nikita Khrushchev during the Cuban Missile Crisis. During this crisis, in which the stakes could not be higher, 'either man could cause the other to fail; each would have to cooperate if they were to succeed'.[24] At the centre of any understanding of the events that sparked the crisis as well as the 'signalling' and 'bargaining' that occurred during the crisis itself were the leaders' perceptions of: one another's motives, their level of control over hardliners in their governments, and likely reactions to particular moves. The questions of how Kennedy perceived Khrushchev, and what the sources of these perceptions were, are therefore rather crucial to understanding the decisions that were made. It is notable that in late 1960, the CIA had sponsored a seminar to examine Khrushchev from a psychological perspective and produced a report, the conclusions of which were later sent to Kennedy prior to the 1961 Vienna summit. The analysis concluded that the Soviet leader was 'predictable', rather than a 'wily communist Machiavelli' as many officials in the Kennedy Administration viewed him, and offered insights into how to deal with him successfully. It remains unknown whether Kennedy had read this profile of Khrushchev, and if so, what influence it may have had on the president's understanding of his Soviet counterpart, relative to other sources informing his perceptions.[25] At the very least, there is no evidence that American policy-makers referred back to the Khrushchev study in their efforts to resolve the missile crisis, even though it might otherwise have provided useful guidance in their dealings with him.

In this regard, a crucial point to note is that leaders' perceptions of their foreign counterparts derive from numerous sources, and that the possession of expertise does not guarantee that it will be utilized. Similar to the public, leaders will have access to news media portrayals and other open sources. They may also rely on accounts from trusted confidantes and possibly their own first-hand experience of dealing with these leaders on a previous occasion.[26] Unlike the public, leaders will have access to other types of information, to include diplomatic reporting and intelligence assessments.

Often, the most comprehensive insights into a foreign leader's personality are the psychological profiles produced by intelligence agencies, such as the Khrushchev study. In the US, the first effort to produce a psychological profile on a foreign leader was the report prepared in the middle of the Second World War on Adolf Hitler by Walter Langer, a psychoanalyst working for the Office of Strategic Services. However, the Langer study suffered from three fundamental problems. First, a great deal of the information on which the conclusions were based came from unreliable sources. There were also important methodological problems of doing 'at-a-distance profiling' compared with having a direct patient–psychologist relationship. Second, the period of time allotted to Langer and his team to conduct the study was too limited.[27] Lastly, and perhaps most crucially, by the time the psychological study had been produced, it was probably too late in the war to have any significant impact upon US policy.

These limitations would also affect other psychological studies of foreign leaders produced with the intent of informing policy-makers. Although the CIA eventually formalized the production of psychological profiles, there would appear to be only a handful of cases in which these profiles have served to inform American leaders. Most notably among these was the CIA profile of Anwar el Sadat and Menachem Begin that was given to President Jimmy Carter in advance of the 1978 Camp David negotiations.[28] As noted in the case of the Hitler study, psychological profiles can take considerable time to prepare, and therefore plenty of lead-time must exist.

In 'crises', such as the death of a foreign leader, where advanced warning is not possible, and profiles for the new leader have not been written, the fall-back option is to rely on 'biographic intelligence'. Usually consisting of a short paper that provides personal details and career highlights, these documents can also include a brief description of the political views of leaders.[29] By their very nature, these documents convey to policy-makers the 'bare essentials' rather than a sophisticated analysis. However, given the time pressures policy-makers are under, especially during crises, their ability to read and comprehend more lengthy analyses is fairly limited. As such, it is fair to assume that as far as the utility of intelligence assessments of foreign leaders is concerned, 'biographic intelligence' documents probably have a greater impact on policy-makers' knowledge of the background of foreign leaders than psychological profiles do.[30] Similarly, mainstream diplomatic reporting and intelligence assessments will normally include their own judgements about a foreign leader's behaviour, and these judgements also probably feed into policy-makers' perceptions.

Regardless of the official sources of information available to policy-makers, it is unclear about the extent to which they influence their views of foreign leaders, especially when compared to non-official sources. In crisis situations, policy-makers simply don't have time to perform rigorous analyses based on all the information they could potentially call on in order to make an ideal judgement. Even in non-crisis situations, despite detailed knowledge being available, experts must still truncate their views in order to convey this knowledge to the non-expert politician, such as by providing a summary or narrative. Yet it is not guaranteed that once politically unbiased expert knowledge is conveyed, it will be understood, believed or able to overturn any pre-existing beliefs of policy-makers. For instance, a political leader who reasons in black-and-white or ideological terms may reject expert knowledge that is highly nuanced. Assuming they have had little or no personal contact, leaders may extrapolate from their own perspectives in trying to understand their counterparts.[31] Furthermore, some leaders will prefer to use their own intuition, whether due to reasons of ego and belief in their superior insight, or even a lack of trust in, or understanding of, official analyses.

Arguably the most notorious case of a leader's intuition of another leader's intent overriding available evidence to the contrary was Stalin's belief that Hitler would not invade the Soviet Union. Thinking that Hitler was a rational leader in the tradition of Bismarck, and that he would not be so foolish as to wage war on two fronts, Stalin dismissed evidence warning of an imminent invasion. After the war, referring to his pre-war views of Hitler, Stalin reportedly remarked, 'When you're trying to make a decision, NEVER put yourself into the mind of the other person because if you do, you can make a terrible mistake.'[32] Political psychologists have also noted that among the reasons why Stalin was unwilling to distrust Hitler's intentions had to do with his own psychological identification with the German leader.[33]

The example of Stalin's perceptions of Hitler raises several points that are applicable to other cases as well. First, although the Soviets possessed hard intelligence of German intentions, this was considered irrelevant. Instead, the Soviet leader trusted his instincts. Second, the source of Stalin's unusual relationship with Hitler could be explained by psychological factors. Third, based on Stalin's view of Hitler, a script was developed that described his likely behaviour. Placed in a more recent context, a similar pattern emerges when examining the case of George W. Bush's views of Saddam. Rather than intelligence informing the president's view, the intelligence was made to conform to the president's view. As noted previously, psychological factors were also crucial to Bush's view of Saddam. Finally, given his views of Saddam, or perhaps of his own destiny, regime change, rather than tolerating the status quo, became the dominant script. Admittedly, many other factors were involved in Bush's decision to invade Iraq. For instance, had 9/11 not occurred, Bush would almost certainly have found it difficult to mobilize support for military action. On the other hand, it is hard to make a case that Bush's views of Saddam were not integral to the decision to go to war.

Conclusion

The concept of 'scripts' provides a useful tool for enhancing an understanding of US and UK policy towards the Middle East, as well as international relations more generally. Although leadership perceptions can hardly be viewed as the only or even the most important factor in determining US–UK policies, they have still played a crucial role in influencing general policy preferences. Unfortunately, the scholarly literature, particularly in the field of political psychology, has limited its focus to studying the psychology of individual leaders, without any significant examination of policy-makers' perceptions of other leaders, much less how those perceptions influenced policy decisions.

The history of US and UK foreign policy in the region has been characterized by an emphasis on dealing with individual leaders, and their dynasties or regimes, while minimizing efforts to promote more pluralistic political systems. Reliance on these leaders is predicated not only on a belief about their stability, but also on beliefs about the nature of the opposition. Indeed, it is common sense that governments will be unwilling to risk backing someone whom they perceive to be a loser, unless the prospect of dealing with an empowered opposition is viewed as a far worse possibility. As has been demonstrated in numerous instances in their relations with

Middle Eastern governments, both the US and UK have entertained certain negative beliefs about many opposition groups, leading them to prefer maintaining the status quo.

In addition to friends, policy-makers have also developed scripts for adversaries. These scripts have been based on assessments about the adversary's intentions, survivability, rationality, trustworthiness, ability to do deals with, the degree of control they exercise, what they value, are they an immediate threat or long-term menace, and whether or not they are amenable to persuasion by means of bribery or coercion. In cases where the adversary was considered a 'known quantity', the idea of 'the devil you know' may have been seen as preferable to disturbing the status quo, thereby risking a potentially worse successor. In some instances, deterrence was deemed preferable to military action. In others, negotiation was viewed as a tenable option. Alternatively, in cases where neither a tenuous peace nor outright war was considered appropriate, covert action, perhaps in conjunction with other policy levers such as economic sanctions, provided the best option. At times, the scripts that policy-makers have of their adversaries may be based on very sketchy, if not outright skewed knowledge of them. In such cases, negative consequences are bound to result. With no shortage of cases where American and British policy-makers keep 'getting it wrong', and the ever-present risk of future war in the region, the need for paying more attention to improving these scripts is a pressing one.

Notes

1   Deborah Welch Larson, 'The Role of Belief Systems and Schemas in Foreign Policy Decision-making', *Political Psychology*, Vol. 15, No. 1, (March 1994), pp. 17–33.

2   Yuen Foong Khong, *Analogies at War: Korea, Munich, Dien Bien Phu, and the Vietnam decisions of 1965* (Princeton, NJ: Princeton University Press, 1992); Keith L. Shimko, 'Metaphors and Foreign Policy Decision Making', *Political Psychology*, Vol. 15, No. 4, (December 1994), pp. 655–71.

3   J. Philipp Rosenberg, 'Presidential Beliefs and Foreign Policy Decision-making: Continuity during the Cold War Era', *Political Psychology*, Vol. 7, No. 4, (December 1986), pp. 749–50.

4   Deborah Welch Larson, 'Trust and Missed Opportunities in International Relations', *Political Psychology*, Vol. 18, No. 3, (September 1997), p. 701.

5   Robert Jervis, 'Deterrence and Perception', *International Security*, Vol. 7, No. 3, Winter 1982–3, p. 3; Barry R. Schneider, 'Deterring International Rivals from War and Escalation', in Schneider and Jerrold M. Post (eds) 'Know Thy Enemy: Profiles of Adversary Leaders and Their Strategic Cultures', USAF Counterproliferation Center, Maxwell Air Force Base, Alabama, (July 2003), pp. 1–15.

6 Lloyd C. Gardener, *Pay Any Price: Lyndon Johnson and the wars for Vietnam* (Chicago, IL: Ivan R. Dee, 1995), p. 197.

7 David Milne, '"Our Equivalent of Guerrilla Warfare": Walt Rostow and the Bombing of North Vietnam, 1961–1968', *Journal of Military History*, Vol. 71, No. 1, (January 2007), pp. 169–203.

8 Fred Kaplan, 'All Pain, No Gain: Tom Schelling's Little-known Role in the Vietnam War', *Slate*, (11 October 2005). Schelling noted that there was 'a poverty of knowledge about Vietnam. ... There was a quality of benightedness, not only among the populace, but even among those in foreign policy. This was almost unique to dealing with North Vietnam.' Quoted in Stanley Hoffmann, Samuel P. Huntington, Ernest R. May, Richard N. Neustadt and Thomas C. Schelling, 'Vietnam Reappraised', *International Security*, Vol. 6, No. 1 (Summer 1981), p. 13.

9 'A Life in Public Service: Conversation with Robert McNamara'. Interview by Harry Kreisler, (16 April 1996). Available at: http://globetrotter.berkeley.edu/ McNamara/mcnamara7.html.

10 Robert S. McNamara, *In Retrospect: The tragedy and lessons of Vietnam* (New York: Vintage Books, 1996), p. 33.

11 Dan P. McAdams, *George W. Bush and the Redemptive Dream: A Psychological Portrait* (Oxford: Oxford University Press, 2010), pp. 3–14, 77–8; Justin A. Frank, *Bush on the Couch: Inside the Mind of the US President* (London: Politico's Publishing, 2006), pp. 113, 146–7.

12 Raymond Birt, 'Personality and Foreign Policy: The Case of Stalin', *Political Psychology*, Vol. 14, No. 4, (December 1993), pp. 618.

13 Nathan Leites, 'The Operational Code of the Politburo', The RAND Corporation, 1951. Can be accessed online at: http://www.rand.org/content/ dam/rand/pubs/commercial_books/2007/RAND_CB104-1.pdf.

14 Birt, pp. 610–11; Robert C. Tucker, *The Soviet Political Mind: Stalinism and Post-Stalin Change* (London: George Allen & Unwin, 1972), pp. 205–5.

15 For a discussion of this point, see Daniel L. Byman and Kenneth M. Pollack, 'Let Us Now Praise Great Men: Bringing the Statesman Back In', *International Security*, Vol. 25, No. 4, (Spring 2001), pp. 115–21.

16 Cited in Walter Isaacson, *Kissinger: A biography* (New York: Simon & Schuster, 1992), p. 13.

17 Ahmed Rashid, 'How Obama Lost Karzai', *Foreign Policy*, March/April 2011; Jackson Diehl, 'Where Are Obama's Foreign Confidants?', *Washington Post*, 8 March 2010.

18 See, for instance, Giles Scott-Smith, *Networks of Empire: The US State Department's Foreign Leader Program in the Netherlands, France, and Britain 1950–70* (Brussels: Peter Lang, 2008). In the case of Britain, members of the Jordanian royal family, to take one example, have been trained at Sandhurst. It was also revealed that the Foreign Office had lobbied for Muammar Gaddafi's son Saif al-Islam to be admitted to Oxford. See: 'The Woolf Inquiry: An inquiry into the LSE's links with Libya and lessons to be learned',

(October 2011), p. 28, Fn. 12. Can be accessed online at: http://www.lse. ac.uk/newsAndMedia/woolf/pdf/woolfReport.pdf. The British Council runs other programmes for 'young leaders'.

19 David. F. Schmitz, *Thank God They're on our Side: The United States and right-wing dictatorships 1921–1965* (Chapel Hill, NC: University of North Carolina Press, 1999); David. F. Schmitz, *The United States and Right-wing Dictatorships, 1965–1989* (Cambridge: Cambridge University Press, 2006).

20 Mark Gasiorowski, *US Foreign Policy and the Shah: Building a Client State in Iran* (Ithaca, NY: Cornell University Press, 1991).

21 Robert Jervis, *Why Intelligence Fails: Lessons from the Iranian Revolution and the Iraq War* (Ithaca, NY: Cornell University Press, 2010), pp. 31–123.

22 Kai Bird, 'Obama's "Shah" Problem', *Slate*, 30 January 2011; Ronen Bergman, 'Lessons on Egypt from Carter and the Shah', *Wall Street Journal*, 1 February 2011.

23 Steven R, Weisman, 'Rice Admits US Underestimated Hamas Strength', *New York Times*, 30 January 2006.

24 Graham Allison and Philip Zelikow, *Essence of Decision: Explaining the Cuban Missile Crisis, Second Edition* (New York: Longman, 1999), p. 355.

25 Bryant Wedge, 'Khrushchev Undergoes Analysis From Afar', *Washington Post*, 27 October 1968. Referring to the Khrushchev study, this participant of the CIA seminar wrote: 'I believe the national leaders should have access to personality judgments of other national leaders, since an adequate understanding of "the other fellow" may determine the fate of mankind.'

26 Following a December 1984 visit to the UK by Mikhail Gorbachev in which he met Margaret Thatcher, the latter famously remarked: 'I like Mr. Gorbachev; we can do business together.' In her memoirs, Thatcher noted of the meeting: 'His line was no different from what I would have expected. His style was. As the day wore on I came to understand that it was the style far more than the Marxist rhetoric which expressed the substance of the personality beneath. I found myself liking him.' Thatcher's description of his visit to Chequers may be found in her autobiography, *The Downing Street Years* (London: Harper Collins, 1993), pp. 459–63.

27 Walter C. Langer, *The Mind of Adolf Hitler: The Secret Wartime Report* (New York: Basic Books, 1972). For a critical view, see Hans W. Gatzke, 'Hitler and Psychohistory', *American Historical Review*, Vol. 78, No. 2, April 1973, pp. 394–401.

28 Jerrold M. Post, *The Psychological Assessment of Political Leaders with Profiles of Saddam Hussein and Bill Clinton* (Ann Arbor: The University of Michigan Press, 2006), pp. 39–61. According to Post, in 1965 the CIA started a pilot programme based in the Psychiatric Staff of its Office of Medical Services to assess the personalities of foreign leaders. This was eventually replaced by the Center for the Analysis of Personality and Political Behavior in the Directorate of Intelligence, and later renamed the Political Psychology Division.

29 An example of this type of intelligence document that includes the biographic data of Chilean leader Augusto Pinochet may be found online at: http://www.

gwu.edu/~nsarchiv/NSAEBB/NSAEBB212/197501%20DIA%20Pinochet%20
bio%20(full).pdf.

30 A search of databases of US declassified documents unearthed hundreds of
examples of 'biographic intelligence' whereas there was a distinct absence
of psychological profiles. From the end of the Second World War until the
early 1960s, for instance, the State Department's Bureau of Intelligence and
Research (the name underwent several changes during this period) maintained
a Division of Biographic Information (later transferred to the CIA) with
specialists who covered Soviet and Chinese leaders, among others. It is unclear
whether the UK government had a similar reliance on biographic intelligence.

31 Margaret G. Hermann and Joe D. Hagan, 'International Decision Making:
Leadership Matters', *Foreign Policy*, No. 110, (Spring 1998), p. 134.

32 Simon Sebag Montefiore, *Stalin: The Court of the Red Tsar* (London:
Phoenix, 2004), p. 357.

33 Birt, pp. 618–19; Robert C. Tucker, *Stalin in Power: The revolution from
above, 1928–1941* (New York: W. W. Norton, 1992), pp. 620–5.

CHAPTER FOUR

Hitler on the Nile?

British and American Perceptions of the Nasser Regime, 1952–70

Nigel Ashton

Introduction

Writing from the British Embassy in Cairo on 25 February 1963, Ambassador Harold Beeley offered British Foreign Secretary Lord Home a sophisticated analysis of 'Nasser and "Nasserism" in Relation to British Interests'.[1] While President Gamal Abdel Nasser was hostile to British interests, he argued, his main purpose was the advancement of his own ambitions. This meant that he did not give top priority to overturning British positions in the region. Attempting to put himself in Nasser's place, an exercise in empathy rarely carried out by British politicians and officials during this period, Beeley wrote: 'I sometimes feel that he approaches us rather like a police officer giving a reformed criminal the benefit of the doubt.' 'Nasser,' argued Beeley, 'will not mount a major offensive against our positions in the Arab world unless his own interests urgently require it.' Nor was he responsible for all instability or the instigation of revolution in the region. Rather, he tended to respond to events where possible to advance his own interests.

If this analysis was correct, Beeley asked, how should Britain frame its policy towards the Egyptian President? Given the central importance of Nasser as an Arab nationalist leader, if Britain continued to pursue a consistent policy of opposing Nasserism, it risked being seen as blankly opposing Arab nationalism in general. What Britain should do instead was to adopt an approach similar to that of the United States, which would involve seeking a 'reasonable working relationship with President Nasser'. This approach would also have the benefit of improving cooperation with the Americans, who might thus be more likely to support Britain in any future regional crisis.

Beeley's dispatch reached the desk of Prime Minister Harold Macmillan on 15 March 1963. One unfortunate effect of the wound in the hand Macmillan had received during the First World War is that his handwriting bears a strong resemblance to the passage of an intoxicated spider across the page. But the annotation he scribbled on Beeley's dispatch is clearly legible: 'For Nasser read Hitler and it's all very familiar.'[2]

Given the apparent disconnection between Macmillan's annotation and Beeley's message, we are left to consider two possibilities. Either the Prime Minister had not read or fully digested Beeley's analysis and thus responded on the basis of preconceived, ingrained prejudices. Or, he had read the paper, but was so out of sympathy with its conclusions that he scribbled an angry dissenting note. Either way, Macmillan's characterization reflected a consistent strand in British thinking about Nasser which transcended the Suez crisis and ran through British analyses well into the 1960s. Nasser was a type of 1930s fascist dictator, with the only point of debate being whether he could more appropriately be termed an Arab Mussolini or an Arab Hitler. In fact, Macmillan's predecessor Anthony Eden tended to prefer the Mussolini analogy, noting in private conversation in January 1956 that, like Mussolini, Nasser's object 'was to be a Caesar from the Gulf to the Atlantic and kick us out of it all'.[3]

British views of Nasser

How can we explain what in hindsight appears to have been an obvious misperception? One part of the explanation for such characterizations lies in the concept of what Donald Cameron Watt termed 'historical generations'.[4] British leaders, such as Anthony Eden and Harold Macmillan, had cut their political teeth during the 1930s. Moreover, both men had established reputations as anti-appeasers. To this extent it is perhaps not surprising that they applied the lessons of the 1930s out of context when confronting the challenge posed by nationalism in the Middle East during the 1950s and 1960s. Further sustenance to this line of argument might appear to be given by the change in tone between the Conservative governments led by Eden, Macmillan and Douglas-Home, and the Labour government of Harold

Wilson with regard to Nasser. The change in government also marked something of a generational shift from governments led by men born before or around the turn of the twentieth century, and who entered Parliament in the 1920s, to those born after the outbreak of the First World War, and who entered Parliament after the Second World War.

While Wilson held Nasser in some distaste this was in large measure a function of his personal pro-Israeli sympathies rather than a legacy of experiences in the 1930s. Successive foreign secretaries in his governments, from Patrick Gordon Walker through Michael Stewart to George Brown, all attempted to promote a thaw in relations with Nasser. Although these initiatives ground to a halt in the face of adverse regional developments, the baggage of the 1930s and the references to Hitler and Mussolini which had been the stock in trade of Eden, Macmillan and to some extent Douglas-Home were largely absent from the Labour discourse about Nasser and Nasserism. So the forces which shape particular historical generations may be part of the explanation for such perceptions.

A second part of the explanation, though, must be cultural. During the 1950s and 1960s Britain underwent a wrenching international transition. The observation that Britain changed from a global imperial power to a regional European power hardly does justice to the wrenching process of adjustment and changing self-perception which these decades witnessed. The frustrations and sense of vulnerability engendered by what was in large part an involuntary process were bound to affect perceptions of nationalist leaders. Nasser was only the most prominent of a series of late imperial 'hate-figures' who came to act as the personification of these British insecurities: others included Mohammad Mossadegh of Iran, Jomo Kenyatta of Kenya and Archbishop Makarios of Cyprus.

But it was Nasser who seemed best to personify what from the British perspective was the inversion of the appropriate order of things. That this jumped-up junior army officer could face down an empire over Suez in 1956 was something for which the Tory establishment at any rate could never forgive him. The continuing references to him in British political discourse as *Colonel* Nasser, rather than *President* Nasser, across the ensuing decade sum up this sentiment. It was as though, by giving him his appropriate army rank, one might yet put him back in his appropriate place. One might here paraphrase the British diplomat Evelyn Shuckburgh's diary comment on the Arabs' view of the British: 'how the Arabs hate us really. ... They will never forgive us Israel.'[5] For Nasser it would be 'how the British hate me really. ... They will never forgive me Suez.'

Third, when considering the cultural context of British perceptions of Nasser, Edward Said's concept of 'orientalism' must of course be taken into account. On one level, Said's thesis gives us a straightforward way of explaining how the British conceptualized Nasser as an Egyptian: 'there are Westerners, and there are Orientals. The former dominate, the latter must be dominated.'[6] For Said, Orientals were attributed the traits of weakness, irrationality and femininity within this hegemonic structure. In fact, a large part of the problem with Nasser was that his apparent strength and masculinity, demonstrated in his success in facing down Britain over the Suez crisis, did not fit with this model. Hence the British search for appropriate analogies from European history in the shape of Nazism and fascism which might combine the traits of irrationality with strength and masculinity.

How then did these perceptions of Nasser affect the course of British strategy across two decades in the Middle East? For the bulk of the period of Conservative government the answer is straightforward. Nasser was central to the framing of strategy in the region, and he was perceived as an inveterate enemy. Eden's private comment to Shuckburgh in March 1956 to the effect that 'it's either him or us, don't forget that' was a particularly extreme illustration of the kind of anti-Nasser paranoia which affected the upper echelons of successive Conservative governments.[7] But the Prime Minister was by no means alone among senior Tories in believing that Britain faced an irreconcilable threat from Nasser.

There were only really two brief periods during the era of Conservative government in which one might qualify this judgement. First, during the final months of 1954 into early 1955 after the signature of the Anglo-Egyptian agreement over the Suez Base a brief opportunity opened up for less hostile relations. The Suez Base agreement removed the largest impediment to an improvement in Anglo–Egyptian relations and at the same time seemed to hold out the prospect of new regional defence arrangements which might include a willing rather than a coerced Egypt.[8] However, this window of opportunity closed quickly in the wake of the signature of the Turco–Iraqi Pact which Britain subsequently joined as the Baghdad Pact in April 1955. The British decision to join the pact was seen by Nasser as part of an imperialist attempt to build up Iraqi leadership in the Arab world at the expense of that of Egypt. The signature of the pact was a crucial milestone in the development of the Anglo-Egyptian antagonism which led to the Suez crisis of 1956.[9]

Second, during 1959 to 1961, as British concerns about a possible Iraqi threat to Kuwait increased, culminating in the military intervention of the summer of 1961, consideration was given to improving relations with Cairo as part of a balance of power strategy in the Arab world.[10] The British government sought to capitalize on the rivalry which had developed between the leader of post-revolutionary Iraq, Brigadier Abd al-Karim Qasim, and Nasser. Diplomatic relations between Britain and Egypt, which had been severed over Suez, were slowly restored. Chargés d'Affaires were exchanged on 1 December 1959, while Beeley was eventually despatched as Ambassador to Cairo on 26 January 1961. But, the thaw in relations was short-lived. With the outbreak of the Yemeni civil war in September 1962, and the subsequent threat posed to the British position in neighbouring

South Arabia by Nasser-backed nationalist forces, the tentative détente was superseded by the reassertion of the Nasser/Hitler paradigm, as witnessed by Macmillan's annotation on Beeley's February 1963 despatch about Nasserism. During the final year of Conservative rule under Douglas-Home, relations deteriorated still further, with incursions by Egyptian aircraft into the airspace of the British-backed South Arabian Federation provoking a severe British retaliatory response on the Yemeni fort at Harib in March 1964. During a visit to Yemen a month later, Nasser made full use of the opportunity to attack British policy and its military presence in the region.[11]

Under Labour, as noted above, with a new generation of politicians in power, repeated attempts were made to initiate a détente in relations with Nasser. Within a week of taking over at the Foreign Office after Labour's election victory, the new Foreign Secretary, Patrick Gordon Walker, despatched a telegram to Cairo expressing a desire for an improvement in bilateral relations.[12] While Nasser welcomed the British approach there remained significant problems to resolve over the civil war in Yemen and the nationalist insurgency in South Arabia. Given that the Labour government was committed to defending British interests in the region and that there was a considerable degree of continuity between its initial approach and that of its Conservative predecessors, the initiative ultimately yielded little in terms of a sustained improvement in relations with Nasser. Indeed, in a speech on 22 July 1965, Nasser was trenchant in his criticism of Labour's policy, noting that: 'when the Labour government was formed we said we were willing to open a new page with them but... Labour adopted the same policy as the Conservative Government.' Nasser went on to warn of a 'conspiracy in the Gulf, and the attempt to keep Arab territories under imperialism'.[13] Despite the Egyptian leader's public criticism, the new Foreign Secretary, Michael Stewart, who had taken over from Gordon Walker in January, continued to pursue the diminishing prospects of détente throughout 1965, all the while recognizing the significant challenges posed by the clash between British and Egyptian interests. In fact, the formal reason for the severing of diplomatic relations between Britain and Egypt which took place in December 1965 was a request from the Organisation of African Unity for member states to protest Britain's failure to prevent Rhodesia's unilateral declaration of independence. Nevertheless, the climate in bilateral relations had become so poor that such a move on Nasser's part was not unexpected.

During 1966, despite the severing of formal diplomatic relations and the inauspicious regional and international backdrop, George Brown, who took over as Foreign Secretary in August, briefly attempted to breathe new life into the strategy of détente. Brown was one of the more fascinating and mercurial figures to have held the post of Foreign Secretary in recent times. While his native intelligence and quick wits were sometimes dulled by his penchant to begin drinking early in the day, those officials who worked most closely with him as Foreign Secretary developed a respect for his abilities.[14] In terms of the framing of British Middle East policy he possessed a unique network of contacts in the Arab world and Israel. His introductions to Arab friends had come mainly during the 1950s through his relationship with the Lebanese businessman Emile Bustani. Meanwhile, on the other side of the Arab-Israeli divide, Brown had also been introduced by the pro-Zionist Labour leader Hugh Gaitskell to key figures including Moshe Dayan and Yigal Allon.[15] Brown sought in particular to use his established friendship with Nasser to rebuild Anglo–Egyptian relations. During November and December 1966, Brown pursued an unorthodox diplomatic initiative which resulted from a chance encounter with Nasser's deputy, Field Marshal Abdel Hakim Amer, when their respective planes were diverted to Leningrad during a visit to the Soviet Union. Subsequently, he exchanged messages with Nasser via intermediaries which seemed to establish a desire for better relations on both sides.[16]

But the dynamics of the continuing Yemeni civil war, the South Arabian insurgency and the Arab–Israeli conflict soon put paid to Brown's attempt to revive détente with the Egyptian leader. The underlying predilection in Whitehall to see Nasser as the enemy reasserted itself against this backdrop. During the crisis which led to the Arab-Israeli war in June 1967, the Wilson government took the lead in international efforts to establish a convoying system in response to Nasser's declaration via Radio Cairo on 23 May 1967 that the Straits of Tiran were closed to Israeli shipping. Even Brown, perhaps chastened by the way in which his détente strategy had backfired, argued for the strongest measures to break Nasser's blockade.[17] In fact, the so-called 'Red Sea Regatta' never came into being. From the outset there were divisions within the Wilson Cabinet about the possible impact on British interests of leading the convoying effort, particularly from the Chancellor of the Exchequer, James Callaghan, who warned of the dangers posed to Britain's fragile economy.[18] Once it became clear that the Johnson administration was unwilling to put its full weight behind the convoying effort, the British government backed off.[19] Nasser's false claim that Britain and the United States had colluded in the subsequent Israeli attack on 5 June 1967, which subsequently became known in London and Washington as the 'Big Lie', underlined the degree of mistrust in Anglo–Egyptian relations.[20] While Brown, with some typically entrepreneurial and unconventional diplomacy, was able to secure the resumption of formal diplomatic relations in December 1967, suspicion remained the keynote of the relationship.[21] It was only after Nasser's death in September 1970 under his successor Anwar el Sadat that a serious reconfiguration of Anglo–Egyptian relations proved possible.

American views of Nasser

Since the theme of this volume is *Anglo-American* Perceptions of Middle East adversaries we also need to consider perceptions of Nasser in Washington, how these changed over time and how they influenced American strategy in the region. From the outset, the United States was far less encumbered by historical baggage than Britain in shaping its relations with the Nasser regime. At an early stage, the concept of cultivating Nasser as what was termed an 'independent ally' gained currency among those charged with handling relations with Egypt whether through intelligence or diplomatic channels. Miles Copeland no doubt overstates the degree of foresight and strategic planning with which the CIA approached its early contacts with Nasser.[22] Nevertheless, the notion that the cultivation of a strong, Arab nationalist leader willing to take difficult decisions, such as making peace with Israel and opposing communism, would be in America's interests found a ready audience in Washington. The theory underpinning the strategy was straightforward: as President Dwight Eisenhower put it in a meeting on 23 December 1958: 'Nasser could oppose Communists better than can the US in the three cornered struggle of the Middle East.'[23] In other words, if the United States could entice Nasser as the most important of the local Arab nationalist leaders into the Western camp in the Cold War then he might prove a potent ally in fighting communism.

There are two important points to note about this strategy, which was also pursued by the Kennedy Administration, but came increasingly to be questioned under the Johnson Administration. It placed the Cold War at centre stage in determining the United States' engagement with Nasser. It was also predicated on an element of pragmatism, of judging Nasser on his actions in particular crises, based on their Cold War implications. This kind of pragmatism was more often lacking on the British side.

One might deduce from this argument that the kind of Hitler/Mussolini historical analogy which was common currency on the British side was absent in Washington. In fact, this was not entirely the case. Of the senior US officials involved in making US policy towards the Middle East, Secretary of State John Foster Dulles in particular did occasionally resort to the Hitler analogy in judging Nasser. 'Nasser, like Hitler before him, has the power to excite emotions and enthusiasm', he commented in the wake of the Iraqi Revolution.[24] However, the crucial difference in his analysis versus that of Eden or Macmillan was that as he put it, Nasser 'was ... an evil', but he was 'a lesser evil than Communism'.[25]

For his part, Eisenhower resorted to more homespun analogies when judging Nasser. When faced with the problem of deciding who was a greater threat to US interests, Nasser or Abd al-Karim Qasim, the leader of post-revolutionary Iraq, Eisenhower noted that 'this seemed to be a case of whether we decided to support a baby-faced Dillinger or an Al Capone'.[26] No doubt Nasser's cherubic features more suited him to the role of 'baby-faced Dillinger', but either way, the comparison with 1930s mobsters placed both Nasser and Qasim in a different league of malfeasance in Eisenhower's perception than the Hitler/Mussolini analogy beloved of Eden and Macmillan.

One element in common between American and British analyses, though, concerns the trait of irrationality attributed to the Arabs in general and to Nasser in particular. This has already been mentioned as one component of Said's concept of 'orientalism'. US official records for this period are littered with what can only be termed an 'orientalist' analysis of the Arab world. For example, Eisenhower, in the wake of the July 1958 Iraqi revolution, argued that the US had to try to understand what he called 'underlying Arab thinking'. He also observed that 'they may act out of violence, emotion and ignorance. Our question is still how to get ourselves to the point where the Arabs will not be hostile to us.'[27]

Dulles, whose opinion on this matter has already been quoted, linked Arab enthusiasm for Nasser to emotion rather than reason. But as relations with the Nasser regime deteriorated under the Johnson Administration this supposed trait of irrationality came to figure more prominently in American analyses. During his final interview before leaving Cairo in 1967, US Ambassador Lucius Battle spoke of Nasser launching into a 'thirty minute tirade [against US policy] of [the] most emotional character yet displayed in my meetings with him'. 'Nasser,' Battle continued, 'was more emotional than I have ever seen him and at moments developed [the] glaze over [his] eyes typical of that we have seen when he makes speeches.'[28]

But how far did this perception of Nasser as the emotional, irrational Arab shape the course of US strategy over two decades? It will be argued here that the answer to this question is rather less in the case of the Americans than that of the British. The strategy which has already been outlined of prioritizing the waging of the Cold War, and dealing with Nasser pragmatically on the basis of whether his actions helped or hindered the Soviet Union, was in essence that adopted by successive administrations.

Under Eisenhower, the first key test of Nasser's willingness to act as a force for regional stability as defined by the United States was provided by the top secret 'Alpha' peace initiative of 1955 to 1956. While the plan was British in origin, Alpha became an Anglo–American peace initiative during the course of 1955.[29] Its essence was to trade off concessions by Israel, in the form of territory ceded to the neighbouring Arab states and compensation for the Palestinian refugees, in exchange for recognition by the Arab states and guarantees of Israeli security from the Western powers.[30] While Alpha aimed to open up a broader Arab–Israeli peace process in the longer run, its immediate goal was to secure an Egyptian–Israeli agreement.

Unfortunately for the putative peace-brokers in Washington and London, Alpha ran into a wall of resistance. In Israel, Prime Minister David Ben Gurion made it clear that he was opposed to the territorial concessions implicit in the plan. In a bid to unlock the process from the Egyptian end, Eisenhower dispatched a covert intermediary, Robert Anderson, to meet with Nasser during January and March 1956. Anderson's missions ended in failure.[31] His inability to secure Nasser's agreement to the 'Alpha' plan made clear the limits of the Administration's 'independent ally' strategy. It was evident in Nasser's negative response that he placed his independence and his Arab nationalist credentials well ahead of any considerations of potential Cold War 'alliance' with the United States.

The response to this setback in Washington was a re-evaluation of relations with Nasser during March 1956. Instead of dangling carrots in front of him in the shape of the offer to aid in the financing of the Aswan High Dam project which had been floated during 1955, sticks would be applied in the form of economic and political pressure on the Egyptian regime. But a crucial element of pragmatism remained in the US approach to Nasser, which was lacking in London: 'we would want for the time being to avoid any open break which would throw Nasser irrevocably into a Soviet satellite status and we would want to leave Nasser a bridge back to good relations with the West if he so desires.'[32]

During the ensuing Suez crisis, US policy was shaped on the strategic level by the continuing Cold War imperative of denying the Soviet Union opportunities to advance its influence in the region with the Arab states. This meant spinning out the diplomatic process in a bid to avoid any resort to war by Britain and France. On the tactical level, domestic political considerations played their part in the shape of Eisenhower's re-election campaign. But in spite of Dulles' private comments to the British, which seemed to encourage the toppling of Nasser, US policy aimed consistently at a peaceful resolution of the crisis.[33] In its aftermath, the strand of pragmatism in judging Nasser based on changing perceptions of his relationship with the Soviet Union remained in evidence. A State Department briefing paper prepared for the Bermuda conference with the British in March 1957 noted that 'our long-term, broad objectives with respect to Egypt are the restoration of close relations with an Egypt which lives up to her international obligations, recognizes the advantages of close relations with the West and is prepared to curtail her relationships with the USSR'.[34]

During the winter of 1957 to 1958, the willingness of the Administration to explore the possibility of working with Nasser to block the advance of communist influence in Syria illustrated the point perfectly. A covert approach by Nasser's confidant, the newspaper editor Mohamad Heikal, to the US Ambassador in Cairo asking for US cooperation in Nasser's attempts to stem the communist advance in Syria met with a positive response: 'we would welcome action designed [to] impede Communist penetration [of]

Syria.'[35] Subsequently, the creation of the United Arab Republic of Egypt and Syria (UAR) in February 1958 was also interpreted in Washington through the same prism as a development which had forestalled a potential communist takeover in Damascus.

While events in Syria had served to breathe fresh life into the Nasser as 'independent ally' paradigm, the revolution which overthrew the Hashemite monarchy of Iraq in July 1958 initially raised fears in Washington that Nasser might have acted at the behest of the Soviet Union in helping to overthrow a key pro-Western regime. With little information about the allegiance of the plotters who had toppled the monarchy, the Cold War reflex in Washington was to assume that they must be Soviet-backed, with Nasser acting as Moscow's puppet in organizing the coup. According to Eisenhower's analysis, Nasser was now 'so small a figure, and of so little power, that he is a puppet, even though he probably doesn't think so'.[36]

As more information emerged about the events which had led to the overthrow of the monarchy and about the complexion of the post-revolutionary regime, it quickly became clear that these Cold War fears in Washington were largely unfounded. The leaders of the Iraqi 'Free Officers' movement who now held power in Baghdad were not communists but nationalists of various hues. The emergence of Brigadier Abd al-Karim Qasim as the paramount figure in the new regime, and the defeat and exile of his rival, Abd al-Salam Muhammad Arif, created the conditions for the swift re-emergence of a community of interest between the US and Nasser. Qasim charted what might be termed an independent Iraqi nationalist course in Arab politics which brought him increasingly into rivalry with Nasser, who had favoured his rival Arif. Meanwhile, to the consternation of Washington, Qasim relied increasingly on the support of the Iraqi Communist Party in a bid to bolster his domestic position against pro-Nasser forces. Qasim's reliance on the communists for support created a potential community of interest between the US and Nasser. As Assistant Secretary of State William Rountree reported to the President after a tour through the Middle East which took in Cairo, where he was welcomed, and Baghdad, where he was threatened by an angry mob: 'Nasser desires to work with us on Iraq. He is much concerned over Communist influence with Qasim.'[37] Rountree's report elicited Eisenhower's previously quoted comment to the effect that Nasser was better able to oppose communists than the United States in the three-cornered struggle in the Middle East. By the end of the year, Nasser as the 'independent ally' had been almost fully rehabilitated in Washington.

During the early part of 1959, concerns in Washington about the rise of communist influence in Iraq increased still further. A special Interdepartmental Group under the chairmanship of acting Secretary of State Christian Herter was established to monitor developments closely.[38] In fact, although it was not clear at the time, by this stage the high watermark of communist influence in Iraq had already passed. Although the group continued to function throughout the rest of the year and into 1960, as communist influence receded so did high political attention in Washington for developments in Iraq. Nevertheless, the improvement in relations with Nasser fostered by the apparent community of interest in blocking communism was sustained through the final stage of the Eisenhower Administration.

Much of the historiography concerning the Kennedy Administration's Middle East strategy suggests that the new President brought a fresh approach to the region and treated it as a test case for his broader approach of pursuing a constructive engagement with the forces of indigenous nationalism. According to Fawaz Gerges, the Kennedy strategy was one of 'co-opting Arab nationalism'.[39] In a similar vein, Douglas Little argues that Kennedy saw engagement with the Nasser regime as the key to the stability of the region as a whole.[40] Both analyses are persuasive to the extent that they emphasize the importance Kennedy attached to improving relations with Nasser. This was mirrored in the personal correspondence Kennedy maintained with the Egyptian President throughout his term of office. However, although there was a change in style and presentation, the substance of the Kennedy approach had much in common with that of Eisenhower. As with much of Kennedy's foreign policy, his administration in effect cleverly rebranded Eisenhower-era ideas as new policies reflecting the 'new frontier'. The Kennedy Administration's strategy of 'co-opting Arab Nationalism' was really only the Eisenhower strategy of building up Nasser as an 'independent ally' repackaged, albeit that Kennedy engaged in more personal diplomacy aimed at cultivating Nasser than had Eisenhower.

It was the outbreak of civil war in Yemen in September 1962 and the subsequent Egyptian military intervention in the conflict which put this improved relationship with Nasser to the test. Nasser backed the new republican regime led by Colonel Abdullah Sallal, while the royalist forces of the ousted Imam of Yemen were supported by Saudi Arabia, Jordan and Britain. In a doomed attempt to preserve good relations with Nasser alongside those with its Saudi, Jordanian and British allies, the Kennedy Administration pursued the policy of disengagement of all outside forces from Yemen. The policy ran into resistance from all sides. By April 1963, the President's increasing frustration with Nasser's role was evident in his reaction to intelligence reports about a putative coup attempt in Jordan which was being framed with the Egyptian leader's full knowledge: Nasser 'was obviously a coming force in the Middle East and we naturally wanted to stay on the right side of him, but what about the growing accusation that our support was helping his to pursue expansionist policies?'[41] Kennedy no doubt had in mind here not only the criticisms of allies such as the Saudis or the Jordanians, but also domestic criticism of the Administration's policy from supporters of Israel. Such critics gained ground as the year progressed and by November 1963 were strong enough to secure the passing of the Gruening amendment to the PL-480 Bill.[42] This blocked aid to any nation engaging in or preparing for aggressive military efforts against the United States or any country receiving US assistance. Although Egypt was not specified in the Bill, much of the debate in the Senate focused on Nasser's role in the Yemen, Algeria and over the Palestinian question. The final Foreign Aid Bill incorporating a slightly revised version of the Gruening amendment was eventually signed into law by Kennedy's successor, Lyndon Johnson, on 16 December 1963.[43]

Johnson's signature of the Bill was indicative of the course which US relations with Nasser would take during his presidency. While a number of officials who had carried over from the Kennedy Administration, including Bob Komer of the National Security Council, continued to advocate engagement with Nasser, relations deteriorated as the Johnson Presidency progressed. During 1966 and 1967 there was a clear tilt in US strategy against Nasser. This was in large measure a function of changing Cold War and regional dynamics and reflected Nasser's move closer to the Soviet Union, the reinvigoration of the Arab Cold War, and the resurgence of the Arab–Israeli conflict, which resulted in the outbreak of war in June 1967. The perception of Nasser as an increasingly irrational, emotional actor, typified by Ambassador Lucius Battle's report of his final meeting with the Egyptian President quoted previously, was part of the explanation for the shift in US strategy. But a much more significant explanation is provided by the failure of the 'independent ally' strategy devised under Eisenhower and rebranded under Kennedy as the strategy of 'co-opting' Arab nationalism. Nasser's interests had simply proven incompatible with those of the United States in the region in the longer run.

Conclusion

Although perceptions of Nasser as an individual mattered in both British and American strategy in the Middle East during the 1950s and 1960s, they appear to have mattered rather more on the British than on the American side. The perception of Nasser as a sort of Arab reincarnation of Hitler or Mussolini was an important theme, particularly under the Conservative governments of Eden, Macmillan and Douglas-Home. For much of this period Nasser was seen in London as an inveterate, irrational enemy. Attempts at fostering détente with him were short-lived and inconclusive. On the American side, meanwhile, perceptions of Nasser as an individual were for the most part subordinated to broader Cold War strategy. Relations with the Egyptian leader were subject to constant reassessment based on whether his actions were helping or hindering the Soviet Union.

In this sense, the historical analogies selected by leaders on either side of the Atlantic do provide some clue as to the likely course of strategy. It was, after all, always more likely that one could cut a mutually beneficial deal with baby-faced Dillinger than it was with Adolf Hitler.

Notes

1 Telegram, Beeley to Home, (25 February 1963), PREM11/4173, United Kingdom National Archives (UKNA).

2 Macmillan's annotation, ibid.

3 Evelyn Shuckburgh, *Descent to Suez: Diaries 1951–56* (London: Weidenfeld & Nicolson, 1986), p. 327.

4 D. Cameron Watt, *Succeeding John Bull: America in Britain's place, 1900–1975* (Cambridge: Cambridge University Press, 1984), pp. 13–20.

5 Shuckburgh (1986), p. 311.

6 Edward W. Said, *Orientalism: Western conceptions of the Orient* (London: Penguin, 1991), p. 36.

7 Shuckburgh (1986), p. 346.

8 For further discussion of the Suez base agreement see W. R. Louis, 'The Tragedy of the Anglo-Egyptian Settlement of 1954' in W. R. Louis and Roger Owen (eds) *Suez 1956* (Oxford: Oxford University Press, 1989).

9 The historiography of the Baghdad Pact is extensive. See in particular: Nigel Ashton, *Eisenhower, Macmillan and the Problem of Nasser: Anglo-American relations and Arab Nationalism, 1955–59* (Basingstoke: St Martin's Press, 1996), pp. 37–60; Ayesha Jalal, 'Towards the Baghdad Pact: South Asia and Middle East Defence in the Cold War, 1947–55', *International History Review*, Vol. 11, No. 3, 1989, pp. 409–33; Richard L. Jasse, 'The Baghdad Pact: Cold War or Colonialism?', *Middle Eastern Studies,* Vol. 27, No. 1, (1991), pp. 140–56; Elie Podeh, *The Quest for Hegemony in the Arab World: The struggle over the Baghdad Pact* (Leiden, 1995); Brian Holden Reid, 'The Northern Tier and the Baghdad Pact', in John W. Young, *The Foreign Policy of Churchill's Peacetime Administration* (Leicester: Leicester University Press, 1988); Behcet Kemal Yesilbursa, *The Baghdad Pact: Anglo-American Defence Policies in the Middle East, 1950–59* (London: Routledge, 2005).

10 On British policy and the Kuwaiti crisis see: Mustafa Alani, *Operation Vantage: British Military Intervention in Kuwait, 1961* (Surbiton: Laam Press, 1990); Nigel J. Ashton, 'Britain and the Kuwaiti Crisis, 1961', *Diplomacy and Statecraft*, Vol. 9, No. 1, 1998, pp. 163–81; W. Taylor Fain, *American Ascendancy and British Retreat in the Persian Gulf Region* (New York: Palgrave Macmillan, 2008), pp. 46–140; Morice Snell-Mendoza, 'In Defence of Oil: Britain's Response to the Iraqi Threat towards Kuwait, 1961', *Contemporray British History*, Vol. 10, No. 3, (1996), pp. 39–62.

11 For further discussion of this incident see: Clive Jones, *Britain and the Yemeni Civil War, 1962–1965* (Brighton: Sussex Academic Press, 2004), pp. 90–1; Spencer Mawby, *British Policy in Aden and the Protectorates: Last Outpost of a Middle East Empire* (London: Routledge, 2005), pp. 113–14.

12 Robert McNamara, *Britain, Nasser and the Balance of Power in the Middle East, 1952–1967* (London: Frank Cass, 2003), pp. 209–10.

13 Nasser's speech quoted in McNamara (2003), pp. 218–19.

14 See, for example, Frank Brenchley's views of Brown in *Britain, the Six Day War and its Aftermath* (London: I.B. Tauris, 2005), pp. xv–xvii.

15 G. Brown, *In My Way: The political memoirs of Lord George-Brown* (London: Chatto & Windus, 1993), pp. 227–32.

16 McNamara (2003), pp. 234–5.

17 Robert McNamara, 'Britain, Nasser and the Outbreak of the Six Day War', *Journal of Contemporary History*, Vol. 35, No. 4, (2000), p. 624.

18 McNamara (2003), p. 625.

19 For the US approach see M. Moshe Gat, 'Let Someone Else Do the Job: American Policy on the Eve of the Six Day War', *Diplomacy and Statecraft*, Vol. 14, No. 1, (2003), pp. 131–58.

20 For further discussion of the 'Big Lie' see: Brenchley (2005), pp. 41–52; Spencer Mawby, 'The "Big Lie" and the "Great Betrayal"', in Nigel J. Ashton, *The Cold War in the Middle East: Regional Conflict and the Superpowers, 1967–73* (London: Routledge, 2007), pp. 167–9.

21 Brenchley (2005), pp. 65–73.

22 Miles Copeland, *The Game of Nations* (London: Weidenfeld & Nicolson, 1969), pp. 63, 78. See also Michael T. Thornhill, *Road to Suez: The Battle of the Canal Zone* (Stroud: Sutton Publishing, 2006), pp. 84–6 for a discussion of Copeland's claims regarding early US contacts with Nasser.

23 Memorandum of a Conference with the President, (23 December 1958), *Foreign Relations of the United States (FRUS)*, 1958–60, Vol. 13, pp. 509–11.

24 Memorandum of a Conference with the President, (24 July 1958), Ann Whitman File, DDE Diary Series, Dwight D. Eisenhower Library (DDEL).

25 Record of a Conversation between the Secretary of State and Mr Dulles, (4 February 1959), FO371/141641, UKNA.

26 Memorandum of discussion at the 393rd meeting of the National Security Council, 15 January 1959 (*FRUS*), 1958–60, Vol. 12, pp. 375–377.

27 Memorandum of a Conference with the President, (24 July 1958), Ann Whitman File, DDE Diary Series, DDEL.

28 Telegram, Cairo to State, (4 March 1967), document 393 (*FRUS*), 1964–68, Vol. 18.

29 On Alpha's British origins see Shimon Shamir, 'The Collapse of Project Alpha', in Louis and Owen (1989), p. 81.

30 Peter L. Hahn, *Caught in the Middle East: U.S. Policy Toward the Arab-Israeli Conflict, 1945–1961* (Chapel Hill: University of North Carolina Press, 2004), pp. 182–6.

31 For further discussion of the reasons for Anderson's failure see Hahn (2004), pp. 190–1.

32 Memorandum from the Secretary of State [Dulles] to the President, (28 March 1956), document 223 (*FRUS*), 1955–1957, Vol. 15, p. 419.

33 Macmillan reported back to Eden that Dulles had discussed with him 'different methods of getting rid of Nasser' and that 'he quite realised that we might have to act by force' (Note of a Private Talk with Mr Dulles, 25 September 1956, PREM11/1102, UKNA).

34 'Long-range Policy towards Egypt', undated [March 1957], White House Central File, Box 9, Confidential Series, Subject Sub-Series, DDEL.

35 Telegram from the Department of State to the Embassy in Egypt, (12 December 1957), document 421 (*FRUS*), 1955–7, Vol. 13, p. 746.

36 Memorandum of a Conference with the President, (15 July 1958), Box 35, Ann Whitman File, DDE Diary Series, DDEL.

37 Memorandum of a Conference with the President, (23 December 1958) (*FRUS*), 1958–60, Vol. 13, pp. 509–511.

38 National Security Council, 402nd meeting, (17 April 1959) (*FRUS*), 1958–60, Vol. 12, p. 436.

39 Fawaz A. Gerges, 'The Kennedy Administration and the Egyptian-Saudi Conflict in Yemen: Co-opting Arab Nationalism', *Middle East Journal*, Vol. 49, No. 2, 1995, pp. 292–311.

40 Douglas Little, 'The New Frontier on the Nile: JFK, Nasser and Arab Nationalism', *Journal of American History*, Vol. 75, No. 2, (1988), pp. 501–27.

41 Meeting with the President on the situation in Jordan, (27 April 1963) (*FRUS*), 1961–1963, Vol. 18, pp. 484–6.

42 Public Law 480 (PL-480), officially known as the 'Agricultural Trade Development Assistance Act', dealt with food aid, and was approved by Eisenhower in 1954. Under Kennedy it was rebranded as 'Food for Peace'.

43 Little, 'The New Frontier on the Nile', pp. 524–5; Bundy to Fulbright, (11 November 1963) (*FRUS*), 1961–3, Vol. 18, pp. 775–6; Abraham Ben-Zvi, *Decade of Transition: Eisenhower, Kennedy and the Origins of the American–Israeli Alliance* (New York: Columbia University Press, 1998), p. 133; Warren Bass, *Support Any Friend: Kennedy's Middle East and the Making of the U.S.–Israel Alliance* (New York: Oxford University Press, 2003), pp. 137–40.

CHAPTER FIVE

Seeing Sadat, thinking Nasser: Political and intelligence assessments of the transition

Dina Rezk

Introduction

The death of ardent nationalist Gamal Abdel Nasser on 28 September 1970 brought an extraordinary epoch of Egyptian history to a close. His successor Anwar el Sadat was an unknown quantity, whose legacy came to be defined by a series of momentous events. From the dramatic military offensive of Yom Kippur to the fundamental reorientation of Egypt's political identity towards the West, eventually culminating in the historic Camp David accords, Sadat's eventful presidency was to change the face of the Middle East.

The archival material now available (some of it only recently declassified) demonstrates the extent to which the histories of the early years of Sadat's leadership have been tainted – on both the Egyptian and the Western sides – by events that would later define him. True admirers of Sadat, most notably Henry Kissinger, concede with regret that the new leader was initially so underestimated, moving the discussion to his later achievements.[1] More frank accounts accurately highlight that Sadat was seen at home and abroad as a 'stopgap leader', marginalized by his reputation as 'Colonel Yes Yes', his Sudanese ancestry (and thus dark skin) and mocked for his repeated yet fruitless professions of the 'Year of Decision' to regain Egyptian land.[2]

Yet few studies have explored in depth the prevailing impressions of this new leader in Britain and America using archival records, and from what these impressions derived. Political and intelligence assessments enable us to address this lacuna from a more historicist perspective, revealing the details and nuance of perceptions that have been either lost or neglected in the recollected accounts. As well as bringing the 'missing dimension' of intelligence to the fore, it becomes apparent that historians of diplomacy can do more with these texts than merely evaluate what predictions emerged to be 'right' or 'wrong' (although that is of course an interesting undertaking in itself). Inspired by our fellow cultural and intellectual historians with their focus on both the 'spoken' and the 'unspoken', we can use political and intelligence documents to unearth how the bureaucracy that produced 'knowledge' for policy-makers actually *thought* about the Arab 'Other'.[3]

In an age where the intelligence community has been accused of 'mirror imaging' or substituting Western rationality in the behaviour of their adversaries, it is striking that assessments of Nasser and Sadat commonly demonstrated a keen appreciation of cultural 'Otherness'. As might be expected, this was frequently tinged with the deprecating 'Orientalism' notoriously coined by Edward Said in his scathing critique of Western stereotypical representations of the Middle East.[4] It is beyond the scope of this chapter to discuss Said's seminal work (save for a brief reflection in the conclusion) but if Western stereotypes of 'the Arab' are to some extent unsurprising, it is revealing how often such representations of Arab culture were validated and at times promoted by the Arab political elite themselves, the 'subjects' of these assessments, both contemporaneously and retrospectively. In the absence of respectively accessible archival material in Egypt, this study has relied on an interview programme with senior surviving Egyptian diplomats in the hope of 'validating' (however imperfectly) Anglo-American perceptions of this formative transition in Egyptian history as well as integrating somewhat the historiographical divide between Arabic and Western narratives.

The first part of this chapter explores initial impressions of Sadat on his rise to power. Was he seen as an improvement to his predecessor, as some accounts suggest? In fact, the archives illustrate a significantly less favourable set of perceptions, often correlating with those of Egyptian diplomats interviewed. Despite the prevailing hostility towards Nasser explored by Nigel Ashton in the previous chapter, upon inheriting the presidency, Sadat was initially perceived to be a temporary figure, an inferior statesman to his formidable predecessor and ultimately a tactical leader rather than one with a strategic vision.

Anglo-American reluctance to regard Sadat strategically may be seen in the analysis of two dramatic and interrelated events which form the second part of this chapter: the expulsion of 15,000 Soviet advisers in July 1972 and Egyptian preparations for war against Israel in 1973. In both cases it can be argued that negative perceptions of Sadat affected analysts' interpretation of these events resulting in and from, a fundamental failure to see Sadat as a 'strategic leader'. This reflected both perceptions of him as a weak politician but also as a Western-centric, linear definition of 'strategy' rather than a more flexible and fluid 'script' which allowed simultaneously for military action alongside a diplomatic solution.

The final section explores how impressions of Sadat changed following the dramatic military and political 'success' of the 1973 war in shifting the balance of power in the region to Israel's disadvantage. As the Egyptian leader made the transition from an 'adversary' to an 'ally' of the West, was he necessarily regarded more positively? Even after Sadat had demonstrated himself to be a statesman in his own right, it is remarkable how enduring the legacy of Nasser proved to be in the minds of Anglo-American analysts.

Early impressions of Sadat

The archival evidence suggests that the first impressions of Sadat by British and American intelligence were considerably less favourable than the recollected histories imply. William Quandt, for example, recalls that Sadat was viewed in Washington 'as a considerable improvement over Nasser'.[5] Similarly, former Egyptian Foreign Minister Mahmoud Riad writes in his memoirs that Nasser's death was met with relief by the Americans, who regarded him as a 'stumbling block on the road to peace'.[6] The political and intelligence assessments show either (and perhaps both) the power of retrospect in skewing historical recollection or the multiplicity of views on the new Egyptian leader. From the assessments of those tasked with analysing Sadat, three dominant impressions stand out. The first was that Sadat was overwhelmingly seen as a weak, temporary figure, deriving the respect and popularity he commanded from Nasser's shadow, which was in turn perceived to be inescapable and overwhelming. The second was an emanating difference between Sadat's priorities and those of his predecessor. The new leader was essentially regarded (particularly in British diplomatic assessments) as much more of an opportunist than Nasser had been. Third, and perhaps a manifestation of the former, was Sadat's considerably less consistent political orientation.

A Central Intelligence Agency (CIA) memorandum produced in the immediate aftermath of Nasser's death noted: 'Sadat does not appear to carry much personal weight in Egyptian political circles, and it is doubtful that he will fill the presidency for more than an interim period.'[7] A telegram from Chief of US interests in Egypt Donald Bergus confirmed to the State Department that 'we believe the interregnum will probably just lose steam'.[8] The CIA felt that Sadat 'owed his position more to his loyalty to Nasir [*sic*] than to his political strength and acumen'.[9] Similarly the immediate impressions by British ambassador Richard Beaumont were that Sadat 'seems to be fairly popular though without the appeal or the intelligence of Nasser. ... His leading position in the 1952 revolution as well as the obvious trust which Nasser placed in him lent respect.'[10] Initially riding on the wave of Nasser's popularity and legitimacy, Sadat's main task would be matching the appeal of his predecessor, in order to consolidate his leadership. With some exceptions, in general it was recognized by the intelligence community on both sides of the Atlantic that Nasser's would be a challenging shadow from which to emerge. Despite the prevalent image of Nasser as a troublesome adversary among policy-makers, by the time of his death, the scholar can certainly unearth more favourable, even deferential perceptions of Nasser with which Sadat would have to compete within the diplomatic and intelligence community.

Here the contrast of intelligence assessments produced by bureaucratic committees like the Joint Intelligence Committee (JIC) against those produced by the diplomatic service (essentially human intelligence) is particularly marked, with the latter at times producing significantly more astute assessments. Men on the ground were able to capture the 'mysteries' of Nasser's appeal in a way that the matter-of-fact JIC struggled to relay. In his seminal work on the JIC, Sir Percy Cradock accuses the British intelligence community of underestimating Arab nationalism.[11] The following JIC assessment of 'Nasser's Prospects' just months before he died substantiates his case:

> Over the last 15 years the regime has managed despite many external setbacks and internal vicissitudes, to retain at least the acquiescence of the broad mass of the population. This has owed much to the traditional passivity of Egyptians and to the lack of any obvious alternatives to President Nasser though there have of course been more positive factors such as the identification of the regime with the struggle to regain Arab land from Israel and to neutralise 'imperialist' influence in Arab affairs and with the goals of social and economic progress.[12]

The reluctant tone of such reports in acknowledging the 'positive factors' – the central features of what defined Arab nationalism – can only be contrasted with the more colourful assessments of Nasser's appeal produced by the diplomatic service. Recording Nasser's funeral, Ambassador Beaumont wrote:

> In the course of a consular and diplomatic career I have had ample opportunity to observe the disarray of families suddenly bereaved, but I cannot recall ever having witnessed a scene of bewilderment and disarray such as was to be seen in Cairo in the days following Nasser's death. It

went from the bottom to the top of Egyptian society. ... Thus the first Egyptian Pharoah was carried to his grave in an atmosphere of grief and devotion such as this country cannot have witnessed since the last of the priest-kings was carried by his awe-stricken subjects to his richly stocked resting place to confer with Horus, Isis and Osiris.[13]

As Nasser's confidant Hassanein Heikal poetically recalled in an interview with the author 36 years later, the response to Nasser's death demonstrated that, 'the sound of music does not lie'.[14] Heikal's allusion to a Weberian identification of the Egyptian masses with the charismatic leadership of Nasser was a significant difference between the two statesmen which analysts were quick to pick up on.[15] Whatever the American and British relationships with Nasser, analysts had long recognized the leader's representative quality. In 1958, the JIC described 'Colonel Nasser' as the 'personification of Arab dissatisfaction with their old corrupt rulers and with their past inferior status'.[16] A National Intelligence Estimate (NIE) in 1961 wrote that 'no Arab leader now on the scene, nor as far as we can tell waiting in the wings' was 'capable of matching Nasser's appeal or achieving a comparable basis of power and authority'.[17] A later JIC report on Nasser's achievements admitted that within Egypt, Nasser had accomplished 'major advances in social justice and health' and built 'a large reservoir of domestic goodwill and a new national pride'. Above all, Nasser's popularity derived from giving 'the Egyptians a new dignity and self-respect'.[18]

It was soon clear that Sadat was a different man to Nasser, with a different temperament and different priorities. Despite a flair for courting the West for which he came to be known, early into his presidency American diplomats noted that Sadat had neither the charm nor the conviction of his predecessor when dealing with Western politicians. It seemed that the new leader lacked Nasser's 'self-confidence' and 'incomparable ability for dealing with Westerners'. They noticed that in discussions:

If Sadat senses scepticism or unreceptivity on the part of his interlocutors, he gets carried away with himself, loses respect for the intelligence of those to whom he is speaking, and ends up with a highly unattractive mish-mash of emotion and twisted fact. In short he falls back on the old Arab habit of playing a phonograph record.[19]

Analysts observed such differences of temperament and charisma not only in Sadat's manner with the West, but also with his own people. As Ambassador Beaumont reflected in 1971,

By temperament he [Sadat] is a very different man from Nasser. There was a certain grim and obstinate determination in Nasser which to the very end encased him in the prejudices and objectives of his youth and tended to demand of the Egyptian people a similar grim dedication of which he himself knew them – as he admitted to me on one occasion – to be temperamentally quite incapable. Sadat has recognised this and has judged that by pandering to the easy going side of Egyptian character, he could in the short term at least both achieve popularity and at the same time establish his personal ascendancy.[20]

Perhaps most interesting is the implicitly critical eye with which British assessments looked upon Sadat's early manoeuvrings. In his valedictory despatch, Beaumont wrote a thoughtful and tentative assessment of the differences between the two leaders over which his ambassadorship had presided:

> I would say that as a man – sincere as his purposes may be – Sadat has not the same vision and does not inspire the same trust. Whatever the twists and turns of Nasser's policies – and there were many – one always had the impression, and, what is more important, the majority of his countrymen had the impression – possibly wrong – that he was tending towards an ultimate goal and that that goal was to their benefit and not to his own. With Sadat the impression has not been the same.[21]

The overwhelming impression on the part of Anglo-American analysts, like much of the political elite in Egypt, was that Sadat's primary concern was that of maintaining his own power. The tone of Beaumont's report reveals an unspoken respect for Nasser and an admiration for the 'ultimate goal' (the good of the Egyptian people) to which his often turbulent decision-making was directed, alongside a corollary and implicit criticism of Sadat. Perhaps most interestingly, Beaumont's analysis has been validated by all the first-hand Egyptians interviewed. That British diplomats were able to see Sadat so accurately through the eyes of the Egyptian political elite is testament to their skill and acuity.

No doubt deriving in part from this opportunism, Sadat's leadership was observed by analysts to be notably less consistent than that of his predecessor. British diplomats watched with concern as student consciousness expressed itself in an unprecedented manner in Egypt in January 1972:

> [The students] have drawn attention to the contradictions underlying Sadat's policies, the contradictions between liberalisation and mobilisation, between calling for war and searching for peace, between military dependence on the Soviet Union and the reopening of links with the West, between placing Egyptian interests first and getting the Arabs collectively to put pressure on Israel.[22]

Observers feared that the ideological inconsistency of Sadat's leadership was breeding an increasing sense of disillusion and disintegration within the

Egyptian people.[23] In a rare instance of explicit Anglo-American analytical engagement, we see that the State Department took a somewhat less pessimistic outlook:

> Although Sadat is broadly criticised for his lack of consistency and amateurishness, there may also be considerable passive acquiescence in Sadat's overall approach, especially since no-one else seems to be coming up with a better idea. The broad lines of Sadat's policy of 'not selling out Egypt's rights,' of avoiding (so far anyway) rash military moves, and of trying to build up the country's strength over the long term, are probably in tune with the way most Egyptians feel. This factor, plus his manipulative skills in creating diversions and keeping his enemies out-manoeuvred, could give Sadat and his regime a longer life-span than the period indicated toward the end of Beaumont's report. But we would agree that Sadat faces formidable difficulties in this respect and that the outcome is by no means certain.[24]

The State Department derived comfort from its belief that Sadat was broadly taking a 'safe' line of rejecting the half-hearted offers of peace put forth by Israel while strengthening Egypt's military and economic might. This, along with some of the more 'manipulative' elements of his domestic leadership, led American analysts to suggest that Sadat might last longer than their British counterparts had prophesied.[25] Their comments concluded with the prediction that 'the likelihood of a coup that brings to power some unknown Egyptian Qaddafi is somewhat less likely than the possibility that at some stage Sadat will stumble seriously enough' and that he will be replaced by 'some other figure as President who could command more widespread support among the populace'.[26] Even the more optimistic assessments thus predicted Sadat's eventual downfall.

Reluctance to view Sadat as a strategic leader: the expulsion of the Soviets and preparations for war

Nowhere was Sadat's apparent opportunism and inconsistency more visible than in his relations with the Soviet Union. The incoherent policy he pursued since assuming the Presidency only seemed to confirm a leadership of 'tactics', rather than one conceived of any firm principles. The CIA noted that 'Sadat is an ardent nationalist who is reportedly opposed to domestic Communism, but he realises the value of both political and military aid from the USSR. Like many Egyptian politicians, he is probably more opportunistic or pragmatic than ideologically motivated.'[27] The *Mitrokhin Archive II* reveals the extent to which the Soviet Union regarded the death of Nasser as an unmitigated disaster. Egyptian intelligence intercepted communications of an impending Soviet plot to oust Sadat by 'Soviet man' Ali Sabri, leading to a bitter purge of the government in May 1971. Only two weeks later however, Sadat signed a treaty of friendship with the Soviets.[28] The expulsion of 15,000 Soviet advisers in July 1972 was the most dramatic twist yet, one only later to be recognized by the world as clearing the decks for war.

Anglo-American analysts had a good understanding of the underlying tensions between the Soviet 'advisers' and their Egyptian counterparts. As historian Christopher Andrew writes, 'the influx of Soviet advisors served only to highlight the gulf between Soviet and Egyptian society', well illustrated by the fact that in stark contrast to their American counterparts, marriage between Soviet advisers and their Egyptian hosts was 'virtually unknown'.[29] British diplomats assessed that the primary motivation behind Sadat's actions was 'that the Soviet Union has refused to supply Egypt with offensive weapons which are needed to reopen hostilities or provide a deterrent against Israel'. Soviet policy, on the other hand, was bound by a 'desire to avoid a military confrontation with the US'.[30] They empathized with the prevailing Egyptian belief that the no-war no-peace situation 'suits the Russians very well since it gives them a continuing opportunity to maintain their position in the Middle East – an opportunity which settlement would remove by ending Egyptian dependence on Soviet support'.[31] In other words, ousting the Soviet Union would break the stalemate, prompting either a diplomatic or a military solution.

A revealing analysis in July 1972 by James Craig, head of the Near East and North Africa Department in the Foreign Office, demonstrates both the strengths and the weaknesses of British 'strategic' assessments on the Soviet expulsion. First it was proposed that perhaps 'Egypt is clearing the decks for a renewal of hostilities'. What made this 'hard to believe' was that even with Soviet support, Egyptian military prospects against Israel looked dismal. How therefore could they win without it? Craig posited that perhaps the expulsion was an attempt to 'declare to the West that if they would support her [Egypt] a little more, she is ready for a rapprochement'. The flaw to this interpretation was the timing. As Kissinger later commented, it surely would have made more tactical sense to make the offer in advance and be sure of a response. The final possibility, 'on a middle ground', was that the Russians were unable to restrain Egypt any longer and so would continue to provide arms but avoid the risk of superpower confrontation. Nonetheless, it was perceived as unlikely that the Soviet Union would agree to supply arms without any dividend in political influence or that she would accept the loss of credibility. Having found flaws in all of Sadat's possible strategic considerations, Craig thus concluded that 'there is so far no plausible explanation!'[32]

The strength of this British assessment lay in an ability to accurately 'imagine' and understand the strategic dimensions behind Sadat's decision-making, i.e. Craig formulated the individual pieces of what would later be recognized to be a strategic puzzle. What he failed to do was envision these pieces *together*, as complementary rather than mutually exclusive options. The 'either-or' approach demonstrated a rigid Western-centric appreciation of strategy as a planned set of movements taken with a clearly defined goal in mind and a binary opposition of war and peace. The 'strategy' in Sadat's mind, however, was that the odds were on getting rid of the Soviet Union. He hoped that a favourable Western response might in turn facilitate a political settlement of the Arab-Israeli conflict, but in the event that this was not forthcoming, Sadat estimated that the Soviet Union would probably seek to salvage relations by continuing its arms supply. The restrictions that the Soviet presence (by this stage actively pursuing Détente) could impose on Egypt's ability to plan a military initiative would be effectively removed.

Yet analysts seemed unwilling to attribute such a multi-faceted dimension to Sadat's thinking. On the British side in particular, he was regarded as taking a rash and ill-planned gamble with his superpower patron to his own detriment, and in the process undermining both Egypt's political and military leverage. Consequently it was concluded that 'the expulsion of the Russian advisors was not part of a strategic plan so much as an isolated act from which Sadat subsequently tried, vainly, to extract advantage'.[33] Instead of granting the possibility that the expulsion might be part of a considered strategy, it was believed to be more probable that Sadat had allowed himself to be carried along by the force of events without much foresight of the consequences.

The overwhelming tendency therefore was to believe that a future Arab-Israeli war would resemble its 1967 predecessor – confused and unplanned. Kissinger would recall, 'not knowing Sadat, I had to conclude that he was still playing Nasser's game'.[34] Similarly, a minute to British Prime Minister Edward Heath in May 1973 reveals the extent to which British assessments also rested on assumptions stemming from the events of 1967:

> The danger is that, in seeking to restore his [Sadat's] credibility, he will not only convince himself that he must do something but will also create a momentum which he will be unable to check.

The minute also warned of the 'dangerous delusion' of limited hostilities with the danger of a 'repeat of 1967, i.e. he will provoke the Israelis into some form of pre-emptive strike'.[35]

In their assessment of war in 1967 Anglo-American analysts appreciated that rhetoric had forced Nasser's hand into provoking a showdown with Israel which he knew he could not win due to a combination of miscalculation, misunderstanding, and above all a dogmatic commitment to save 'face'.[36] This precedent loomed large in the minds of analysts. The danger was that Sadat was backing himself into a corner, as Nasser had done, which would once more put the onus of unrestrained action on Israel. This implied passivity was reinforced by Sadat's own rhetoric and the frequent references to the 'Year of Decision' which never seemed to come.

In fact, Sadat's notorious wolf cries appeared to confirm a long-standing observation made by the political and intelligence community over the years, which the tragic example of the Six-Day War served only to reinforce: the Arabs do not always mean what they say and often what they do say is in fact a substitute for, rather than an indicator of, any real action. This idea was developed and explained by anthropologist Raphael Patai in a book entitled *The Arab Mind*, which was reviewed by the CIA upon publication in 1973 and controversially remains part of the US military curriculum.[37] Patai argued, among other things, that '*mubalagha*' (exaggeration) was a cultural phenomenon of the region with socio-economic foundations: essentially a verbal compensation for a material deficit.[38] In an assessment of Sadat's use of war-mongering rhetoric as early as 1969, State Department Arabist Richard Parker wrote,

> of course with Arabs, words are often as important as deeds. Sometimes more so. Having uttered these warlike cries Sadat can now go back to whatever he was doing, confident that he has done his duty for the war effort. It was through a similar process of bluster that Egypt got itself into such a mess in 1967.[39]

The risk of another war with Israel had thus for a long time been framed in this way: a bumbling rhetorical accident rather than something strategic and planned.

This explicit 'Orientalism' is perhaps best demonstrated in a peculiar exchange between British Ambassador Glen Balfour Paul in Amman and James Craig at the Foreign Office less than two months before the war. Herein Balfour Paul cites a 'thesis' relayed to him by Jordanian Foreign Minister Zaid Rifai advising that the 'Arabs must be dealt with as children'.[40] Rifai explained to Balfour Paul that

> governments in other Arab countries maintained two quite separate levels of policy – 'the Declared and the Real' and that consequently Sadat and Hafez Asad were able to exploit 'their restored partners' [Jordan's] military inability' to join in hostilities towards Israel, 'as a pretext for calling them off, or deferring them.[41]

The analytical endorsement of these 'cultural observations' as implicit confirmation of the unlikely possibility of hostilities is significant. What is more surprising is the fact that such explicit cultural stereotypes about the Arab world were actually being *advanced* by the Arab political elite themselves. Such an exchange illustrates how cultural knowledge can be used by the 'Other' both to justify and perhaps even conceal a strategic goal. When presented with these documents in a recent interview, Sir James Craig resolutely differentiated between ignorant cultural stereotypes and 'valid' cultural knowledge and understanding born of exposure to, and immersion in, the Middle East.[42] The exchange certainly makes a fascinating contribution to Said's contentions about the role of the 'Other' in perpetuating Western stereotypes of the 'Arab' and why they might choose to do so.

The post-1973 assessment of Sadat

The war of 1973 is clearly a turning point in the historiography of Sadat, not only marking [the first (albeit limited) military victory of Egypt over Israel, but also the first time since the days of the Crusades that Arabs managed to gain the upper hand in open, large-scale armed conflict with a non-Muslim Western-trained and equipped force. As Avi Shlaim writes, the successful surprise attack 'radically changed the whole political and psychological balance of power in the Middle East to Israel's disadvantage'.[43] It was from this point that Sadat came to be considered a true 'statesman', going on to declare '*infitah*' (the economic 'opening' of Egypt to the world), rendering the Suez Canal open to international navigation (thereby pressuring Israel to come to the second Sinai disengagement agreement), followed by his unprecedented trip to Jerusalem. Kissinger describes Sadat's actions as demonstrating, 'the transcendence of the visionary'.[44] President Carter's recollection is a little more guarded, describing Sadat as a character 'extraordinarily inclined towards boldness'.[45] Ismail Fahmy, Egyptian foreign minister between 1973 and 1977, attributed Sadat's achievements to an 'impulsive style' of 'split-second decision making' and a quest for personal fame.[46]

The diplomatic and intelligence documents allow us to dig deeper into how and why perceptions of Sadat changed. Only three months after the invasion British Ambassador Phillip Adams assessed the consequences of this momentous achievement from multiple perspectives. He wrote that, 'as a direct consequence of Egypt's crossing of the Suez Canal the Arab oil weapon has been unsheathed for the very first time'. In inter-Arab relations, 'Egypt's stock has risen to the point where she can again fairly claim the leadership of the Arab world' although he qualified, 'she is now content to share that doubtful privilege with Saudi Arabia.' In her relations with Israel, Egypt was 'self-confident enough to face Israel across the conference table in Geneva'. Most significantly, Adams reflected that crossing the Suez

Canal 'proved to herself and the world at large that Egyptian patriotism can produce deeds as well as words and that the despised Egyptian army can fight with fervour and determination'. Adams therefore concluded that within Egypt, 'Sadat is now undisputed master and looks like remaining so, provided that the process of Israeli withdrawal is not too long delayed'.[47]

In Egypt's changed relations with the West, the themes of friendship, equality and interdependence emerge strongly from Adams' analysis:

> We must accept that this part of the world and our relations with it will never be the same again. President Sadat ... wants our friendship on the basis of a partnership based on equality of status and interest. The Arabs have found that they can exploit us just as effectively as they claim we have exploited them. The era of patent interdependence has arrived.[48]

Adam's musings reflect not only a more complimentary portrayal of Sadat and the significance of what he was able to achieve, but also a certain anxiety about the future of the West. No longer should, or indeed could, the West look upon this particular Arab leader as an inferior 'Other' since he had patently demonstrated a military and political strength worthy of equality.[49]

Other British analyses revealed an unmistakable degree of surprise and cynicism with a reluctance to renounce entirely their earlier negative assessments of Sadat. 'It is curious', wrote James Craig, 'how he has blossomed into such a potentate; but there was not room for two potentates when Nasser was alive.' Ultimately Craig does not seem to foresee even the victory of Yom Kippur sustaining Sadat's presidency. He goes on, 'I would not like to guess how long he will bear the strain, mentally or physically. At least his past career has given him plenty of opportunities to develop self-control and he does not yet seem to have lost touch with reality.'[50] There is clearly some concern here and a hint of the denigrating descriptions associated with Sadat before the war: a fundamentally weak leader, lacking self-control and potentially delusional.

And yet this is perhaps not surprising since perceptions of individuals tend not to change overnight. What is more interesting is that even after Sadat had apparently proven himself to be a statesman in his own right, the comparisons with Nasser prevail. Indeed to some extent, Sadat's pro-Western shift was considered to be merely a continuity of Nasser's natural inclinations. A despatch in 1974 reflected,

> Egyptians are so used to alien power that they tend to display an exaggerated reverence for it; for them the USA is quite simply the most powerful and richest nation on earth. Even Nasser was not immune from this obsession and at first turned instinctively to the Americans for his economic and political salvation.[51]

The CIA expanded on the comparisons between Sadat's and Nasser's foreign policy in a fascinating and more recently declassified intelligence memorandum in April 1975 with the revealing title: 'A Coming of Age: The Foreign Policy of Anwar Sadat'.[52] The piece begins by reinforcing the continuity between the two leaders, suggesting that Sadat introduced a revolutionary 'flexibility' to foreign policy which 'Nasir [sic] might have introduced ... himself had he lived'.[53] The memorandum goes on to place the 1973 war as a 'striking example' of politics previously practised by Nasser: 'Like Nasir [sic], Sadat knows the politics of confrontation and the tactics of a leader who can force attention to his country's interest by an adventurist foreign policy.'[54] The notion that in fact a limited war had been planned by Nasser himself prior to his death has been confirmed by senior Egyptian diplomats in interviews with the author.[55]

According to the CIA, the main difference between the two leaders was that Sadat knew 'the limits of confrontation and the advantages of co-operation'. The memorandum contrasted Sadat's 'flexibility' to Nasser's 'inflexibility' which in turn was the result of the latter's 'concern for appearances', and 'rigidity' which 'precluded even an exploration of areas of compromise'. The memorandum explained, 'like most revolutionaries he [Nasser] was unwilling to adapt his policies and concepts to changing circumstances around him ... unable to view the interests of the outside world except in terms of Egypt's interests, and more particularly in terms of his narrower vision of himself.' While Nasser's 'own tendency toward conflict ultimately caused him to overplay his hand', Sadat, on the other hand, 'is aware of the interests of other states and realizes that some accommodation must be made if Egypt's own interests are to be furthered'. Consequently he has 'consciously eschewed the revolutionary tactics, the appeals to emotionalism, and the invocation of "principle" in defence of inaction that have heretofore brought popularity but few foreign policy successes for progressive Arab leaders'. The analysis goes on:

> Sadat's concept of foreign policy is unremarkable by pragmatic Western standards, but by the standards of the Arab world it is revolutionary. Sadat himself describes it as a new maturity. It is a positive policy undertaken on behalf of a people imbued with a negative attitude toward the non-Arab, non-Islamic world. It is a planned, action orientated policy imposed where ad hoc essentially reactive decisions have been the norm.[56]

There is a clear contrast here of Sadat's rational, mature, practical, strategic and Western (both in nature and orientation) foreign policy in comparison to Nasser's youthful, impetuous, negative and reactive foreign policy. Yet this is not merely a comparison of two leaders; the loaded language used by the intelligence analysts also reflects their political thought about the Arab world – the discourse of a 'passive', 'reactive' Arab world, 'coming of age' to the political maturity of their Western counterparts, by adopting and conceding to Western rationale and moderation. It is once again notable that they quote Sadat himself encouraging this comparison.

At the same time there are some serious qualifications to this newfound admiration of Sadat. Of Egypt, the CIA clearly posited that 'Nasir [*sic*] made it the leader and political centre of the Arab world by the forces of a personality that Sadat cannot equal and by tactics that he does not choose to match.' Nasser maintained his edge by being 'more radical than the radicals ... whilst Sadat has adopted a style that is attuned more to the moderation of the outside world than to the radicalism of the Arabs. ... To win acceptance of his policies among the Arabs, he must present them in a language the other Arabs understand.'[57] This is an introduction to a barely disguised word of warning: the popularity that Sadat gained gave him the ability to frame negotiations as an extension of war. The 'Westernization' of his politics should not alienate him from his Arab constituency. Analysts predicted that Sadat's popularity would inevitably wane unless 'he demonstrates to the Arabs by practical results that his pragmatic approach to leadership produces more than radicalism can'.[58]

The JIC were also cautious about Sadat's prospects for success:

> It is difficult to predict when Sadat might decide he has no option but to return to war. ... The breaking point of Arab patience could come after a few weeks if the Israelis remained intransigent. ... The timescale could possibly be much longer; it is even possible that Sadat or Asad will be able and willing to spin out diplomatic option long enough to see what the next American administration has to offer them but we doubt it.[59]

One senses an underlying sympathy for Sadat. Now a man of action, their presumption is that hostilities will inevitably resume, it is merely a question of when. Arab '*patience*' is favourably contrasted to Israeli '*intransigence*' giving the historian a crucial insight into perceptions and discourse surrounding the Arab-Israeli conflict. The language suggests that the JIC seemed to be less optimistic as to the long-term success of Sadat's strategy than their American counterparts. Sadat or Asad 'might' be able to make a diplomatic gain but they 'doubt it'.

Only a few months later, the diplomatic option was indeed successfully spun with a second Sinai agreement, but the JIC were still not convinced that this was enough to preserve Sadat's presidency – in fact rather the opposite: 'Criticism of his policy could mount if he is seen to be politically isolated in the Arab world and if the Israelis make it clear that the Sinai agreement was not a step towards a final settlement but their last concession.' Rather prophetically they predicted as early as 1975 that 'there is a heightened risk of Sadat's assassination'.[60]

A curious paradox is thus revealed: despite the fact that Sadat's policies were 'now directly in line with vital Western interests', the British Embassy's appraisal was that nonetheless the present state was 'not encouraging'. While Sadat's policy of 'Egypt first' was positively contrasted with Nasser's 20 years of 'hungry Arab heroes', the assessment also identified economic and social dangers in the new economic policy of '*infitah*' which produced benefits for a narrow group at the expense of the vast majority of the population. It was clear to all that the achievements of Nasser's socialism were being eroded.[61] As the Editor of *Al Ahram al-Iqtisadi* (the economic journal of the newspaper) Dr Loutfi Abdul Azim wrote sarcastically in 1976:

> With every step I take my eyes are dazzled by the glitter of the open door policy. I need only to walk into any grocery store to breathe a sigh of relief and to thank God that he has compensated us so well for the long period of frustration and deprivation.

He was of course talking about the masses of unaffordable imported goods that crowded Egyptian products off the shelves.[62] Analysts rightly demonstrated some unease about the social and economic implications of Sadat's turn towards the West.

Conclusion

Consider this final description of Sadat by Ambassador William Morris shortly after his arrival at the British Embassy in 1976:

> His personality still mystifies me ... he has given the impression of a warm, engaging, mellow and rather simple personality, relaxed and confident – altogether too relaxed and confident considering the problems that face him – but without any philosophical depth or detailed grasp of economic questions: he paints with a very broad brush ... he enjoys relaxing in a variety of presidential residences, and watching films for an evening. (That at least is one thread in a continuity otherwise difficult to trace between the young revolutionary and conservative president: he had to be fetched out of the cinema to be told the coup was about to be launched in 1952.) ... He seems to be unaware of or unconcerned about, any ill effects that his and his family's rather monarchical lifestyle, contrasting so much with the ostentatious austerity of Nasser may have on his position. He can act and react emotionally – calculation seems sometimes to be subordinated to emotion.[63]

This rather naive, childlike portrayal of Sadat is a revealing prelude to some concluding comments. Before 1973 the images of Sadat were of a weak, tactical and inconsistent leader (although the Americans were more inclined to see his strengths). After the war and the political successes that followed it, the images shifted somewhat to a more positive hue; 'tactics' were perceived to be part of a grand 'strategy', what was once 'inconsistency' came to be formulated as 'flexibility'. Yet this view was not without concern or reservation. Sadat seemed to be moving unilaterally to the West, towards peace with Israel and economic liberalization. But despite some flattering comparisons with Nasser, Western analysis seemed not entirely convinced that this was a good thing. Analysts were quick to identify the contentious legitimacy of Sadat's leadership and there was almost a sense that a strong adversary might be preferable to a weak ally. The ghost of Nasser, troublesome antagonist that he was, nevertheless endured in the psyche of the Western world well beyond his death. We need only to look at the recurring images of Nasser in the recent 'Arab Spring' to confirm the strength and depth of his legacy in the Arab world.[64]

Attempts to understand and sometimes deprecate both leaders were often framed in 'Orientalist' language about Arab behaviour. This was arguably more marked in periods of uncertainty, transition or crisis. When faced with a frustrating or incomprehensible cognitive scenario, Western analysts relied on cultural preconceptions: the 'typical Arab' trait of 'rhetoric', 'emotion', 'passivity' or 'irrationality' as an explanatory factor. Often these observations were confirmed, even advanced, by Arabs themselves. This in turn raises a complex yet crucial question that goes beyond a study of these two Arab leaders: at what point does cultural knowledge become deprecating 'Orientalism'? Or as Said's work implies, is the West in fact incapable of portraying 'the Arab Other' without an underlying and inherent hostility or condescension? In fact my archival research suggests a more complex plethora of spoken and unspoken perceptions of both leaders ranging from admiration to empathy.

A final word on some 'lessons learned'. It is clear that in order for cultural knowledge to be a help rather than a hindrance in political and intelligence analysis we need to be aware of and explicit about our beliefs and presumptions about the 'Other'. So frequently were cultural beliefs lightly scattered throughout political and intelligence documents on Egypt as natural or immutable truths, so rarely were such beliefs made transparent and explicit in such a way that rendered them easily amenable to questioning, debate and therefore change. Using cultural knowledge to understand and predict the behaviour of individuals or nations requires a recognition that 'culture' is not a passive, static and deterministic force but rather a fluid and contradictory frame of reference, often constructed and actively relayed for a variety of purposes. Hence, this frame of reference that constitutes 'culture' is continually subject to change and manipulation.

Despite astute analysis of both leaders and their influence, it was (perhaps unsurprisingly) such self-conscious awareness of both the uses and limitations of 'culture' that was most consistently lacking in Anglo-American assessments of the Nasser–Sadat transition.

Notes

1 Henry Kissinger, *The White House Years* (London: Weidenfeld & Nicolson: Joseph, 1979), p. 1294.

2 David Reynolds, *One World Divisible: A Global History since 1945* (London: Allen Lane, Penguin Press, 2000), p. 370.

3 Dina Rezk, Forthcoming PhD thesis, Cambridge University.

4 Edward Said, *Orientalism* (London: Routledge & Kegan Paul, 1978).

5 William Quandt, *Decade of Decisions: American Policy towards the Arab-Israeli Conflict 1967–1976* (Berkeley: University of California Press, 1977), p. 123.

6 Mahmoud Riad, *The Struggle for Peace in the Middle East* (New York: Quartet Books, 1981), p. 169.

7 CIA memorandum, 'Nasir's Death: The Immediate Aftermath', (29 September 1970). *Declassified Documents Reference System (DDRS).*

8 Telegram from US interests Cairo (Bergus) to Secretary of State, (November 1970). Country Files UAR, Vol 5. National Security Council Files, Box 636, Nixon Presidential Materials, National Archives College Park, College Park, MD.

9 CIA memorandum, 'Nasir's Death: The Immediate Aftermath', (29 September 1970). *DDRS.*

10 Telegram, 'President Nasser's Death', from Ambassador Beaumont to FCO, (29 September 1970), The National Archives (TNA), FCO 39/737.

11 Percy Cradock, *Know your Enemy: How the Joint Intelligence Committee saw the World* (London: J. Murray, 2002), p. 111.

12 JIC Report, 'Nasser's Prospects', (13 January 1970), TNA, CAB 186/3.

13 Diplomatic report no. 108/71, 'United Arab Republic: Annual Review for 1970', from Ambassador Beaumont to Secretary of State for Foreign and Commonwealth Affairs, (25 January 1971), TNA, FCO 39/961.

14 Interview, Mohammed Hassanein Heikal, Cairo, (1 March 2006).

15 Max Weber, *From Max Weber: Essays in Sociology* (New York: Oxford University Press, 1946). Weber established the concept of 'charismatic leadership' as the emotional bond between a heroic leader and his followers.

16 JIC report, 'Nationalist and Radical Movements in the Arabian Peninsula', (10 Februrary 1958), TNA, CAB 158/31.

17 National Intelligence Estimate Number 36–61, 'Nasser and the Future of Arab Nationalism', (27 June 1961). http://www.foia.cia.gov/docs/DOC_0000012085/DOC_0000012085.pdf.

18 JIC report, 'The Outlook for the United Arab Republic During the Next Two Years', (2 February 1966), TNA, CAB 158/59.

19 Telegram from Bergus in Cairo to Sisco at State Department, (22 February 1971), *DDRS*.

20 Despatch, 'Arab Republic of Egypt: Annual review for 1971', by Ambassador Beaumont in Cairo to FCO, (7 January 1972), TNA, FCO 39/1200.

21 Diplomatic report no. 161/73, 'Sir Richard Beaumont's Valedictory Despatch' from Ambassador Beaumont to Secretary of State for Foreign and Commonwealth Affairs, (18 January 1973), TNA, FCO 93/74.

22 Telegram no. 139, 'Student Disturbances', from Ambassador Beaumont to FCO, (17 January 1972), TNA, FCO 39/1203.

23 Despatch, 'Egypt in the Doldrums', from British Ambassador Beaumont in Washington to the Foreign Secretary, (28 November 1972), TNA, FCO 39/1207.

24 State Department's Comments on Beaumont's despatch, 'Egypt in the Doldrums', relayed by Moberly in British Embassy in Washington to Near East and North Africa Department in FCO, (28 December 1972), TNA, FCO 39/1207.

25 Ibid.

26 Ibid.

27 CIA memorandum, 'Nasir's Death: The Immediate Aftermath', (29 September 1970). *DDRS*.

28 Christopher Andrew and Vasili Mitrokhin, *The Mitrokhin Archive II: The KGB and the World* (London: Penguin, 2006), p. 156.

29 Ibid., p. 153.

30 Report, 'Egypt and the Soviet Union' by A.J.M. Craig of the Near East and North Africa Department to Private Secretary, (18 July 1972), TNA, FCO 39/1264.

31 Ibid.

32 Ibid.

33 Despatch, 'Sadat's Long Haul', from Ambassador Adam Phillips to Sir Alec Douglas-Home at FCO, (7 September 1973), TNA, FCO 93/236. Phillips also explains the unlikely possibility of war to be the result of his assessment of Sadat 'as a man of peace'. Phillips seems to have regarded Sadat more highly than most of his counterparts.

34 Kissinger (1979), p. 1285.

35 Minute from A.D. Parsons to Private Secretary for Prime Minister Heath, (3 May 1973), TNA, PREM 15/1764.

36 Dina Rezk, *British and American Political and Intelligence Assessments of the Nasser–Sadat Transition: From the Six-Day War to Yom Kippur*. Unpublished M.Phil. thesis (Cambridge: Cambridge University, 2006).

37 Patrick Porter, *Military Orientalism: Eastern war through Western eyes* (London: Hurst, 2009), p. 60. Patai's book was reviewed by Lloyd F. Jordan at the CIA's in-house journal *Studies in Intelligence* (Fall 1974). https://www.cia.gov/library/center-for-the-study-of-intelligence/kent-csi/vol18no3/html/v18i3a06p_0001.htm.

38 Raphael Patai, *The Arab Mind* (New York: Charles Scribners & Sons, 1973).

39 Memorandum, 'New Egyptian Vice-President', from Parker to Sisco, 23 December 1969. File Chron 1969 Office Memoranda, Records relating to Egypt 1967–75, Bureau of Near Eastern and South Asian Affairs, Office of Egypt Affairs, Box 11, General Records of the Department of State, Record Group 59, National Archives at College Park, College Park, MD.

40 Memorandum from Glen Balfour Paul in British Embassy Amman to James Craig in FCO, (27 August 1973, TNA), FCO 93/82.

41 Ibid.

42 Interview with Sir James Craig, Oxford, (24 October 2011).

43 Avi Shlaim, 'Failures in National Intelligence Estimates: The Case of the Yom Kippur War', *World Politics*, Vol. 28, No. 3, (1976), p. 349.

44 Henry Kissinger, *Years of Upheaval* (New York: Little Brown, 1982), p. 647.

45 Jimmy Carter, quoted in Ibramin Karawan, 'Sadat and the Egyptian-Israeli Peace Revisited', *International Journal of Middle East Studies*, Vol. 26, No. 2, (1994), p. 249.

46 Ismail Fahmy, quoted in ibid.

47 Diplomatic report no. 125/74, 'The Fourth Arab-Israeli War: Political Results', from Phillip Adams to FCO, (16 January 1974), TNA, FCO 93/561.

48 Ibid.

49 Ibid.

50 Memorandum, 'Wielders of Power in Egypt', from James Craig to Robert Faber, (27 February 1974), TNA, FCO 93/379.

51 Despatch 2/4, 'Egypt Between the superpowers', from Richard Faber in British Embassy, Cairo to James Callaghan in FCO, (12 August 1974), TNA, FCO 93/383.

52 CIA memorandum, 'A Coming of Age: The Foreign Policy of Anwar el Sadat', 9 April 1975 [electronic record]; CIA Records Search Tool (CREST), National Archives at College Park, College Park Maryland (NARA II).

53 CIA memorandum, 'A Coming of Age', (9 April 1975), CREST database, NARA II.

54 Ibid.

55 Various interviews with senior Egyptian diplomats, Cairo, April 2006.

56 CIA memorandum, 'A Coming of Age'.

57 Ibid.

58 Ibid.

59 JIC Report, 'Arab/Israel the Prospects', 20 June 1975, TNA, CAB/186/20.

60 JIC Report, 'Arab/Israel: The Effects of the Sinai Agreement', (12 September 1975), TNA, CAB 186/20.

61 Despatch from Ambassador William Morris in British Embassy, Cairo to James Callaghan, (9 February 1976), TNA, FCO 93/847.

62 Raymond Baker, 'Sadat's Open Door: Opposition from Within', *Social Problems*, Vol. 28, No. 4. (1981), p. 380.

63 Despatch from Ambassador William Morris in British Embassy Cairo to James Callaghan, FCO, (9 February 1976), TNA, FCO 93/847.

64 Images of Nasser in Arab Protests of 2011 available to view at http://www.daylife.com/topic/Gamal_Abdel_Nasser/photos?__site=daylife (last accessed 6 December 2011).

CHAPTER SIX

Three images of the Ayatollah

David P. Houghton

Introduction

On New Year's Eve 1977, President James Earl Carter famously raised a glass of champagne in Tehran, toasting the Shah's leadership and praising Iran as 'an island of stability in one of the more troubled regions of the world'. Rather foolishly – Iran was of course an Islamic state even then – the Shah reciprocated, doing so on live television. The intelligence upon which this overly fulsome praise was based was, of course, incorrect, and it was followed by yet more optimistic reports. In September 1978, for instance, a US Defense Intelligence Agency (DIA) report suggested the Shah was good for another ten years.[1] The Central Intelligence Agency (CIA) felt the same way. 'Iran is not in a revolutionary or even a pre-revolutionary condition', claimed an August 1978 report.[2] Warnings about the Shah's political vulnerability were isolated, vague and did not predict an Islamic revolution as such. If there was to be a revolution in Iran, critics of the Shah believed, such opposition was unlikely to come from theocratic sources. And later British ambassadors like Sir Anthony Parsons seem to have had far more confidence in the Shah. Parsons opined in January 1978 that the Shah remained in a strong political position, and his advice was mirrored around that time by that of the US Ambassador William Sullivan.

Tempting though it may be, it is difficult to fault the British and US intelligence communities – or anyone else – for failing to predict an Islamic revolution, however. Revolutions in general are notoriously difficult to predict, and we still have no satisfactory social scientific or academic theory capable of predicting tumultuous events in advance.[3] The simple fact is that nobody in the West, either inside or outside the US or UK governmental systems, predicted an Islamic revolution in Iran or the rise of the Ayatollah Ruhollah Khomeini; if the Shah fell, practically everyone expected that some kind of military government or nationalistic coalition would replace him (and in fact this was, from the perspective of all past experience, by far the most likely outcome).

There was a general but understandable failure within the West to consider that an elderly man in a turban who wore women's perfume could be a powerful political player in Iran. Khomeini simply did not look like the Western idea of a politician, and he did not fit our cognitive image or stereotype. And yet even those who were better informed about Khomeini were fooled by him as well: the Iranian clergy had long been dominated by the quietist, non-interventionist tradition within Shia Islam, and in modern times no member of the Iranian clergy had played a forceful role in politics. The opposition was almost all secular. One would have to admit, then, that the rise of Khomeini was very unlikely from the perspective of 1978 or 1979 – this was quite simply outside anyone's experience. The Islamic revolution was in effect what Nassim Taleb has termed a 'Black Swan'. These are momentous but very unlikely and highly unpredictable events which only seem to have been inevitable in retrospect.[4] It has been argued that revolutions occur when not only the necessary social, economic and political preconditions are present, but when a sufficient number of bystanders begin to 'think the unthinkable', that is, they come to believe that large numbers of people will act in concert with them (a mass psychological perception).[5] But this is of course inherently difficult or impossible to predict in advance. Only afterwards did what happened in Iran appear likely or 'inevitable' (what psychologists call the hindsight bias or the 'I knew it all along' effect).[6]

In order to appreciate the difficulties for the intelligence analyst or policy-maker in predicting the events that eventually unfolded, it is worth considering the following. First, it would need to be predicted that the Shah, in power for the best part of 40 years, must suddenly fall. He must be pushed out in part by a groundswell of support for an exiled clergyman in his late seventies. That man must then set up a system which emasculates not only the remnants of the Shah's political forces but the whole liberal, nationalist, socialist and Marxist opposition in Iran. Having outmanoeuvred the secular forces, he must then outmanoeuvre the moderate clergy completely, establishing sharia law in a country that had been undergoing modernization programmes since the 1920s. You would have been called crazy if you had predicted in 1978 that all this would soon come to pass, and yet it happened. Nobody – apart perhaps from Khomeini himself – actually predicted it in advance, and it is questionable whether even he knew the course events would take.

None of this means, however, that US intelligence was satisfactory or that the crisis from a Western perspective was well handled. Even though our miscomprehension of what was occurring was in many ways understandable, it is nevertheless possible in retrospect to chart three general misperceptions which existed at various times within the Carter Administration which affected US decision-making. Misperceptions about Khomeini went through three phases between 1977, when the West first began to take any notice at all of the man, and 1989. First of all, he was regarded between 1977 and mid-1978 as a figure of irrelevance, as someone who could not possibly influence the course of events inside Iran; second, many Western policy-makers were inclined after the middle of 1978 to regard Khomeini as a 'Gandhi-like' figure, a cognitive image which persisted right up until the seizure of American hostages in Tehran in November 1979; and in the third phase, he became a 'Mad Mullah' and an irrational ideologue, a perception popular from November 1979 until his death in 1989. His very physical image seemed to convey some sort of unreasoning, even demonic force. As one observer later put it: 'to Westerners, his hooded eyes and severe demeanor, his unkempt gray beard and his black turban and robes conveyed an avenger's wrath.'[7] All three images were misleading at best, however, and at worst simply wrong.

Khomeini as a 'figure of irrelevance'

The important Iran scholar James Bill has noted that there still existed in early 1979 what he calls a 'supershah myth' among Western intelligence operatives and embassy officials.[8] In other words, there was a widespread notion that the Shah was simply invincible and could not fail. As a result, the non-collection of intelligence on Iran hampered any understanding in Western capitals of what was really happening in the country. The Shah himself seems to have encouraged this: prickly and prone to paranoia and conspiracy theorizing, there was a tendency to rely on his own estimations of where he stood, and a consequent deference to and reliance on his own secret police, SAVAK, for intelligence. This tendency also led to an over-reliance upon the inevitably idiosyncratic impressions of the British and US ambassadors in particular, impressions which may have been rooted in a long experience of diplomatic activity but were certainly not based upon any real experience of intelligence-gathering. There appears to have been a deliberate decision made on the part of US intelligence that 'the Shah is OK', and since the wheel which does not squeak rarely gets the oil, understaffing and budget-cutting during the 1970s tended to deprioritize the Iranian situation (only a small handful of CIA people remained in the Tehran Embassy by the time the hostage crisis began). American reliance on one man for intelligence, Ambassador William Sullivan, meant that when he gave no hint until November 1978 that anything was wrong, President Carter was essentially compelled to rely on this judgement.

The CIA failed to predict the downfall of Mohammed Reza Pahlavi, the Shah of Iran, a leader allied with the United States who for a number of years had found it increasingly difficult to maintain his grip on the country. The Shah had been placed in office following a CIA-inspired coup in 1953 which deposed the democratically elected Mohammed Mossadegh. Although by the 1970s the Shah's hold on the country was getting more and more tenuous – he had resorted by this time to the use of brutal secret police tactics to maintain that slippery hold – many in the US intelligence community apparently believed up until the very last moment that the Shah would survive the profound undercurrent of discontent with his leadership. On 12 December 1978 – relying of course on bad intelligence – President Carter stated: 'I fully expect the Shah to maintain power in Iran ... the predictions of doom and disaster that come from some sources have certainly not been realized at all.'[9] On 16 January 1979, however – barely one month after Carter's 'doom and disaster' quote and less than 13 months after the President's 'island of stability' speech – the Shah would flee the country and go into exile. On 1 February, the Ayatollah Khomeini arrived at Tehran airport to the jubilation of a fanatical welcoming crowd, estimated by some to number six million people. Khomeini's arrival signalled the emergence of a new chapter in Iran's history and the beginning of what is now commonly known as the Islamic Revolution in the region.

Decision-making about the Shah was characterized by flawed and dysfunctional interagency processes, and Carter generally received poor and intermittent advice on Iran.[10] And if the President did not exhibit much understanding of what was transpiring within the country, neither, it must be conceded, did the US intelligence community. As then CIA Director Stansfield Turner later admitted:

> We let him down badly with respect to our coverage of the Iranian scene. We had not appreciated how shaky the Shah's political foundation was; did not know that the Shah was terminally ill; did not understand who Khomeini was and the support his movement had; did not have a clue as to who the hostage-takers were or what their objective was; and could not pinpoint within the embassy where the hostages were being held and under what conditions. As far as our failure to judge the Shah's position more accurately, we were just plain asleep.[11]

Many American intelligence officials who had spent time in Iran came to see Pahlavi as a permanent and unmovable fixture within the Iranian political system. To those who had done several tours of Iran and had seen the Shah shake hands with US presidents from Eisenhower to Carter, Bill notes, 'the Shah seemed to have been around forever. They had witnessed his many close brushes with disaster and had come to view him as indestructible. They could not envisage an Iran without the Shah.'[12]

Perhaps the most significant by-product of this 'cult of the Shah' was a widespread ignorance of Khomeini and his objectives, which seems to have been common even among US-based academics working on the Middle East. While some of them knew something about Khomeini, others had absolutely no idea who he was. Bernard Lewis, a Professor of Middle Eastern Affairs at Princeton University later to achieve renown as an informal adviser to Vice-President Dick Cheney, has admitted that he knew very little about Khomeini before the latter's return to Tehran. Lewis recalls that in early 1979 he went straight to his university library to look Khomeini up, finding a book by Khomeini he had never read before called *Islamic Government*.[13]

More importantly, US intelligence on Khomeini was practically non-existent before the middle of 1978. Although a June 1963 CIA study had noted that Khomeini potentially represented a dangerous threat to the Shah's regime, personnel turnover and Khomeini's exile from Iran meant that the US government had all but forgotten him by the late 1970s.[14] The head of the Iran desk at the State Department, Henry Precht, recalls that 'in May of 1978, there was a secret cable from the Embassy referring to Ayatollah Khomeini which had to identify him for readers. We were ignorant about the political potential of the clergy or even the National Front and their respective influences in the Iranian society.'[15] Moreover, there was no full-time expert on Iran within the National Security Council until Gary Sick was appointed to the job in 1978. Carter's late Press Secretary, Jody Powell, remembers memoranda about Khomeini circulating in the White House prior to 1979, and everyone of course eventually did come to hear of the Iranian cleric; nevertheless, few knew anything very substantive about him early on. There were no governmental-level contacts between the Carter administration and either moderate or radical opposition members in the 1970s, and the opposition in general was, as we have noted, considered of little consequence in any case. Although a number of people became convinced by late 1978 that the Shah's rule would soon end, the general assumption continued to be that liberals or moderates of some kind would prevail. Those who suggested that Westerners should talk to Khomeini, already isolated in number, were marginalized by fears that doing so would weaken the Shah. In addition, why talk to someone who probably would not be a major player anyway? Why take the risk? Having gone 'all in' on the Shah, however, the United States was left with nothing when he fell.

Within the lower levels of the CIA, there were certainly voices warning that Khomeini was becoming the most important player within the opposition movement to the Shah. A report at the end of November 1978, for instance, warned that Khomeini was xenophobic, anti-American and a threat to US interests in the region. He now represented a genuine threat to the Shah's rule, and was determined to topple him. One 'Alert

Memorandum' even warned that the actions of Khomeini would be 'the single most important factor in determining what will happen within Iran'.[16] But there were many who could not or did not wish to heed such dire predictions. As Bruce Riedel (a CIA officer working on Iran at the time) recalls, 'our bosses couldn't cope with the idea of an 80-year old Ayatollah, which they didn't even know what an Ayatollah was, who lived on garlic and onions and yoghurt, directing a revolution that was about to topple America's most important ally'.[17]

Khomeini as a 'Gandhi-like figure'

Western disregard of Khomeini began to change in late 1978 when the ageing but charismatic cleric arrived in Paris, and the Western media descended upon him in their hundreds. The Ayatollah had been living in the holy city of Najaf in Iraq since 1964, but was exiled by Saddam Hussein in 1978.[18] He was then refused admission to Kuwait, but in retrospect this turned out to be a blessing in disguise. Invited to stay at a villa just outside Paris, Khomeini was for the first time in his life accessible to the world's media. Journalists who would not have dreamed of flying to Iraq or Iran all of a sudden could visit the man just miles outside a fashionable Western European city. Many in the West began to realize that this oddity was actually playing a role in Iranian politics from afar, and he became a figure of great interest for the world's press. As Richard Cottam, a Professor of Political Science at the University of Pittsburgh who had visited Khomeini in Paris before the fall of the Shah, noted, 'there was a growing fascination in the media with this new and exotic world figure who gave interviews sitting on the floor of a modest house outside Paris, speaking with simple force and bluntness'.[19]

In late 1978 and early 1979, there was a great deal of optimism about Khomeini's intentions among the mass media. Dorothy Gilliam, for instance, described Khomeini as 'the man of the hour, a holy man in waiting'.[20] In early 1979, *Time* magazine wrote of 'a sense of controlled optimism in Iran'. It expressed the view – exceptionally commonplace at the time – that

> those who know [Khomeini] expect that eventually he will settle in the Shi'ite holy city of Qum and resume a life of teaching and prayer. It seems improbable that he would try to become a kind of Archbishop Makarios of Iran, directly holding the reins of power. Khomeini believes that Iran should become a parliamentary democracy, with several political parties.[21]

Even well into 1979, there was more than a little wishful thinking among scholars of Iran on this score as well. Cottam described Khomeini as courageous and possessed of a 'simple dignity'.[22] More strikingly, Richard Falk, a noted Professor of International Law at Princeton University who had also visited the Iranian cleric in France, wrote in a February 1979 Op-Ed piece in the *New York Times* that Khomeini had been 'defamed' by the news media, not least because he had in fact given 'numerous reassurances' to non-Muslims that they would not be persecuted in his Iran. Falk cast doubt upon the idea that Khomeini himself was some sort of devious Machiavellian, and on the notion that life under him would be unbearable for its citizens. 'To suppose that Ayatollah Khomeini is dissembling seems almost beyond belief. Khomeini's style is to express his real views defiantly and without apology, regardless of consequences. He has little incentive to suddenly become devious for the sake of American public opinion', he argued. In a highly optimistic claim which he would later come to regret, Falk added that

> the depiction of him as fanatical, reactionary and the bearer of crude prejudices seems certainly and happily false. ... Having created a new model of popular revolution based, for the most part, on nonviolent tactics, Iran may yet provide us with a desperately-needed model of humane governance for a third-world country.

Khomeinism, moreover, was distinctive as a revolutionary movement for 'its concern with resisting oppression and promoting social justice', Falk maintained.[23] In the spring of 1979 he spoke of 'Khomeini's promise', expressing a similar view in the pages of *Foreign Policy* while castigating the Carter Administration for not being more proactive in reaching out to the Iranian cleric.[24]

One can easily dismiss Falk's statements about Khomeini as atypical, or at least unrepresentative of the thinking of those inside the Carter Administration (Falk was of course an outsider). Nevertheless, he did capture a view that was all too common at the time inside the American government as well. Most notably, US Ambassador to the United Nations Andrew Young famously called Khomeini 'some kind of saint', suggesting that 'it would be impossible to have a fundamentalist state in Iran' because Western influence was supposedly too strong there, and Ambassador William Sullivan explicitly compared Khomeini to Gandhi in a famous memorandum called 'Thinking the Unthinkable' sent to Washington from Tehran on 9 November 1978.[25] Sullivan – who had earlier been seen as pro-Shah by many – advocated opening talks with the Iranian cleric. As Gary Sick later related, from Sullivan's perspective 'Khomeini could be expected to return to Tehran in triumph and hold a "Gandhi-like" position in the political constellation'.[26]

In similar vein, State Department Iran expert Henry Precht is said to have often described Khomeini as 'another Gandhi' during the same period.

Ledeen and Lewis relate one especially revealing story in which Precht is supposed to have attacked members of the media who had claimed that Khomeini would be a despot:

> There was considerable consternation and disgruntlement in the State Department and the CIA when three American newspapers published extensive accounts of Khomeini's writings. The articles showed that Khomeini's books revealed him as a violently anti-Western, anti-American, anti-Zionist, and anti-Semitic individual, who offered an unattractive alternative to the shah. Yet as late as the first week in February 1979, when Khomeini was returning in triumph to Tehran, Henry Precht [head of the State Department's Iran desk] told an audience of some two hundred persons at the State Department 'open forum' meeting that the newspaper accounts were severely misleading, and he went so far as to accuse *Washington Post* editorial columnist Stephen Rosenfeld of wittingly disseminating excerpts from a book that Precht considered at best a collection of notes taken by students, and at worst a forgery. Precht was hardly an isolated case, for the conviction was widespread that Khomeini's books were either false, exaggerated, or misunderstood.[27]

This view was not shared by Gary Sick or by his boss, National Security Adviser Zbigniew Brzezinski; the latter openly doubted, as he later put it rather sarcastically, that the Iranian cleric would return to Iran as some sort of 'venerable sage'.[28] Nevertheless, the Gandhi analogy was extraordinarily popular at the time. This kind of cognitive error may occasionally derive from straightforward ignorance, and statements like Young's about Khomeini's supposed 'sainthood' have long provided fodder for right-wing commentators in the United States attempting to show that the Carter administration was simply incompetent. However, cognitive science has shown us that such mistakes also commonly derive from the way in which the human mind works. We put people, places and objects into categories, employing simple scripts, schemas and analogies to cope with the often bewildering amount of information with which ordinary people are bombarded every day.

Ambassador Young was also possibly comparing Khomeini to Martin Luther King (MLK) in his own mind. If so, Young was simply doing what we all do; he was making sense of something novel and unprecedented by falling back on what he knew. As a young man, Young had been a close associate of MLK and had played a prominent role in the Civil Rights Movement, a factor which doubtless contributed to Carter's decision to make Young the US Ambassador to the United Nations. Unfamiliar as he undoubtedly was with Iranian politics, it must have been all too tempting to see Khomeini as 'another MLK', another religious figure who would promote all that was right and decent in the world. We also know from cognitive consistency theory and other motivational approaches that wishful thinking is a very human tendency; we see what we want to see, not necessarily what is actually there. Having been divided over what to do about the Shah and then 'losing' Iran, many in the Carter administration desperately wanted to believe that his replacement would be a friend to the West. Having agitated for an end to the Shah's regime, surely Khomeini could not be any worse than the man he had replaced.

In retrospect, it is fairly clear that comparisons between King/Gandhi and Khomeini were almost entirely inapt, of course. Most obviously, the Ayatollah condoned (and probably explicitly ordered) the execution of large numbers of his political opponents, especially anyone who had supported the Shah or been associated with SAVAK, while violence of this sort was anathema to King or Gandhi. MLK, for instance, deplored the killing on all sides during the Vietnam War. While both Khomeini and Gandhi were motivated by religious factors, the former believed that Islam was the one true faith to which all must adhere, while the latter sought peace between the Hindus and the Muslims in India. King was similarly tolerant of other religions in a way that Khomeini patently was not. For Gandhi, human rights and social justice were just as important as religion, while Khomeini showed little concern with issues like these or with equality in general. King was explicitly focused on the latter, of course, marching for peace and calling for racial equality.

One cannot fully understand Carter's outrage at Khomeini's behaviour in endorsing the Embassy takeover in November 1979 without first comprehending the source of his original hopes and expectations about the Ayatollah's likely conduct as Iran's de facto leader. Carter's presidential memoir *Keeping Faith* is unfortunately not very forthcoming on this issue – like many such memoirs, cognitive errors tend to get airbrushed out of the story – but it is likely that Carter's initial perceptions of Khomeini derived from two main sources. First of all, stock images about the behaviour of 'holy men' in general tend to reinforce the notion that such figures largely confine themselves to spiritual rather than temporal matters; there is often widespread consternation in the United Kingdom when the Archbishop of Canterbury occasionally speaks out on what are seen as partisan issues, for instance, and there are role expectations in the West which tend to circumscribe the political activism of religious figures. Probably more important than such stock characters in Carter's case, however, were those religious/political figures who had spoken out on temporal matters and had an impact on Carter's own political thinking, most notably King and Gandhi. King in particular had played a formative role in Carter's own attitudes as a relatively progressive young legislator in Georgia, and the Carter family had espoused the cause of civil rights for black Americans at a time when such positions were deeply unpopular in the South. Both King and Gandhi evoked liberal cognitive scripts, in which a religious figure pushes hard for social justice and progress. The notion that a religious leader might advocate something other than the progress of mankind in a Western or liberal sense was simply outside of Carter's experience.

Deborah Larson notes that Harry Truman was initially fooled into thinking that Stalin could be trusted in the aftermath of the Second World War, in part because the Soviet leader physically resembled his own mentor from Missouri politics, Boss Pendergast. Truman apparently reasoned that Stalin would be a man of his word, just like Pendergast had been – a kind of cognitive process similar to analogical reasoning which Larson terms a 'persona'.[29] In similar fashion the use of the Gandhi persona had a significant cognitive impact. While there was no real physical resemblance between Gandhi and Khomeini, those who used this image reasoned that the Iranian leader would be a force for peace and non-violent change. He would also play a symbolic role in politics like modern European monarchs, but would not try to shape policy in an instrumental sense. The Iranian cleric might even preside over an Islamic democracy which would in the end be relatively friendly to the United States and the West in general.

The image of Khomeini as a benign apolitical figure was probably not purely cognitive but emotional as well; those who bought into it wanted it to be true in a motivational sense. This kind of wishful thinking was not shared in the National Security Council as we have already noted, but it probably was in the Oval Office. Like many former state governors with little or no foreign policy experience and relatively little knowledge about this domain, Carter frequently fell back on intuitive but stereotypical images about how given actors could be expected to behave. Carter undoubtedly felt a kinship or link with Khomeini as a fellow spiritualist and knew that Islam is a religion of peace, so he probably expected the Ayatollah to behave like his own cognitive image of how Western 'holy men' typically conduct themselves.

While it is easy to be wise after the event – an instance of hindsight bias again, perhaps – it is worth noting that this image of Khomeini was widely shared in 1978 not just among ordinary Iranians but among the Iranian leader's own immediate circle. Many around Khomeini both in Paris and in the early months after his return to Iran have confessed that they were essentially duped by the Iranian cleric in this respect. For instance, Mansour Farhang, the revolutionary government's first Ambassador to the UN, has confessed that 'at the time, I saw him as the Mahatma Gandhi of Iran'.[30] What most did not appreciate at the time (or even now) is that Khomeini was deliberately cultivating this image. Knowing that the source of his political power lay in being all things to all men, a sort of anti-Shah about whom people would assume the best, he quite consciously made himself an empty vessel, helping to fashion the misperception himself.[31] Since the Shah had been an autocrat, the anti-Shah must be a democrat. In his messages from Paris, he focused on attacking the incumbent Shah without saying much about what he stood for himself (rather similar, ironically, to standard US presidential campaign strategy). Even moderate figures like Abdolhassan Bani-Sadr, Ibrahim Yazdi and Sadegh Ghotzbadeh – those seemingly closest to Khomeini in Paris – were completely fooled by this, and Bani-Sadr admitted as much many times in later interviews. Khomeini deliberately lied to Bani-Sadr in Paris, for instance, saying that he had abandoned the doctrine of *velayat-e-fakir*. He later admitted that he had told a 'white lie'.[32]

The Western intelligence community admittedly should have known what *velayet-e-fakir* was, not least because it formed the core of Khomeini's political and religious viewpoint as articulated in his book *Islamic Government*. This collection of the Iranian cleric's lectures had been in the public domain since 1970. *Velayet-e-fakir* – which literally means 'rule by the jurisprudent' – was essentially a justification for political rule by the clergy. Derived more from Plato's *Republic* than it was from the *Quran*, the doctrine was especially radical in Iran, where a long-established quietist tradition had generally refrained from political activities; indeed, Khomeini's doctrine had often been rejected by most other ayatollahs as virtual heresy. Many of the students who seized the Embassy in 1979 were largely ignorant of who Khomeini was, however. We possess no reliable polls on this point, but Michael Metrinko (a former teacher in Iran and one of the hostages himself) discovered that most younger people had little idea in 1978 who Khomeini was, though older Iranians had certainly heard of him.[33] The Shah's secret police had banned Khomeini's writings, and so even an Iranian who wanted to read *Islamic Government* would have found it difficult to do so in the 1970s.

In this sense, the Shah's restrictive political laws played directly into the Ayatollah's hands. Being an empty vessel was politically useful, and it caused Iranian moderates who should have been wary of the old cleric – and who perhaps wanted to believe that the Khomeini of 1979 was not the Khomeini of *Islamic Government* – to let down their guard. It is said that moderates like Ibrahim Yazdi – acting as interpreters outside the house in Paris – would routinely 'soften' the words of their leader for Western ears, making them sound more diplomatic than they in fact were. If even those around Khomeini were deceived by the man, it is perhaps little wonder that several key Carter officials (and, indeed, Carter himself) were as well.

Khomeini as a 'Mad Mullah'

If it is not entirely clear just how long the misperception that Khomeini was 'another Gandhi' reigned in the corridors of Foggy Bottom and the White

House, it is relatively easy to pinpoint the precise moment at which that particular illusion ended. When the US Embassy was seized in November 1979 precipitating the 444-day-long hostage crisis – or, more precisely, when the Ayatollah sided with the students who had taken the Embassy – President Carter and many of his colleagues shifted 180 degrees, and began to see Khomeini as an entirely irrational figure. The most common response within the Carter Administration initially was to dismiss both the radical students, and the Ayatollah in whose name they were acting, as insane: what could they possibly hope to achieve by such an action? In his memoirs Carter claimed that the Iranian leader 'was acting insanely', though he notes that 'we always behaved as if we were dealing with a rational person'.[34] It is at about this time that the all-too-familiar 'Mad Mullah' stereotype was invented and took hold of the popular imagination in the West.

William Beeman has provided an apt description of the 'Mad Mullah' image, which has its parallel in the 'Great Satan' image held by many Iranians:

> Suddenly, in 1979 Tehran seemed filled with turbaned, bearded, old men espousing a combination of religious and political philosophy that was strange to Westernized ears. When confronted with individuals whose actions are incomprehensible, the natural human tendency is to assign them to a 'residual' category within the culture. 'Crazy', 'irrational', 'evil', 'incompetent', 'moronic', and 'incomprehensible' are just a few of these categorizations. ... Just as the Great Satan was born, so was the Mad Mullah, whose crazed and wild-eyed image became the stuff of editorial cartoons.[35]

Why is the Mad Mullah stereotype wrong, though, or at least misleading? In short, because it downplayed or simply misunderstood Khomeini's vast pragmatism and ruthless determination to succeed. If anything is clear about the man with the hindsight of 30 years or more, it is that Khomeini was highly political and highly rational about the goals he wanted to achieve. He was especially adept at turning crises to his advantage. Ironically, it was the State Department – many of whose members had earlier engaged in wishful thinking about Khomeini – who saw what the Iranian cleric was doing most clearly. Secretary of State Cyrus Vance argued that the hostage taking was being manipulated for domestic political reasons; the Ayatollah was by no means fully in control of Iranian politics in the immediate aftermath of the Shah's fall, and so he took advantage of what the students had done in order to mobilize Iranians against the common foe, the 'Great Satan'.[36] The hostages, in other words, were simply useful pawns in an internal power struggle. Gary Sick has similarly argued that Khomeini consciously exploited the hostage crisis for his own domestic political purposes, since 'the real issue was Khomeini's constitution and the realization of his vision of an Iranian republic'.[37]

Khomeini knew how to seize the moment. Far from being an unrepentant ideologue, he often bent ideology to the needs of the situation (purchasing arms from the Americans during the Reagan Administration in 1985–1986, for instance, when they were needed to fight the war against Saddam). Far from being trapped in the seventh century, Khomeini was more than willing to use Western twentieth-century technology when it suited him. While in Paris, he proved technologically savvy, using cassette tapes and modern communication systems to broadcast his ideas and send out messages to his followers. And when he confronted the problem of how to get back into Iran from exile in Paris – members of the military still loyal to the Shah had vowed to shoot his plane down – Khomeini rather cleverly decided to take along a number of Western television and print journalists, including the late Peter Jennings of ABC, Elaine Sciolino then of Newsweek and a German TV crew. Khomeini correctly calculated that the Iranian military would not shoot down a plane full of Western civilians. The plane was allowed into Iranian airspace, and then landed without a hitch.

Domestically, Khomeini then played an especially skilful and savvy role in manoeuvring his rivals out of the way. He knew that his government would have to include a large number of moderate figures who did not agree with *velayet-e-fakir* at all; indeed, he would have to include a number of members of the nationalist and pro-democracy movements. He did just this, but at the same time he put his own man in each ministry. Rival institutions holding the real power were created alongside the official ones. Alongside the army, for instance, was the Revolutionary Guard. Alongside the police force were the Komitehs. Alongside the provisional government was the Revolutionary Council, which exercised the real power. Eventually, the Guardian Council would vet candidates for office, ensuring that only 'sufficiently Islamic' figures could run for office and vetoing 'unIslamic' legislation. More generally, Khomeini created a system of parallel government with many superficial trappings of democracy but where real power resided with one man, the Supreme Leader. Khomeini also later used the failed US rescue mission, the 1980 invasion by Iraq, and the Salman Rushdie affair to strengthen the revolutionary government and rally his forces.

The 'Mad Mullah' image was misguided not just because it failed to see the element of strategic thinking behind Khomeini's actions, but because it also failed to recognize the historical grievances which had given rise to the students' actions in seizing the US Embassy in 1979. Massoumeh Ebtekar's explanation for why the hostage crisis began in the first place is especially useful to historians. Ebtekar, who acted as the spokeswoman for the students through most of the hostage crisis, emphasizes the overriding importance of the 1953 analogy as a determining force behind the embassy takeover:

When the man whose long rule had brought riches beyond all description to his immediate family and associates, and impoverishment and cultural subjugation to the Iranian people, was welcomed in the United States, we believed that the West was once more determined to subvert our newly won independence. Were the fate and future of our country once again going to be decided in Washington D.C., which had first brought him to power in its 1953 coup? How could we voice our concern, our indignation? To whom could we protest? From the media establishment and from international bodies, the response was a deafening silence. Iranians, whose immense sacrifices had finally brought down a corrupt dynasty, were once again being ignored.[38]

Later on in her book, Ebtekar recalls that

this was not the first time Iran had lived through harrowing times. In August 1953, a coup d'etat engineered by the CIA that overthrew the democratically elected government of Dr. Mossadegh and restored the Shah to power had dashed all hopes of establishing an independent democratic system. The price of genuine independence was heavy.

She insists that 'our reading of our own history told us that we had to act quickly ... action was our only choice'.[39] She is suggesting, in other words, that the students genuinely believed that the United States was about to mount another coup – this time against the Ayatollah Khomeini. Generations of Iranians were brought up in the shadow of 1953, and it became a defining experience and national rallying point – a mixture of historical fact and exaggeration – in their lives. Consequently, when another Iranian leader whose political priorities clashed markedly with Western interests appeared on the scene after the fall of the Shah, it is easy to see why that historical script should have become activated in such a striking way.

There was little concrete evidence at the time (and none has emerged since) to suggest that Carter himself had any serious plans to mount a second coup; according to available records, Brzezinski was alone among the president's advisers in seriously considering such an action.[40] Moreover, even if Carter had wished to take this action, the CIA lacked the human assets on the ground to make this viable, and the records show that the president strongly resisted pressure for the Shah's admission into the US initially (something which is hard to explain if his admission on medical grounds was in fact the pretext for a second coup).[41] Nevertheless, perceptions mattered as much as, if not more than, reality. To expect that history would repeat itself was, moreover, an understandable position for the students to take at the time, given the fact that none of this information was available to them. We are now fairly certain that Khomeini had no foreknowledge of the students' actions, and he apparently debated whether to support it afterwards; nevertheless, he came to see the political utility of what the students had done, and capitalized on this in order to solidify his revolution.

Conclusion

Many things had to come together to produce Khomeini's rise, but it was very unlikely in the sense that any one of 10 or 15 slight changes to history could have altered the outcome, and it was very hard to imagine in any case at the time. There was apparently a substantial increase in religiosity in Iran during the 1970s. According to one estimate, more mosques were built between 1968 and 1978 than in the previous 200 years. The number of Iranians visiting Mecca for pilgrimage rose from 12,000 to 100,000 during the same period. The Shah's modernization efforts were seen as having failed, and other projects (notably Panarabism, socialism and Marxism) were seen as having failed elsewhere in the Middle East. And yet none of this preordained a political role for Islam in Iran or the emergence of a politicized clergy in a country which lacked a tradition of this. Hardly anyone at all predicted this turn of events, and it took an extraordinary series of events to bring it about.

It was, in that sense, one of those 'Black Swans' of which Taleb talks. It was the outcome of an incredible mixture of Machiavellian fortuna, skill and sheer luck on Khomeini's part, but it could so easily not have happened. For instance, in 1978 Saddam Hussein offered to assassinate Khomeini. What if the Shah had said yes? It could easily have happened. What if the Shah had not miscalculated and ordered the publication of a defamatory article about Khomeini in early 1978? This single act drew more attention to a 'forgotten man' than Khomeini himself ever could. What if Khomeini had remained in Najaf – or gone to Kuwait – and had not attracted the attention of the world's media? That too could have happened. What if the Iranian military had gone ahead and shot down Khomeini's plane? Again, by many accounts it almost happened.

If the failure to anticipate the Islamic revolution in Iran was partly a failure of the imagination, the question becomes whether it will ever be possible to predict Black Swans. This question probably misses the central point that Black Swans are never anticipated because they are inherently unpredictable, but some misperceptions on the American side were probably avoidable. For instance, of the three images of Khomeini presented here, the second ('Gandhi-like figure') was undoubtedly the most damaging of all to the Carter Administration. The first ('Figure of irrelevance') seemed reasonable at the time, and by the time the third emerged ('Mad Mullah') it was too late to avert the course of events in Iran; the hostage crisis had begun, and there was little that Carter could do to get the US diplomats back until their political utility to Khomeini had dissipated and circum-stances changed. However, the second image led the administration down a disastrous course. Until November 1979, it led Carter and others to believe that normalization of relations with Iran, now led by a fellow 'holy man', was a real possibility. It led Embassy officials to put out feelers to moderate Iranians in a way which provoked suspicion that the destruction of the revolution by a foreign power was again imminent. Unwittingly, this played directly into Khomeini's hands, but his real views – especially his virulent anti-Americanism – should have been known to the CIA from his actions in 1963, when he led protests against the US presence in Iran which eventually led to his exile by the Shah. His views should have been known from the doctrines espoused in *Islamic Government*, and they should have been known from the cassette lectures he was circulating in Iran. Why none of this ever really percolated up to the top levels of government in 1978–1979 after it became clear that Khomeini was a force to be reckoned with is still a mystery, but we do know that wishful thinking is a powerful and very human failing.

Notes

1 See Stansfield Turner, *Burn Before Reading: Presidents, CIA Directors, and Secret Intelligence* (New York: Hyperion, 2005), p. 180.

2 Quoted in William Daugherty, *In the Shadow of the Ayatollah: A CIA Hostage in Iran* (Annapolis, MD: Naval Institute Press, 2001), p. 74. For a good general analysis of US intelligence failure and the Shah, see Robert Jervis, *Why Intelligence Fails: Lessons from the Iranian Revolution and the Iraq War* (Ithaca, NY: Cornell University Press, 2010).

3 It is in that respect similar to failure to predict the end of the Cold War, or the precise manner in which 9/11 occurred.

4 Naseem Nicholas Taleb, *The Black Swan: The Impact of the Highly Improbable* (New York: Random House, 2007).

5 Charles Kurzman, *The Unthinkable Revolution in Iran* (Cambridge, MA: Harvard University Press, 2004).

6 Baruch Fischoff and Ruth Beyth, '"I Knew It Would Happen": Remembered Probabilities of Once-future Things', *Organizational Behavior and Human Performance*, Vol. 13, No. 1, 1975, pp. 1–16.

7 See Milton Viorst, 'Ayatullah Ruhollah Komeini', *Time*, (13 April 1998).

8 James Bill, *The Eagle and the Lion: The Tragedy of American–Iranian Relations* (London: Yale University Press, 1988).

9 Quoted in Bill (1988), p. 259.

10 Alexander Moens, 'President Carter's Advisers and the Fall of the Shah', *Political Science Quarterly*, No. 106, (1991), pp. 211–37.

11   Turner (2005), p. 180.

12   Bill (1988), p. 403.

13   Quoted in the documentary *The Road To 9/11* (PBS Videos, 2006).

14   See Doug MacEachin and Janne Nolan, 'Iran: Intelligence Failure or Policy Stalemate?', Working Group Report No. 1, Edmund Walsh School of Foreign Service, Georgetown University, p. 5. Available at: http://www12.georgetown.edu/sfs/isd/Iran_WG_Report.pdf.

15   Interview with Henry Precht conducted by Fariba Amini, (17 June 2003). Available at: http://www.iranian.com/FaribaAmini/2003/June/Precht/.

16   MacEachin and Nolan, 'Iran', p. 15.

17   Bruce Riedel, quoted in the BBC documentary *The Man Who Changed The World*, BBC Iran and the West Series, first broadcast 7 February 2009.

18   The cleric was considered a nuisance by Saddam and apparently offered to assassinate Khomeini, but the Shah turned this down.

19   Richard Cottam, 'Goodbye to America's Shah', *Foreign Policy*, Vol. 34, spring 1979, pp. 3–14. See also Charles Peters, 'The Khomeini Corollary: Take the Revolution to Where the Reporters Want To Be and You'll Get Worldwide Exposure', *Washington Post*, (4 March 1979), p. C8.

20   Dorothy Gilliam, 'The Optimism of a Holy Man in Exile', *Washington Post*, (15 November 1978), p. D1.

21   *Time* magazine, (12 February 1979).

22   Cottam (1979), p. 11.

23   Richard Falk, 'Trusting Khomeini', *New York Times*, (16 February 1979), p. A27.

24   Richard Falk, 'Khomeini's Promise', *Foreign Policy*, Vol. 34, (spring 1979), pp. 28–34.

25   Quoted in John Stempel, *Inside the Iranian Revolution* (Bloomington, IN: Indiana University Press, 1981), p. 176.

26   Gary Sick, *All Fall Down: America's Encounter With Iran* (New York: Random House, 1985), p. 95.

27   Michael Ledeen and William Lewis, *Debacle: The American Disaster in Iran* (New York: Vintage Books, 1982), pp. 129–30. For a rare example of this more pessimistic but nevertheless realistic view of Khomeini from this period, see 'The Darker Forces of Islam: The Vision of Ruhollah Khomeini', *Washington Post*, (5 January 1979), p. A19.

28   Zbigniew Brzezinski, *Power and Principle: Memoirs of the National Security Adviser, 1977–1981* (New York: Farrar, Straus & Giroux, 1983), p. 381.

29   Deborah Welch Larson, *Origins of Containment: A Psychological Explanation* (Princeton, NJ: Princeton University Press, 1985), pp. 55–6.

30   Quoted in the Al Jazeera documentary *I Knew Khomeini*, first broadcast on 21 January 2009.

31   This argument is similar in some ways to that made about Dwight Eisenhower by Fred Greenstein. See the latter's *The Hidden-hand Presidency:*

Eisenhower as Leader (Baltimore, MD: The Johns Hopkins University Press, 1994).

32 Quoted in the Al Jazeera documentary *I Knew Khomeini*.

33 Quoted in the BBC documentary *The Man Who Changed The World*.

34 Jimmy Carter, *Keeping Faith: Memoirs of a President* (New York: Bantam, 1982), p. 468.

35 William Beeman, *The 'Great Satan' vs. the 'Mad Mullahs': How the United States and Iran Demonize Each Other* (London: Praeger, 2005), p. 69.

36 Cyrus Vance, *Hard Choices: Critical Years in Americans Foreign Policy* (New York: Simon & Schuster, 1983), p. 376.

37 Sick (1985), p. 251.

38 Massoumeh Ebtekar, *Takeover in Tehran: The Inside Story of the 1979 US Embassy Capture* (Vancouver: Talonbooks, 2000), p. 37. See also David Patrick Houghton, *US Foreign Policy and the Iran Hostage Crisis* (New York: Cambridge University Press, 2001), esp. pp. 46–74.

39 Ebtekar (2000), p. 52.

40 Brzezinski (1983), pp. 382–98.

41 Kenneth Pollack, *The Persian Puzzle: The Conflict Between Iran and America* (New York: Random House, 2004), p. 163. The Shah was finally admitted to New York for hospital treatment on 22 October 1979.

CHAPTER SEVEN

Skewed perceptions: Yasir Arafat in the eyes of American officials, 1969–2004

William B. Quandt

Introduction

Yasir Arafat dominated Palestinian politics for most of a generation, from 1969 when he took over as Chairman of the Palestine Liberation Organization (PLO) until his death in November 2004. During this time, seven American presidents, ten Secretaries of State and countless other high-ranking American foreign policy officials tried to figure out the enigmatic Palestinian leader, but only rarely were their views based on direct contact with Arafat. Instead, perceptions of the Palestinian leader were almost always skewed by prior policy commitments, or by highly politicized accounts of Arafat, his policies and his personality by both his friends and his enemies.

For much of the period from the rise of Arafat – and with him the phenomenon of contemporary Palestinian nationalism – until the end of 1988, most American officials were wedded to a view of 'the Palestinian problem', as it was usually termed, that envisaged an eventual political arrangement between Israel and Jordan that would somehow take care of the Palestinians. This so-called 'Jordan option' was occasionally questioned by those who thought the Palestinians would have to be given a voice in any eventual peace settlement, but on the whole it was King Hussein, not Arafat and his colleagues, who was viewed in Washington as the proper address for dealing with the thorny issues of the future of the West Bank, refugee claims, Jerusalem and security. The fact that the Israeli Labour Party was known to also look to Jordan rather than to the Palestinians as partners for any peace deal – and that they maintained covert ties with King Hussein – added weight to the idea that Arafat should be ignored, marginalized, and possibly even replaced. But Arafat had a way of challenging American preferences, so over time Washington did find ways to deal with him and even to try to decipher his often complex political manoeuvring.

The Nixon-Kissinger period

If the dominant view of Arafat during much of this period was that he was a radical, anti-Western terrorist, as well as pro-Soviet, anti-Israeli, or beholden to one or another Arab regime, there were alternative views that occasionally gained traction. In early 1970, the American Ambassador in Amman began to speak of King Hussein as a wasting asset and urged Washington to look seriously at the PLO and its claim to speak for most Palestinians.[1] But when King Hussein ousted the PLO from Jordan after 'Black September' of that year, this particular dissident view faded away, to be replaced by concern for the PLO role in Lebanon.

Before long, the United States found itself obliged to deal with the PLO in Beirut, since its embassy was right in a part of town where the PLO held sway with its armed militias. In one of the odd dimensions of the US–Palestinian relationship, it was the PLO that helped provide security for the American embassy in Beirut, and a liaison relationship was established between the CIA and Arafat's own intelligence chief, Ali Hassan Salameh (this latter relationship almost certainly led to Salameh's recruitment by the CIA and to a very valuable channel of intelligence over a period of years that only came to an end when Israel assassinated him in early 1979).[2]

In short, during this early period of US–Palestinian relations in the 1970s there was something of a gap between the political level – Presidents, top officials, most members of Congress, much of the foreign policy establishment – which saw Arafat and the PLO as little more than terrorists that should be contained or eliminated – and a part of the bureaucracy (State, CIA), a few academics and journalists, and some Arab-Americans who began to see Arafat as the strongest voice for the growing phenomenon of Palestinian nationalism. Whether one liked Arafat or not – and few Americans ever knew him well on a personal level – it was hard to deny, according to this minority view, that he was the leader of a movement that had to be taken seriously.

During the 1970s there were several moments when the US–PLO relationship was given serious high-level attention in Washington. The first of these moments took place during the Jordan crisis of September 1970 when President Richard Nixon and his National Security Adviser Henry Kissinger decided to throw their weight solidly behind King Hussein. Some may have thought at this point that with the PLO out of Jordan it was no longer much of a force to be reckoned with, but its re-emergence in Lebanon over the next decade was a reminder that it could not be so easily ignored.

After the October 1973 War, Nixon urged Kissinger to tackle the diplomacy of the Arab-Israeli conflict. Very quickly, Egypt's president, Anwar el Sadat, became an important partner of the United States. One of his ideas was that the Palestinians should be drawn into the peace negotiations. His own relationship with Arafat was generally good and he tried to persuade the Americans that Arafat, despite his prickly persona, should be seen as the only Palestinian leader capable of eventually making a deal with Israel that would bring the conflict to an end. American officials were not quick to adopt this view, but they heard it first and most consistently from Sadat.

Two major incidents coloured the views of top American decision-makers concerning Arafat. First was the Black September Organization's operation in Munich in September 1972, followed by another terror attack in March 1973 that resulted in the murder of two American diplomats in Khartoum. While Arafat maintained that Black September was not under his control, this was not believed to be true by American officials. In fact, they had considerable evidence that Arafat himself had given the order for the American diplomats to be executed.[3]

Despite a deep aversion in Washington at this time to Arafat as a person, there was nonetheless a realization that the Palestinian issue needed to be treated seriously if there were to be a chance of achieving an Arab-Israeli peace. Perhaps it was with this in mind that Kissinger authorized the CIA to hold talks with a high-ranking PLO official, Khalid al-Hassan, in early 1974. The talks did not really produce any long-lasting results, but over the years this channel remained open and would be used on occasions to clarify issues and to communicate on sensitive matters.

Whatever chance there might have been for some sort of official US–PLO dialogue came to an end in fall 1975. As part of the Sinai II agreement, Kissinger agreed to an Israeli request that the United States would not 'recognize or negotiate with the Palestine Liberation Organization as long as the Palestine Liberation Organization does not recognize Israel's right to exist and does not accept Security Council Resolutions 242 and 338' (Congress passed a law to this effect in 1985). Although Kissinger himself did not believe that this placed serious limits on the US's ability to deal with the PLO if it needed to do so – the commitment did not rule out all forms of communication, after all – it did mean that no high-level American politician met with PLO officials until 1993.

Carter makes overtures

The next moment in US–PLO relations that deserves some attention began in late 1975 and ended two years later. During this period, a number of American foreign policy experts began to develop the idea that the time was nearing when the United States should aim for a comprehensive settlement of the Arab-Israeli conflict. This took the form of a short policy paper entitled 'Toward Peace in the Middle East', more commonly referred to as 'The Brookings Report'.[4] The Report endorsed the concept of 'Palestinian self-determination' and noted that this might take the form of an independent state or 'entity' affiliated with Jordan. One of the signatories, Zbigniew Brzezinski, subsequently became Carter's National Security Adviser, and another, myself, became Brzezinski's staff person on the National Security Council with responsibility for the Middle East.

Early on in the Carter Administration, efforts were made by the president and his aides to signal an openness to Palestinian aspirations. Carter spoke of a 'Palestinian homeland' in March 1977, much to the consternation of the Israelis. During a visit to Israel a month earlier, Secretary of State Cyrus Vance had been told by the Israeli Foreign Minister that a PLO that accepted UN Resolution 242 would no longer be the PLO. With that degree of encouragement, the US had tried through numerous channels to see if the PLO might be willing to accept the 'land for peace' resolution, with its explicit recognition of the right of all states in the region, including Israel, to live in peace and security. The initial PLO reply was that 242 made no mention of the Palestinians by name, and therefore offered them nothing. This led Carter to suggest that the PLO should accept 242, but could then add a 'reservation' that would say something about the PLO's view that 242 was incomplete because it did not address Palestinian national rights.

Trying to communicate all of this through multiple Arab channels became very confusing, and Arafat was getting mixed messages. Consequently, Carter asked a private American, Landrum Bolling, to go to Beirut to meet with Arafat. Brzezinski met with him on 6 September 1977 and told him that if Arafat would accept 242 the United States would be open to Palestinian participation in peace negotiations and would begin a dialogue with the PLO. He explained that Arafat could make a statement of his reservations concerning 242, provided that those did not contradict his acceptance.

A few days later Bolling met with Arafat in Beirut. The PLO chairman had many of his colleagues with him, and made a strong case that he was trying to prevent his own hardliners from rejecting 242. Based on what they had heard from Arab regimes, the US plan for the Middle East did not seem to offer much to the Palestinians, but he did say that he wanted to keep channels open to see if a way forward could be found.[5]

When Bolling returned to Washington, he met with Brzezinski and described his meetings. He said that Arafat was under severe pressure from extremists in his own organization and especially from Syria. He would only be able to accept 242 if he had a direct guarantee from the United States that it would support an independent Palestinian state with himself as president. This went so far beyond anything that Carter was prepared to offer that the effort to bring in the PLO was essentially put on ice. In any event, the Israeli government, now under Menachem Begin's leadership, had no interest whatsoever in seeing the PLO accept UN Resolution 242. Although Carter and his team continued to look for ways to bring Palestinians into the negotiations, this episode clearly influenced their already sceptical view of Arafat.

Reagan turns to Jordan, then to the PLO

For the next decade, Arafat remained on the margins of American diplomacy. When Ronald Reagan replaced Jimmy Carter as president in January 1981, there was almost no one left in official Washington who was inclined to try to work with Arafat or the PLO. In fact, when Secretary of State Alexander Haig was told early in 1982 by Ariel Sharon that Israel was contemplating a major operation in Lebanon against the PLO, Haig expressed considerable interest. He did add a cautionary note – any attack should be in response to an 'internationally recognized provocation' and should not be disproportionate in size. Sharon seems to have correctly read this as a 'green light'.[6]

In June 1982 the Israeli War in Lebanon began. When it was over, a battered but not entirely defeated PLO agreed that its armed fighters would leave Lebanon. Arafat himself took up residence in Tunis. For many in Washington this meant that the PLO was part of the past and that they could once again pursue the Jordan option. This was the basic meaning of President Reagan's major speech on the Middle East on 1 September 1982.[7]

It is fair to say that the Reagan Administration was one of the most pro-Israeli in its basic orientation of any. And yet, it was Reagan and his Secretary of State George Shultz, in his last months in office, who finally opened the way to a direct US–PLO dialogue. How, one may ask, did that happen?

Within months of the outbreak of the Palestinian *intifada* in late 1987, it was clear to all that the Jordan option, so central to official US planning, was no longer a viable strategy. King Hussein had no influence over events in the West Bank and Gaza, a fact that he recognized and acted upon. In summer 1988, the king announced that Jordan was going to end its claim to the West Bank and that henceforth the PLO was the proper address for anyone wanting to deal with Palestinian affairs. This historic decision by Jordan opened the way for an effort to see if the PLO might be willing, under these new circumstances, to accept UN Resolution 242.

By September 1988, a non-official initiative had attracted the attention of the State Department. It consisted of a direct statement the PLO would make accepting 242, Israel's right to exist, and renouncing terrorism, coupled with a response from the United States that would recognize the PLO as spokesman for the Palestinians and an offer to open a dialogue with it. The point was to get both sides to agree on the content of the two statements, so that each party could know in advance the position of the other. The PLO would not move without knowing what the response of the United States would be, and vice versa.

Somewhat surprisingly, Secretary Shultz said that he was interested, but he first wanted to be sure that the PLO would be prepared to make such a statement. He also noted that the US would not be in a position to make its full circumstances known until after the presidential election in November, but that it could conceivably take action in the period following the election and preceding the inauguration of a new president.

Before long, Arafat had given the green light to this initiative and had confirmed that he was now ready to accept 242, but he still wanted to know precisely how the US would respond before he went public with his commitment. Shultz was determined not to make this easy for Arafat, and it is clear that he did not like Arafat as a person.[8] However, Schultz was a pragmatist, and after the election of George H. W. Bush in November 1988 he was given strong encouragement to see if this effort could be concluded before the new administration came to office.

The Swedish foreign minister then stepped in to help clarify the nature of the impending deal. Arafat told him that he was ready to make the public statement that the Americans needed, and Shultz authorized the Swedes to explain to Arafat how the US would respond. Arafat then announced that he intended to come to New York to give a speech at the United Nations. Shultz, however, said he would not give him a visa to enter the US. So Arafat went to Geneva in early December and gave a long and convoluted speech in which he seemed to meet most of the American demands. But he spoke in Arabic, and seemed to be saying that he 'condemned' rather than 'renounced' terrorism. Shultz felt that he had not met the American terms and that was conveyed to Arafat. The next day, Arafat spoke again, this time in English, and said that he accepted 242, recognized Israel's right to exist, and renounced terrorism, although many who were listening thought it sounded as if he had renounced 'tourism'. This was good enough for Shultz, who said that the US was now ready to deal with the PLO and would open an official dialogue. He would not support a Palestinian state or Palestinian self-determination, as the PLO had hoped, but he did allow his spokesman to say that the PLO would have the right, in the context of negotiations, to seek a Palestinian state. And so the taboo was finally broken.

Bush, Baker and Madrid

The Bush Administration may have wanted a dialogue with the PLO, but once faced with the actual prospect they were extremely cautious in the way in which they pursued it. No senior official in Washington was ready to meet with Arafat, who was to remain off limits for several more years. Instead, the American Ambassador in Tunis met with mid-level PLO officials in what soon became rather pointless discussions. By early 1990, Secretary of State James Baker authorized higher level contacts, not including Arafat himself, but with his right-hand man, Salah Khalaf (Abu Iyad).

The enhanced US–PLO dialogue did not last long. It was exposed in a Kuwaiti newspaper and the Americans were embarrassed to be found talking with a man whose reputation as a terrorist was second only to Arafat's among PLO leaders. Yet the dialogue did not cease immediately. Instead, it was brought to an end when a faction of the PLO led by Abul Abbas tried to carry out a military operation against Israel.[9] It was not a success, but it was nonetheless considered by Washington as a violation of the PLO promise not to engage in terror attacks. Arafat was told to denounce the operation and the Iraqi-supported group that launched it. However, by this time Arafat was being courted by Saddam Hussein, who clearly hoped to have the Palestinians in his corner when he launched his August invasion of Kuwait. Arafat hesitated, and Bush, under political pressure, publicly announced the suspension of the US–PLO dialogue – adding that he did so 'more in sorrow than in anger', an odd way of saying that he did not actually think it was such a great idea.[10] For the next three years, the PLO, and Arafat in particular, were back in the doghouse.

Interestingly, it was Abu Iyad who had tried to avoid the breach with the United States. He was concerned that Arafat was getting too close to Iraq, and that Iraq had 'something big' in mind. By this time Abu Iyad seems to have established contact with the CIA to carry out a joint operation against the Abu Nidal network. This led to a significant and successful operation to split the Abu Nidal terrorist organization. Many of those who defected from Abu Nidal came to Tunis and the PLO took them into the fold. One of those, however, was a plant, and he took revenge on Abu Iyad by assassinating him – probably on Saddam Hussein's orders – in January 1991, just on the eve of the US-led war to expel Iraqi forces from Kuwait.

The United States emerged from the Gulf War in early 1991 in a very strong position internationally. The Cold War had come to an end on terms that were hugely advantageous for the United States. It had expelled

Saddam Hussein's troops from Kuwait at minimal cost to itself, and with the backing of the United Nations and several key Arab partners. Those in the Arab world who had seemed to side with Saddam when he intervened in Kuwait – most notably Jordan, the PLO and Yemen – were now in the bad graces of Washington.

Bush and Baker decided to follow up their Gulf War victory with a bold diplomatic initiative to jump start Arab–Israeli peace talks. The core idea was to get all of the parties to an internationally supported conference, and then to launch a series of bilateral and multilateral talks that would involve a wide range of parties in the 'peace process'. The first leader to agree to Baker's proposed 'Madrid Conference' was Syria's Hafiz al-Asad. With his acceptance in hand, Baker set off to gain Israeli agreement, which was soon forthcoming, albeit with the condition that Prime Minister Yitzhak Shamir would not participate if the PLO was invited.

By this time Baker had begun to cultivate relations with Palestinians in the West Bank who were close to the PLO, but who were not part of its leadership structure. Eventually he got everyone to accept the idea that Palestinians would participate at Madrid as members of a joint Jordanian–Palestinian delegation. All of the Palestinian members were approved by the PLO, but none crossed the line of being obvious members of the leadership of the organization. Shamir was not happy with the outcome, but he grudgingly went to Madrid in October 1991. This set the stage for what eventually became a bilateral Israeli–Palestinian track of negotiations, mostly played out during 1992–3 in Washington, DC.

Clinton and Arafat

It is hard to escape the feeling that if Bush and Baker had remained in charge of US policy after January 1993 the results might have been different. But instead, a new president, Bill Clinton, with a partly new foreign policy team, arrived at the White House after a surprising victory over Bush in the November 1992 election. A former governor of Arkansas with relatively little foreign policy experience, Clinton was largely an unknown quantity when it came to the Middle East. But he inherited the most promising negotiating environment of any president, and even some of his top advisers were carry-overs from Baker's team.

Early in 1993, it was apparent that the Israeli–Palestinian talks in Washington were going nowhere. Even with Yitzhak Rabin as prime minister, the situation seemed frozen. Rabin appeared to be more interested in doing a deal with Syria. When the American side was urged to think of dealing with Arafat directly in order to try to break the stalemate in the talks in Washington, the reply was a predictable roll of the eyes. Clinton was not going to get out of step with Rabin, with whom he had almost immediately formed a real bond of friendship.

The Americans were aware that talks were going on in Oslo between Israelis and Palestinians, and that over time they had become more than the normal track-two exercise involving academics and independent personalities. But they did not think that there was much of a chance of success, and Secretary of State Warren Christopher and his main aide, Dennis Ross, seemed to think that Rabin was most interested in the Syrian track. So it was with considerable surprise that they learned the news in September that an agreement had been reached between Rabin and Arafat in Oslo that included mutual recognition.[11]

Clinton had already begun to define the US role in the negotiations as one of facilitation, and now that the Israelis and the PLO had broken the ice he was more than happy to give the effort his blessing. He offered to host the signing ceremony for the Oslo Accords, and immediately the issue of who would actually show up to do the signing arose. Rabin initially thought that his foreign minister, Shimon Peres, should sign with his Palestinian counterpart, Mahmoud Abbas. But here Clinton's political instincts kicked in and he argued that Rabin and Arafat should come to Washington to sign the historic agreement, which they memorably did on 13 September 1993. Clinton could hardly hide his pleasure at being the master of ceremonies when the two old enemies reached over and shook hands.

Clinton thus became the first sitting American president to meet Arafat face-to-face. Over the next seven years, Arafat become one of the most frequent visitors to the Clinton White House, and Clinton even accepted Arafat's invitation to visit him in Gaza in December 1998, where he received a standing ovation after addressing the Palestine National Council. All of this might make one think that Clinton and Arafat must have developed some sort of personal relationship based on a degree of mutual respect. That did indeed seem to be the case up until the very end of the Clinton presidency.

Insofar as there was a genuine shift on the American side in perceptions of Arafat, those changes were heavily dependent on the prior judgement made by Rabin that Arafat, despite his militant past, was the only Palestinian leader with the strength to deliver on an agreement with Israel. Many other Palestinians struck both Americans and Israelis as more admirable, more reasonable, more sophisticated, but none could deliver the way Arafat could, none enjoyed his stature in the Arab world, and no one was as skilful, on a purely tactical level, at the game of politics. So, whatever reservations Americans had about Arafat's personality – he was often seen as extremely manipulative, self-referential, duplicitous, and he loved to present himself as the victim – he was also shrewd, sometimes charming and humorous, and he famously always left the impression that the door was open for one more round of talks, one more exchange of views, one more secret initiative.

As long as Rabin was alive, Clinton and his team deferred to Israel on how to move forward with the Oslo process. After all, it was their agreement, not one made in the USA. It was not until after Rabin's assassination that Clinton and his team became more directly involved in the negotiations, first with the Hebron Accord, and then, more substantively, with the Wye River negotiations in late 1998. By this time Bibi Netanyahu was prime minister in Israel, and it is probably fair to say that for the first time ever Clinton found himself on more cordial terms with Arafat than with the difficult American-born Likud leader.

By 1999, when Netanyahu was finally replaced by Ehud Barak, widely seen in Washington as Rabin's natural successor, pressure was mounting to do something on the Palestinian front. The Oslo Accord had envisaged the end of the transitional period in May 1999, but there was no agreement on what would happen at that point. Arafat began to make noises about a unilateral declaration of statehood in September 1999. But whatever sympathy Clinton may have felt for Arafat at this point, he was not about to second guess the new Israeli prime minister, and Barak decided to try first to get an agreement with Syria, leaving the Palestinians to wallow in their frustration for another year.

Clinton's last engagement with Arafat began in inauspicious circumstances. Clinton had managed to be re-elected in 1996, so was presumably free of the normal political concerns that seem to paralyse American presidents when they think of doing anything that Israel might dislike. But then he nearly got impeached over the Monica scandal, and by the time he had recovered from that traumatic development he was nearing the end of his term, the classical lame-duck period of American politics. In addition, just to add to his complex political calculus, his wife was planning to run for Senator for New York state, and, to put it mildly, he owed her, big time.

Then, much to Clinton's frustration, his serious effort to broker an Israeli–Syrian deal ended in failure in spring 2000, and many on the American side felt that Barak was partly to blame. And yet Barak, now sinking in the polls at home, desperately wanted to make a final stab at Israel–Palestinian negotiations, and he urged Clinton to invite Arafat and himself to a summit meeting at Camp David.

Arafat was reluctant to say yes. He felt that the gap between the two sides was too large, that they needed more time to prepare, and that if the talks failed he would be the one to be blamed. Clinton urged him to come nonetheless and promised that he would not be blamed if it failed.

The accounts of what actually happened at Camp David II cover a wide spectrum, but all of the key players, Barak, Clinton and Arafat, seem to have behaved strangely. Barak, the one who had sought the summit, initially isolated himself and seemed not to want to have anything to do with Arafat. Arafat himself was in a grumpy mood, and generally refused to put forward any ideas, simply adopting a passive and ultimately negative position on ideas put forward by others. Clinton, who initially was inclined to put forward an American proposal, decided not to do so when Israel objected. Then, after about ten days, he left for a trip to Japan, and returned to find that the talks were still stuck, mainly on the issue of the future of the Temple Mount/Haram al-Sharif in Jerusalem. Clinton, towards the end, was intensely frustrated, and resorted to the not very helpful tactic of shouting at Arafat's aides, and sending his translator to shout at Arafat on his behalf. By the time the summit ended in failure, Clinton was angry, and he directed that anger primarily at Arafat. Despite his pledge not to do so, he publicly placed the blame for the failure of the summit primarily on the Palestinian leader.

One might have thought that the failure of the summit would bring to a close this period of sustained US–Palestinian engagement, but talks resumed in the autumn, and Barak even invited Arafat to what seemed to be a cordial dinner meeting at his home. The next day, however, Ariel Sharon went onto the Temple Mount/Haram, setting off a firestorm of angry Palestinian protest. The Al-Aqsa *intifada* was soon in full swing, and Palestinian and Israeli casualties were mounting. Barak's political fortunes were in free fall, and even Arafat did not seem to be clear on where things were heading. Some in Washington began to think that he was giving encouragement to the *intifada*, and at a minimum he was not doing much to rein in the violence. Still, contacts continued.

Normally, Americans – and the rest of the world – know who the next president will be on the eve of the election in November. But not in 2000. The vote was so close, especially in the state of Florida, that the certification of the election did not actually take place until early December. During this period it was possible to imagine that Clinton's vice-president, Al Gore, who had won the popular vote, might well be the next president, in which case US policy on the Middle East might not change very much. Or the electoral college might tip to George W. Bush if the vote in Florida went in his favour. And in parts of the Arab world the name Bush was associated with a relatively 'even-handed' approach to the Arab–Israeli conflict. Visions of Baker returning to play a role were entertained.

During this very uncertain period, the Americans approached Arafat in late November and said that Clinton was willing to make one more effort before he left office.[12] However, he would only do so if Arafat gave them a fairly strong commitment that he would be willing to consider American proposals seriously and favourably. Ross reviewed the general outlines of what Clinton might propose and Arafat expressed his general support for the initiative.

As it turned out, the so-called 'Clinton parameters' were not put forward until 23 December 2000, by which time it was clear that George W. Bush would be the next president. It was also beginning to look as if Barak, who was obliged to call early elections, would lose to his arch-rival Ariel Sharon.

In short, it was an odd time to be trying to finalize an Israeli–Palestinian peace when at least two of the three leaders were about to leave office. Still, Clinton finally put forward a substantive proposal and told the parties that they would have to take it or leave it. Within a short period, Barak said that he was willing to accept the proposal in principle, but he then sent a list of reservations.

The next move was up to the Palestinians. Arafat wrote to Clinton on 28 December spelling out some of his concerns, pleading that he needed to see a map and to get answers to some of his questions. The letter was polite, even deferential in tone.[13] His legal team sent a follow-on memo full of lawyer-like concerns.[14] Finally, Arafat met with Clinton on 2 January 2001. Under considerable pressure from the Saudis and the Egyptians to give Clinton a favourable response, Arafat raised two relatively minor issues, and then said that the formulation on refugees was not acceptable as it stood. It required more work and he was prepared to keep talking, but he could not accept the formula as proposed. Clinton's initial response was to see Arafat's reply as somewhat similar to Barak's – yes, with reservations. But Ross convinced him that Arafat's objection was 'outside the parameters', and that the Palestinian leader was therefore responsible for the failure of the entire initiative.[15]

Clinton apparently came to share Ross's view. When Arafat called Clinton to wish him well at the end of his term, the president angrily told Arafat that he was responsible for him being a failure. In addition, when Clinton met with the new president and his foreign policy team on inauguration day, he told them that Arafat was the reason for the collapse of the peace initiative, that he was a liar who could not be trusted. Whatever sympathy he may once have had for the man was gone.

Bush and the neo-cons

Arafat never had much of a chance with George W. Bush. The new president came to office with a particularly jaundiced view of the Arab–Israeli peace process. At his first NSC meeting, he opined that Clinton had tried too hard and had made things worse. He noted that he had met Sharon, the newly elected Israeli Prime Minister, and was inclined to give him the benefit of the doubt. He doubted that much could be done about the Palestinian issue. When his Secretary of State, Colin Powell, expressed the opinion that things could get worse, especially for the Palestinians, unless the US took some sort of initiative, Bush shrugged and said maybe that would be for the best.[16]

From his own account, Bush had three telephone conversations with Arafat in his first year. He describes them as cordial.[17] But on the one occasion when he and Arafat were in the same room during a UN reception in fall 2001, Bush deliberately avoided meeting him. Soon thereafter 9/11 brought to the fore a new and more assertive American policy – 'with us or against us', 'axis of evil', the 'global war on terrorism' – and in this frame of mind it was impossible for Arafat to avoid being consigned to the enemy camp. In any event, that is where many of Bush's advisers, especially those drawn from the neo-conservative ranks, had always consigned him.

Only Powell tried to make the case for dealing with Arafat, and he was unable to persuade Bush to take the Arab–Israeli conflict seriously in any event. Whatever lingering inclination to see Arafat as a possible interlocutor there may have been was abruptly brought to an end with the Karine A affair in January 2002. A ship that was supposedly carrying arms for the PLO was intercepted at sea by the Israelis. Arafat denied having anything to do with the Karine A, but the Americans had information to the contrary. In Bush's view, Arafat bluntly lied to him, thereby confirming Clinton's parting belief as to the untrustworthiness of the Palestinian leader.[18]

When Bush finally spoke out on the Palestinian issue in June 2002, he coupled his support for a Palestinian state with a demand that the Palestinians reform their political institutions. This meant, as the Americans were quite willing to say, that Arafat had to go, or at least his role had to be radically circumscribed. Barring that change, they could not count on any serious consideration from Washington. That was how things remained until the day of Arafat's death a little more than two years later. No one from the Bush Administration attended Arafat's massive funeral in Cairo. No one regretted his passing. After more than 30 years of interactions with the Americans, Arafat was still shunned and demonized by those whose support he had sought in vain.

Conclusion

Even Arafat's closest friends and colleagues would probably acknowledge that he was not the easiest person to deal with. He could be mercurial, devious and often indulged in conspiratorial thinking. But even his adversaries acknowledged a shrewdness and a remarkable energy that he used on behalf of a cause in which he seemed totally consumed – that of Palestinian nationalism. For those who sympathized with that goal, Arafat's foibles and character flaws were less important than his success in reviving the Palestinian cause. His failures were overlooked or blamed on others. His value as a symbol of his people made up for a lot. Even today he is viewed as an iconic figure by many Palestinians.

Much of Arafat's problem with successive American officials was that the cause he represented was not one that they endorsed. For those who were particularly sympathetic to Israel – and there were many among American officialdom – Arafat at his worst was leading a movement to destroy the Jewish state, and even when he had apparently disavowed that goal he was suspected of encouraging acts of violence and attempts to weaken and delegitimize Israel. Not surprisingly, those who saw the world through this optic viewed Arafat in the most negative possible terms.

There was another category of American officials – neither particularly pro-Palestinian nor pro-Israeli – who thought of themselves as pragmatists who wanted to find a compromise solution to the Arab–Israeli conflict because American national interests in the Middle East would thereby be advanced. For those with such an orientation, Arafat was a trouble-maker. He challenged the status quo, he sowed chaos in Jordan and the Lebanon, and he could not compete in personal charm with the well-mannered King Hussein, the most obvious alternative to Arafat, in the minds of many Americans.

Only after King Hussein withdrew his claim to the West Bank were these Americans forced to take seriously that they might have to deal with Arafat, and they approached the prospect gingerly. Bush I and Baker were open to dealing with the Palestinians, but never took the plunge to meet with Arafat directly. Not until the Israelis had made contact with Arafat acceptable by means of the Oslo Accords did an American president ever meet Arafat face to face. Then, for a frustrating seven years, Clinton and his top advisers engaged with Arafat and his colleagues. It was not a success.

Arafat professed to like and admire Clinton, but he had grave reservations about Ross. Some on the Clinton team seemed to believe that Arafat was the only Palestinian leader who could have delivered a deal, but that circumstances and poor diplomacy compromised the effort in Clinton's final year. But the collective judgement of the Clinton team, from the president on down, is that there was something about Arafat that made it impossible for him to bring the conflict to an end. Ross, who knew Arafat as well as anyone on the American side, went to great lengths in his memoir to develop a psychological portrait of a leader incapable of giving up the conflict that had given his life meaning.[19] The only Arabic speaker in Clinton's entourage, the interpreter Gemal Helal, did not share that view and believed that the Americans were never able to see that Arafat was first and foremost a politician who needed to show his people some tangible gains for all the sacrifices he had demanded of them. He balked at the end because the offer on the table was not good enough, not because he was pathologically wedded to endless conflict with Israel. Perhaps Arafat also hoped, wrongly, that the new president would be more forthcoming.[20]

In short, Americans at the official level never connected in a meaningful way with Arafat. He was too different, too anti-Israel, too flamboyant – and he was asking for more than they could squeeze out of their Israeli ally. In the end, there was probably never really a chance for Arafat to be seen as Sadat, another self-dramatizing Arab leader, but one who came to be viewed as a true statesman by a whole series of American leaders. Partly it was no doubt the difference in the two personalities, but more importantly it was the causes that they embodied. Americans were much more ready to work with Sadat for the restoration of his territory as the quid pro quo for peace with Israel than they were to make the same effort on behalf of a Palestinian state in the West Bank and Gaza with east Jerusalem as its capital.

If more proof were needed that Arafat's personality was not the primary obstacle to peace in 2000, one could note that the much more 'moderate' Palestinian leaders, namely Mahmud Abbas and Salam Fayyad, have achieved little more in terms of concrete support from the Bush II or Obama administrations, despite the complimentary words they hear from time to time about how much more pragmatic they are than Arafat. But since they adhere basically to the same goal of a Palestinian state and some justice for refugees, they too have been disappointed in the degree of real American support for their cause. So perhaps personalities are less important than policy and politics.

Notes

1 Avi Shlaim, *Lion of Jordan: The Life of King Hussein in War and Peace* (New York: Vintage, 2007), pp. 326–7.

2 David Ignatius, *Agents of Innocence* (New York: W.W. Norton, 1997) provides a thinly disguised fictional account of the CIA's relationship with Salameh.

3 David Ottaway, *Washington Post*, (5 April 1973).

4 'Toward Peace in the Middle East', (Washington, DC: The Brookings Institution, 1975). Available at: http://www.jstor.org/pss/2535521.

5 From notes of the Bolling–Arafat meetings of 9–10 September and 11–12 September 1977, Beirut, copies in my possession.

6 Ze'ev Schiff, 'The Green Light', *Foreign Policy*, Vol. 50, (spring 1983), pp. 73–85.

7 For the text of the speech, see: http://www.brookings.edu/~/media/Files/Press/Books/2005/peaceprocess3/peaceprocess_appendixH.pdf.

8 William B. Quandt, *Peace Process: American Diplomacy and the Arab–Israeli Conflict since 1967* (Berkeley: University of California Press, 2005), pp. 277–85.

9 The Abul Abbas faction was supported by Iraq. It tried to carry out an attack on the Israeli coast by sea, but was intercepted by the Israelis. While there were no casualties, it was clear that the Abul Abbas group was acting in violation of the PLO's 'no terrorism' pledge. Arafat was urged to denounce

the attack, but was in Baghdad at the time, where he was being courted by Saddam Hussein in what seems to have been part of the Iraqi leader's political planning for his soon to be launched attack on Kuwait. Counting on Arab support against Kuwait, he wanted Arafat on his side, and a rupture in US–PLO relations would help ensure that outcome. Or so it seemed to many observers at the time.

10 Quandt (2005), p. 301.

11 Ibid., p. 328.

12 Dennis Ross, *The Missing Peace: The Inside Story of the Fight for Middle East Peace* (New York: Farrar, Strauss & Giroux, 2004), pp. 746–747.

13 For the text, see: http://www.brookings.edu/~/media/Files/Press/Books/2005/peaceprocess3/peaceprocess_appendixAC.pdf.

14 See: http://www.brookings.edu/~/media/Files/Press/Books/2005/peaceprocess3/peaceprocess_appendixAD.pdf.

15 Ross (2004), p. 757, with additional detail on p. 11.

16 Ron Suskind, *The Price of Loyalty: George W. Bush, the White House, and the Education of Paul O'Neill* (New York: Simon & Schuster, 2004), p. 71.

17 George W. Bush, *Decision Points* (New York: Crown, 2010), p. 400.

18 Ibid., pp. 400–1.

19 Ross (2004), pp. 761–769.

20 Clayton Swisher, 'Investigating Blame: US Mediation Of The Arab-Israeli Conflict From 1999 To 2001' (MA thesis, Georgetown University, 3 December 2003), interviews with Gemal Helal, pp. 153–61.

CHAPTER EIGHT

Saddam Hussein and US foreign policy: Diabolical enemy images, policy failure and the administrations of Bush Senior and Junior

Toby Dodge

Introduction

From the moment he ordered the invasion of Kuwait, until the day he was hanged in December 2006, the spectre of Saddam Hussein both haunted and defined US foreign policy towards the Middle East. The invasion, on 2 August 1990, was a powerful repudiation of US relations with Baghdad that had sought to 're-socialize' Saddam in the aftermath of the 1980–1988 Iran–Iraq war.[1] Although the 1991 war to eject Iraq's army from Kuwait was seen at the time as a triumph of US military strategy, its mastery of new technology and as a defining moment in a new world order, Saddam's suppression of internal revolts in its aftermath and his continued survival was a potent reminder of the limits of American power in the Middle East. In the aftermath of the attacks by al Qaeda on 11 September 2001, the administration of George W. Bush used American popular outrage to eliminate the spectre of Saddam once and for all. However, the removal of Saddam in April 2003 did not deliver a triumphant victory in Baghdad or the transformation of the wider region that the Bush Administration had been expecting. Instead it saw Iraq descend into an insurgency and bloody civil war that tied down US forces and delivered the worst strategic defeat America has suffered since the Vietnam War. The problems that the US has faced in its long and troubled interaction with Iraq have sprung directly from the perception that key foreign policy-makers in both 1990 and 2003 had of Saddam Hussein and his relationship with Iraq's population.

On a superficial level, the two US-led wars against Saddam in 1991 and 2003 share certain similarities. The most obvious is the familial one, with father and son both launching wars against Saddam. Second, both wars were embarked upon by Republican administrations, seeking military solutions to the crises they faced: the invasion of Kuwait and the aftermath of the 9/11 attacks. Third, there were notable continuities in the personnel involved in the foreign policy decision-making surrounding both events; Richard Cheney, Colin Powell, Richard Haass and Paul Wolfowitz all occupied positions of varying influence.

Beyond these commonalities, however, the governments that Bush Senior and Junior presided over were divided by the ideological influences that shaped their foreign policy decision-making, their war aims and their approach to the international community. By invading Kuwait, Saddam unambiguously breached the United Nations Charter and challenged the very foundations of the Westphalian system. He achieved this during a time of unprecedented international cooperation brought about by the end of the Cold War. This allowed George Bush Sr. to define the war to liberate Kuwait as one of 'necessity'. He gained the backing of the United Nations Security Council and established a broad multinational coalition to drive Iraq out of Kuwait. It was consequentially a war fought to restore the status quo, to re-establish the Westphalian notion of sovereignty and place the Kuwaiti ruling family back in power. By contrast, the invasion of Iraq in 2003 has been labelled 'a war of choice'.[2] At the time, Iraq posed no military threat to either the United States or its allies in the Middle East. Instead, regime change was undertaken as the centre-piece of the 'Bush Doctrine'. It marked a radical and largely unilateral attempt to reform the Westphalian system, to rework and drastically limit the notion of sovereignty, especially in the post-colonial world.[3] If Bush Sr. in 1991 is understood as a Realist, reacting to an unexpected crisis by striving to re-establish the guiding principles of international relations, then his son, George W. Bush, in 2003, is a revolutionary, attempting to radically change those very same principles, breaking open the sovereign state autonomy of Iraq and hoping this would spread across the Middle East.

That said, beyond the radical discontinuities that separate US foreign policy towards Iraq in 1991 and 2003, there is one major and striking similarity, namely how Saddam himself was perceived. Both Bush Sr. and

Bush Jr. used a specific understanding of Saddam to impose ideational order on the situation. Both men highly personalized each conflict and demonized the adversary. The construction of Saddam as a 'diabolical enemy image' imposed a cognitive consistency, and led directly to a marginalization of the political complexities and risks surrounding the consequences of going to war. The conflict was rendered as a simple fight between the US, its allies and Saddam and his Ba'ath Party. Second, the demonization of Saddam radically reduced the moral complexities involved in war. The US was unassailably on the side of good and Saddam represented all that was wrong with the world. For those working within this construct, the moral superiority of American actions was thus assured. Finally, the deployment of a diabolical enemy image led directly to the major policy failures of both wars, namely the assumption in 1991 that Saddam would be swept away by a coup after the ceasefire, and that the occupation and transformation of Iraq in 2003 would be straightforward, welcomed by Iraqis and relatively cost-free.

Cognition, enemy images and Saddam Hussein

In spite of the ideological differences between the two US administrations, the dissimilar international circumstances they were operating in and the different goals they were in pursuit of, both presidents shared a similar perception of Saddam and used this to organize their understanding of the wider crises they faced. What tools may be found within international relations theory to usefully explain this consistency?

Within international relations and foreign policy analysis, two separate and distinct approaches, the cognitive and constructivist, have sought to understand the consistent influence of the ideational on decision-making. The combination of both approaches may yield a coherent explanation of why both Bush Sr. and Bush Jr. deployed the figure of Saddam as the key organizing trope of their policy towards Iraq.

At first glance, the combination of cognitive and constructivist approaches would appear intellectually counter-intuitive. The cognitive approach to foreign policy decision-making sprang from the so-called 'behavioural revolution' that swept the study of international relations in the 1960s. This divided the study of individual decision-making at the state level from the study of the structural dynamics that were thought to shape the international system.[4] The legacy of this divide leaves cognitive approaches with an individualist ontology and a rationalist epistemology. Constructivism, on the other hand, is concerned with what Roxanne Lynn Doty has termed the 'how-possible question'.[5] This seeks to uncover the socially produced structures and processes through which foreign policy decision-makers come to attach meaning to the various objects they encounter within the international system and how relations of hierarchy are established between these objects. Constructivism, in its various forms, stresses the causative power of ideational structures and the 'co-constitutive' relationship between structures and agents.[6]

Though different, both approaches suffer from their own intellectual lacuna. The cognitive study of decision-making, because of its individualist ontology, finds it difficult to factor in the societal dynamics that ultimately structure collective meaning and shape an individual's approach to information processing.[7] On the other hand, within constructivism, the individual level of analysis tends to be marginalized or disappear altogether, with its tendency to focus on the causative powers of ideational structures.[8] The utilization of insights from both approaches, while recognizing the ontological and epistemological tensions inherent in this, would allow for the study of ideational influences on foreign policy decision-making while tracing those influences back to the socially produced structures and processes that give those ideas intersubjective meaning.

At the decision-making level, the cognitive school argues that individuals are 'cognitive misers', enforcing a stable meaning on a highly complex and over-determined reality by subconsciously filtering out data that is considered superfluous. This involves the mind deploying categories and stereotypes and simple causal inferences.[9] The cognitive school understands these amalgamated processes to form an individual's unique belief system.[10] Belief systems not only filter and prioritize information, they also impose normative appraisals on situations, enabling coherence through ideologically shaped judgement.[11] Once a belief system has been formed, it solidifies around the defence of 'cognitive consistency'.[12] The individual defends the internal consistency of their belief system by discrediting information that does not make sense within its own boundaries. A person will actively seek out information that supports their belief system, reinterpreting discordant information to support dominant suppositions, and downgrading or ignoring data that cannot be made to fit.

Ironically, this process of 'cognitive consistency', the exclusion of discordant information in defence of a belief system, is likely to be much more rigid in an expert policy-maker like Bush Sr. The many years he spent at the highest level of policy-making trained him to quickly process large volumes of information at speed. This ability was facilitated by a rigid belief system developed over a long professional career.[13] Experienced foreign policy decision-makers, Bush Sr. in 1991 and Cheney and Wolfowitz in 2003, are likely to have a complex but also more exclusionary belief system than less experienced politicians or laypeople. In spite of the time spent by the cognitive school mapping the role and complexity of belief systems, the analytical dominance of an individualist ontology and rationalist epistemology means that belief systems are understood to be highly individualistic and idiosyncratic, the product of a person's specific life experiences and education.

On the other hand, the constructivist approach, concerned as it is with the mutually constitutive relationship between structure and agency, is focused on how intersubjective meaning is created among a group of decision-makers, and beyond them within a society and across the globe. The categorization of the units that make up the international system is the first step within this process. This breaks the international system into states, placing them within a hierarchy and assigning characteristics to them, such as 'ally', 'enemy' or 'rogue'. Consequently, a series of quasi-causal relationships between these units will be established, thus defining what constitutes the 'national interest'.[14] Jutta Weldes stresses the role of articulation in this process where:

> particular phenomena, whether objects, events or social relations, are represented in specific ways and given particular meaning on which action is then based. With their successful repeated articulation, these linguistic elements come to seem as though they are inherently or necessarily connected and the meanings they produce come to seem natural, to be an accurate description of reality.[15]

In between the individualist approach of the cognitive school and the constructivist approach that sees meaning as produced intersubjectively, is the category of the enemy. The cognitive school places the enemy at the centre of a belief system and the system's defence of cognitive consistency. It helps reduce cognitive dissonance as the moral juxtaposition between the self and the enemy simplifies information about other entities, categorizing them not only as 'allies' or 'foes', but as 'good' and 'bad'.[16] However, constructivism would focus on intersubjective processes where the enemy becomes the 'antithesis of core values and beliefs'.[17] This allows for a whole society to be celebrated as morally superior, acting with unquestionable motives. This is contrasted with the 'diabolical enemy image', the 'other', whose motives are always self-serving and negative. For this basic dualism to be ideationally sustainable, its meaning has to be anchored into a society's morality, its collective perception of itself, its place within international politics and its relations with the 'other'. Brett Silverstein and Robert R. Holt have labelled this 'folk theory', where:

> there is only this one type of war. There is always one right, justified, and innocent side – ours, even if we are committing unprovoked genocide – and the other side is always actuated by evil motives.[18]

Following the cognitive school, the placing of a 'diabolical enemy image' at the centre of a belief system leads to an aggressive defence of cognitive consistency. Once it has been processed from within an unchallenged and highly rigid belief system, the enemy will appear to possess all the traits of an 'ideal-typical enemy', with a denial of discordant information.[19] Negative information or accusations about enemies are likely to be more readily accepted than either positive or ambiguous information, whereas negative information about allies is suppressed. The current and future actions of enemies will be perceived to be hostile by default. If the enemy is seen to be acting in a positive way this will be explained by situational pressures, not because of agential intent; in other words, they did not choose to act in a positive way but were forced to do so.[20]

George H.W. Bush, Saddam and the Kuwait crisis of 1990–1991

Iraq's invasion of Kuwait on 2 August 1990 flew in the face of the assumptions that guided the Bush Administration's approach to Iraq up until that point. Bush's National Security Adviser, Brent Scowcroft, was 'astonished' by the invasion.[21] Both he and Bush had struggled to understand the 'bewildering foreign policy moves' that the Iraqi regime had undertaken since the start of 1990. No senior member of the administration believed that Iraq's campaign of negative propaganda and threats against Kuwait would actually lead to an invasion because, as Secretary of State James Baker argued, 'no realistic calculation of his interests could have foreseen a full-scale invasion of Kuwait'.[22]

As the quote from Baker suggests, until August 1990, US policy towards Iraq was shaped by the core assumption that Saddam was a rational foreign policy decision-maker. US policy-makers thought they could ascertain what that rationality would direct Saddam to do and then reshape his calculations in ways that would suit American objectives. The US government placed the damage done to Iraq during its eight-year war with Iran at the centre of this analysis. Their working hypothesis assumed that Iraqi foreign policy would be constrained, since the government needed to devote its attention and resources to reconstruction. The Bush Administration's transitional policy document on Iraqi policy, National Security Directive (NSD)-26, thus focused on using American diplomatic leverage and economic resources to encourage Iraq to become 'a more responsible status-quo state working within the system and promoting stability in the region'.[23] US policy in the Persian Gulf was still embroiled in the aftermath of the Iranian revolution and the hostage crisis. Against this background, although Saddam was an unsavoury dictator with a dreadful human rights record, he was still judged to be rational and malleable, especially when compared to his revolutionary neighbours in Iran.

The invasion of Kuwait certainly put the core working assumptions of the administration in doubt along with the cognitive structures that shaped them. After the initial shock of the invasion, ideational order was restored to US foreign policy by demonizing Saddam. The cognitive structures that gave coherence to Bush Sr.'s foreign policy were defended by classifying Saddam as beyond the pale of civilization; his actions could thus not be assessed within the rationalist framework used to understand 'ordinary' or 'normal' decision-makers. Saddam was thus deemed to possess all the traits of an 'ideal-typical enemy'; he could not be trusted, would never be consistent enough to abide by agreements and would only act in what he judged to be his own immediate personal interests. Beyond expelling him from Kuwait, policy goals were hence easily definable. Iraq's military machine was to be destroyed, to the extent that he could no longer threaten those of his neighbours that were US allies.[24] This all had to be achieved while ensuring that the Iraqi state remained intact so that it could offset America's other irrational enemy in the region: Iran.[25]

However, from a constructivist perspective the creation of an enemy image has another wider role within foreign policy. The enemy becomes the craven 'other' against which your own country's motives and morality are positively juxtaposed and hence defined. As the Cold War ended, US foreign policy was going through what could be described as a 'crisis of purpose'. In 1990, the Soviet Union was still a world power, but under Mikhail Gorbachev it was committed to international cooperation and internal transformation. Almost as soon as the Kuwait crisis erupted, Bush and Scowcroft began to plan how its solution would act as a model for America's new role in the world. According to them:

> The United States had recognised and shouldered its peculiar responsibility for leadership in tackling international challenges, and won wide acceptance for this role around the globe. American political credibility and influence had sky-rocketed.[26]

The rendering of Saddam as a 'diabolical enemy' gave ideational clarity to the foreign policy choices facing the US in the aftermath of August 1990, but at a time of wider strategic uncertainty offered the Bush Administration a renewed sense of its own moral purpose; anchored initially in the expulsion of Iraq from Kuwait, and then in the construction of a new world order based on that precedent.

However, the clarity and morality supplied by this definition of Saddam may well have been achieved at the expense of a coherent foreign policy-making process. Intriguingly, in comparison to the administration of Bush Jr. where the majority of key decision-makers shared the diabolical enemy image of Saddam, in 1990–1 it seems that it was primarily Bush Sr. who promoted this perception of the crisis.

The enemy image and the belief system of George H. W. Bush

Even before the invasion of Kuwait, Bush Sr. indicated that he was 'baffled' by Saddam, specifically the mismatch between the Iraqi President's public rhetoric and his private explanations of his motivations and goals.[27] Although the administration moved quickly to impose sanctions on Iraq, the President's initial reaction to the invasion, the regional instability it caused but more importantly the challenge it posed to his belief system, was cautious if not incoherent. In comments to the press at the start of the first National Security Council (NSC) meeting on the crisis, Bush appeared to rule out intervention or sending troops. In these comments and those made later that day in Aspen, Colorado, the President studiously avoided criticism of Saddam.[28] This sense of analytical uncertainty and policy drift personified the NSC meeting on the morning of 2 August 1990. Bush took control of the meeting but his National Security Adviser Scowcroft, Chairman of the Joint Chiefs of Staff Colin Powell, and the NSC's Senior Director for Near East and South Asia Richard Haass, all came away from the meeting worried that policy formation towards the invasion was ill-defined and 'missed the point about the larger foreign-policy questions'.[29] To quote Haass, there was an:

> apparent readiness of some in the room to acquiesce in what had taken place. They seemed to suggest there was nothing we could do about it and that instead the focus of US policy ought to be on making sure Saddam did not go any farther and do to Saudi Arabia what he'd done to Kuwait.[30]

Bush overcame the incoherence of his initial reaction to the invasion, its consequences for the US and the development of policies to deal with it, by recalibrating his belief system and placing an enemy image of Saddam at its centre. Bush himself describes how the change in his own understanding of the crisis took place in August and September 1990. This is when he moved from perceiving the crisis as 'a dangerous strategic threat' to a 'moral crusade'.[31] This move enabled Bush to impose cognitive consistency on his understanding of the invasion and his response to it.

Bush's creation of Saddam as 'diabolical enemy image' had three distinct aspects. First, Saddam was transformed into an 'ideal-typical enemy'. Before the invasion, he was president of a country the US hoped would become a status quo power, and a vehicle for regional stability. No longer trustworthy, there could be no negotiations. As Bush observed, 'we have seen what his promises mean: His promises mean nothing.'[32] Now Saddam was capable of unlimited acts of barbarity, not as a response to threats to himself or his state but as a central character trait. He was deemed responsible for the deaths of half a million of his fellow Muslims during the Iran–Iraq War, the use of chemical weapons against his own population and finally the plundering of Kuwait.[33] Bush would not accept any other explanation for Saddam's actions than his own personality, chastising King Hussein of Jordan, when he met him in mid-August 1990, for his denial that Saddam was a madman and his assertion that wider socio-economic explanations were possible.[34]

The construction of Saddam as an 'ideal-type enemy' also served to cast America's actions in the noblest moral light. For Bush, there were no longer shades of grey; it was good versus evil, right versus wrong. Saddam had become the epitome of evil in taking hostages and in his treatment of the Kuwaiti people. Recasting Saddam in a diabolical enemy image enabled Bush to impose analytical certainty upon a fast-moving and complex situation. Saddam's demonization solidified Bush's belief system, allowing him to marginalize or exclude any discrepant information, thus bringing cognitive consistency to the policy-making process. By perceiving the conflict through an unambiguously dichotomous moral lens, Bush believed this 'made the choices before me clearer'.[35]

During August and September, as Bush reconstructed Saddam as an 'ideal-type enemy', he added to the coherence and power of this schema by marrying it to what Yuen Foong Khong has labelled an analogical explanation. Khong argues that analogies are more specific and concrete than schemas. By comparing the unfamiliar crisis to a stable and familiar historical analogy, the decision-maker can impose greater analytical meaning upon it. The use of historical analogies allows them to assess what is at stake and to evaluate alternative options while judging the chances of success and the dangers involved.[36]

George H.W. Bush, in his first television address to the nation on the Kuwait crisis four days after the invasion, invoked one of the most common, powerful but also misleading historical analogies within foreign policy decision-making, the resolution of the Munich Crisis in September 1938, stating 'appeasement does not work'.[37] Bush consciously evoked Hitler's defiance of the Treaty of Versailles, seeing 'a chilling parallel with what the Iraqi occupiers were doing in Kuwait'.[38] He then continually deployed this historical analogy both in public and in private.[39] However, both Khong and Steve Yetiv highlight the damaging effect on policy-making of the Munich analogy. Khong argues that people generally draw the wrong lessons from the historical analogies they deploy. The use of the Munich analogy is likely to lead decision-makers to view the stakes involved as extremely high, comparable to the outcome of appeasing Hitler in the 1930s. The conclusions drawn would see democracies use collective violence to repel the aggression of a dictator with the chance of success and the morality of the action being very high.[40]

Intriguingly, nearly all the major players in the Bush Administration were distinctly uneasy about the President's demonization of Saddam and his deployment of the Munich analogy. Powell maintained that Saddam was certainly ruthless 'but not irrational'.[41] Moreover, Powell made a conscious point of tempering his own negative references to the Iraqi regime. He became uneasy about Bush's own description of Saddam as 'a tyrant removed from human decency' and asked if Cheney and Scowcroft could persuade the President to 'cool the rhetoric'.[42] Cheney and Scowcroft agreed, worrying about Bush's personalisation of the conflict.

Policy implications of ideal-typical enemies and Munich analogies

Domestic American opposition to US military action against Iraq focused on the speed with which the Bush Administration moved towards war, arguing that sanctions should have been given much more time to work, and that an invasion would be costly and unpredictable. Given the speed with which victory was secured and the ability of the Iraqi regime to survive under sanctions, subsequent academic discussion has focused on the way the Bush Administration made it impossible to engineer a negotiated settlement.[43] The Soviet Union made two major attempts at brokering a peace settlement: one in October 1990 prior to the air war and one in February 1991 ahead of the land invasion. The first initiative saw Gorbachev send Yevgeny Primakov to Washington, DC with a proposed set of 'face-savers', which would allow Saddam to move his troops out of Kuwait. Both Baker and Bush forcefully deployed the Munich analogy to dismiss the plan. Baker denounced the move as 'a formula Neville Chamberlain might have approved'. Bush, if anything, was more explicit, telling Primakov:

> They're just like Nazis. They go in there and they loot and they pillage, and we're not going to accept it. You give facer-savers to someone who's part of the civilised world. We will not accept this kind of uncivilised behaviour in this day and age.[44]

The second initiative saw Gorbachev send Primakov to Baghdad in February 1991. This was rejected by Bush much more succinctly: 'No way, José.'[45]

However, given the speed with which victory was achieved after the land war started, the most important area for examination is not the influence of the Munich analogy but the way the construction of Saddam as an 'ideal-type enemy' shaped plans, or the lack of them, for the war's aftermath. Famously, Bush terminated the ground war after 100 hours, with the agreement of his military commanders Powell and Norman Schwarzkopf, and key cabinet members Cheney, Scowcroft and Baker. However, planning dedicated to realizing the war's broader aims was negligible.[46] Baker is clear why: 'Much of our planning in this regard was predicated on the assumption that Saddam would not survive in power.'[47]

This working assumption, or what Haass described as 'gut-int', became apparent 11 days before the ceasefire was announced when Bush declared:

> there's another way for the bloodshed to stop, and that is for the Iraqi military and the Iraqi people to take matters into their own hands, to force Saddam Hussein, the dictator, to step aside, and to comply with the United Nations resolutions, and then rejoin the family of peace-loving nations.[48]

Since that speech, a number of the major players in Bush's war cabinet (Scowcroft, Baker, Cheney and Haass) have all confirmed that not only was there a strong working assumption that Saddam would be removed in the aftermath of military defeat but this in fact shaped the planning and policy post-war. It is the false premise that Saddam would not survive that kept post-war planning to a minimum and ultimately undermined a stunning military victory won on the battlefield. This assumption was rooted in the diabolical enemy image that dominated Bush's analysis of Iraq from August 1990 onwards. Bush perceived Saddam's rule to be anchored in nothing more than his ability to suppress his population. The major target of the war was Saddam's military capacity. Once that had been degraded, either his own troops would move against him or the population, freed from his despotic rule, would rise up. As Bush wrote in his diary during the war:

> I have in my own mind that Saddam Hussein, in decline, will be like Ceausescu was in decline. There will be dancing in the streets, and they will rejoice when he's gone – I'm confident of that.[49]

But once Saddam survived the war, managed to rally his forces and secured his grip on power, the Bush Administration had no Iraq policy options left to deal with him.

Bush Jr., the National Security Strategy and the Bush Doctrine

The roots of Saddam's demonization by George W. Bush Jr.'s Administration are to be found in the ideological vision laid out in the *National Security Strategy of the United States* (NSS) published in September 2002. This grand strategy was given ideational coherence by the juxtaposition of liberty and totalitarianism. The NSS argued that the struggle to overcome totalitarianism had dominated the twentieth century. In the twenty-first century this struggle would be won by 'a single sustainable model for national success: freedom, democracy, and free enterprise'. The United States was now in a position to 'extend the benefits of freedom across the globe' and to 'actively work to bring the hope of democracy, development, free markets, and free trade to every corner of the world'.[50] At the centre of this ideological vision, giving it coherence and certainty, was a powerful if simplistic contrast between the United States, nobly pursuing the goals of liberty and freedom against malign enemies, versus those who used terrorism in the fight to preserve tyranny and totalitarianism across the globe.

It is no surprise that this vision was applied to Iraq after the regime change, since Saddam personified the tyranny and totalitarianism America was now fighting.[51] In Iraq, the US used overwhelming military force in an attempt to transform economic, political and social structures, 'to bring the hope of democracy, development, free markets, and free trade' to the country. In 2003, the war aims of the US involved nothing less than the complete socio-political re-engineering of an entire society. The target of this plan, the malign forces of tyranny and totalitarianism, gave it its intellectual coherence and, for the US government, its moral certainty. In Iraq, this clarity was provided by what were seen as the barriers to and central targets of transformation, namely Saddam and his Ba'ath Party acolytes who had run the state from 1968 until 2003. The military defeat of Saddam's regime was the first and most straightforward part of the plan. In the aftermath of formal hostilities, the US then set about the wholesale removal of the old ruling elite. However, basing the exogenous transformation of the country upon the demonization of one group had profoundly negative consequences for Iraq, directly propelling it into civil war.

The enemy image and the belief system of the Bush Jr. Administration

The role and power that the Iraqi dictatorship as a 'diabolical enemy image' occupied in the administration's belief system underpinned the Bush presidency's reaction to the attacks in September 2001. Although it was quickly apparent that Osama bin Laden at the head of al Qaeda had been responsible for the attacks using a base within Afghanistan, Iraq was ushered into the policy discussions surrounding how the US should respond. By 21 November 2001, Bush had already asked Secretary of Defense Donald Rumsfeld what plans he had in hand to invade Iraq.[52] By January 2002, Bush lumped terrorists and their state allies into one 'axis of evil'.[53] In Bush's memoirs, he makes it plain that it was Saddam Hussein who gave coherence to his perception of Iraq as an enemy image. However, it was not simply Saddam that personified Iraqi 'evil' in Bush's mind. It was also 'his henchmen' and government that 'tortured innocent people, raped political opponents in front of their families, scalded dissidents with acid, and dumped tens of thousands of Iraqis into mass graves'.[54] He then quotes discussions with Elie Wiesel, a holocaust survivor, in which he compared Saddam's brutality to the Nazi genocide, with Wiesel concluding, 'Mr. President, you have a moral obligation to act against evil'.[55]

Unlike Bush Sr.'s administration, we find the construction of both Saddam and the Ba'ath Party as a 'diabolical enemy' reproduced in a remarkably similar fashion across the decision-making elite in Washington, DC. By 2002, Iraq planning was dominated by the Department of Defense. Within the Pentagon, Rumsfeld designated the office run by Under Secretary of Defense for Policy Douglas Feith as responsible for all post-war planning and security.[56] This was formalized in an executive order issued by Bush in January 2003.

For Rumsfeld, like Bush Jr., the Ba'ath Party was best understood through historical comparison to the Nazi Party in Germany and the Communist Party in the Soviet Union.[57] In the autumn of 2003, this historical analogy was powerfully deployed by Rumsfeld's deputy, Wolfowitz, to stop attempts at softening the victors' peace by reaching out to the Sunni community in Iraq. He wrote three words on the policy proposal before returning it to Rumsfeld: 'They are Nazis!' One of Rumsfeld's senior assistants described Wolfowitz's attitude to the Sunni population in Iraq as 'unbalanced':

> You couldn't deal with them. He always described them as 'Nazis'. The word was almost a personal tick. When anyone talked about this he would get so angry he would start shaking.[58]

Feith was the most important man within the US government handling Iraq policy. It was his office that drafted government policy for post-regime change Iraq and ensured it was implemented. In his memoirs, written shortly after leaving government in 2005, Feith laid out what is probably the most coherent description of the Ba'ath Party as a 'diabolical enemy image' placed at the centre of the administration's belief system, giving it both coherence and cognitive consistency. First, as with Bush, Rumsfeld and Wolfowitz, the Ba'ath Party was compared to the Nazis in Germany. It 'had become a synonym for the Iraqi regime, more or less as the Nazi Party was the German regime under Adolf Hitler'. However, in Feith's mind, its sins were even greater because, whereas the Nazis 'had run Germany for a dozen years; the Ba'athists had tyrannised Iraq for more than thirty'.[59]

American decision-making power on the ground in Baghdad was even more concentrated than in Washington, DC. For the first 12 months of the occupation, from May 2003 to April 2004, L. Paul Bremer III, head of the

Coalition Provisional Authority (CPA), had paramount authority across the country.[60] His instructions before leaving the US were minimal, nearly all oral and were not augmented while he was in Baghdad.[61] The enemy image at the centre of Bremer's own belief system, laid out in his memoir of the year he spent ruling Iraq, is built around the same central schema that shaped the perceptions of Bush, Rumsfeld, Wolfowitz and Feith. The Ba'ath Party is repeatedly compared to both the Nazis and the Communist Party of the Soviet Union, with Saddam playing the role of Hitler but for three times as long.[62]

It was through these assertive, coherent, intersubjective schemas that the most influential American decision-makers understood Iraq. The enemy image of Saddam and the Ba'ath Party was total in its construction. By repeatedly comparing the Ba'ath to the Nazis in Germany, there was no room for ambiguity; Ba'ath Party members had no redeeming features. At best, they had been the knowing and willing vehicle through which Saddam had unleashed horror on the Iraqi population. At worst, their active involvement in torture, rape and murder went beyond complicity. Saddam and the Ba'ath, as constructed within American decision-makers' belief systems, gave US policy towards Iraq its coherence.

The reform programme put in place in 2003 and 2004 was targeted against a party membership no better than the Nazis in Germany, and their removal from power was deemed a moral necessity. Once Saddam was removed from power, the Ba'ath Party became the main obstacle to re-engineering Iraq. It was likewise the Ba'ath Party who were blamed for the rising insurgency. However, the damming of a party whose membership, at its peak, contained over two million Iraqis was in itself highly problematic for US policy in Iraq. How do you interact with a state infrastructure populated, at its higher echelons, with a majority of former party members? Indeed, how do you understand a society ruled by such a party for 35 years, what level of complicity does that bring to ordinary citizens beyond the two million people who joined? However, as the quote from Wolfowitz above indicates, the Ba'ath Party and its membership were not the only ones understood in morally absolutist terms. Party membership, or at least sympathy and fellow travelling were extended, explicitly and by inference, to Iraqi Sunnis as a whole. Bremer, when briefing Bush on declining security in June 2003, describes the 'Sunni heartlands' of west and north Iraq as containing 'lots of sore losers'.[63] Feith was repeatedly critical of those he saw adopting 'the Sunni perspective' that was 'inclined to look somewhat benignly on Ba'athists'. In Feith's view, adopting this position was equated with a willingness to do deals with Ba'athists.[64]

It was these dominant perceptions of the Ba'ath Party, central to the belief system of the major American decision-makers working on Iraq, which laid the groundwork for the victor's peace. Key administration officials gained cognitive certainty about Iraq from within their own belief systems by utilizing both Saddam and the Ba'ath Party as 'diabolical enemy images'. As the examples of Wolfowitz, Feith and Bremer indicate, policy was drafted, accepted, or in this case rejected, by using the enemy image of the Ba'ath Party to gain coherence and defend cognitive consistency. However, it was not only the two million members of the Ba'ath Party who were dammed and hence cognitively fixed and coercively persecuted. There is clear evidence that Iraq's Sunni community were cognitively categorized with the Ba'ath Party and dammed accordingly. The ramifications for American policy-making and its effects in Iraq are clear. Not just the former ruling elite but members of a mass party and a large religious group were to be actively excluded from power as a central pillar to the US plans to transform Iraq and 'let freedom reign'.

Policy implications: de-Ba'athification and a victor's peace

It is the centrality of the 'diabolical enemy image' to decision-makers that shapes what Astri Suhrke has categorized as a victor's peace. In a victor's peace, the winner of a conflict continues to deploy coercion after an official ceasefire with the aim of solidifying and guaranteeing the dominance of the war's winning side. With the 'diabolical enemy image' at the centre of the victor's belief system, the conflict arising from the victor's peace is perceived by its protagonist in totality, an ideological struggle between good and evil with success only achieved by total victory. Once the initial military struggle is over, state power is deployed to 'cleanse' society of the vanquished foe, purging the societal and political organizations associated with the old order.[65] The loser's peace, on the other hand, is a direct result of the 'enemy's' exclusion. It is marked by an upsurge of grass-roots, non-state asymmetrical violence. Here local elites, excluded by the victor's peace, have little choice but to deploy violence in an effort to gain a place at the governing table or to overthrow the post-victory settlement in its entirety.

Given the central role that the demonization of the Iraqi Ba'ath Party played in the belief system of key members of the Bush Administration it is little surprise that their political exclusion was the first policy to be enacted once the CPA was created. The one explicit order Bremer took with him from Washington for implementation in Baghdad was the de-Ba'athification of Iraqi society. The document was drafted by Feith in the Pentagon and banned the top four levels of the Ba'ath Party's membership from holding any government job. It also banned *any* former member of the Ba'ath from occupying jobs in the top three management levels of government institutions.[66] When Feith gave Bremer the order, he stressed its political importance by saying, 'We've got to show all the Iraqis that we're serious about building a New Iraq.' The policy was to be implemented 'even if it causes administrative inconvenience'.[67] For Feith, de-Ba'athification was the cornerstone of building a new Iraq. The central role that the Ba'ath played in his belief system meant that the damage caused by purging them from the Iraqi state was of little concern compared with the greater moral good of their exclusion.

The de-Ba'athification of Iraqi society was specifically designed to drive the old ruling elite and those associated with it out of office and place them on the margins of society. In an economy dominated by state employment, excluding large numbers of individuals from working for the government was tantamount to legislating for their forced impoverishment. The effects of this went well beyond the costs of the 'administrative inconvenience' Feith was happy to pay. First, to quote Lieutenant General Ricardo Sanchez, commander of Coalition Forces in Iraq when the order was issued, de-Ba'athification essentially:

> eliminated the entire government and civic capacity of the nation. Organizations involving justice, defense, interior, communications, schools, universities, and hospitals were all either completely shut down or severely crippled, because anybody with any experience was now out of a job.[68]

The second consequence had an even greater impact on Iraq. In May 2003, just after the de-Ba'athification edict was issued, I carried out a series of interviews with mid-level and senior Ba'athists in the Baghdad suburb of Ghazaliya. The effects of the edict were easy to detect. At first there was bewilderment. A senior Ba'athist exclaimed, 'why can't he leave us alone? We are like the Communist Party of the Soviet Union, worn out and ideologically defeated.' But within days of General Order No. 1, this sense of defeat quickly mutated into defiance and reorganization. De-Ba'athification was seen as a needless and vindictive persecution that went well beyond the party into the Sunni heartlands. It triggered a concerted attempt at organization and violent confrontation; the fight for a loser's peace had begun.

Conclusion

Policy-making towards Iraq in the administration of Bush Sr. was clearly dominated by a diabolical enemy image, but that image was largely held by one man, the President himself. Others within the administration largely supported the President's policy towards Saddam but remained uneasy about the personalized tone Bush Sr. adopted in his struggle to drive Iraq out of Kuwait and his frequent comparison of Saddam to Hitler. The

Munich analogy propelled the US to war with Iraq and also precluded any negotiations between Baghdad and Washington that might have averted the conflict. A swift and apparently decisive military victory was squandered, however, by the assumptions that underpinned planning for the aftermath. Bush Sr. had clear and justifiable reasons for not occupying Baghdad, but the dominant assumption that Saddam would be removed by his own army, or failing that, by his own population, stultified any sustained thinking for what would happen if he survived.

The Munich analogy played a much smaller role in Bush Jr.'s understanding of the 2003 invasion of Iraq. The 2003 conflict was a 'war of choice', justified in terms of 'pre-emption'; a regime change to stop what *might* happen. However, a diabolical enemy image also shaped Bush Jr.'s understanding of Iraq. The ideal-type enemy in 2003 was expanded beyond Saddam Hussein to explicitly include all the members of the Ba'ath Party, and to taint Sunni Iraqis by association. After another swift military victory against the Iraqi armed forces, the influence of this enemy image led the American occupation to impose a victor's peace upon Iraq in which former Ba'ath Party members were forcibly excluded from the country's public sphere. This attempt at mass exclusion ignited the insurgency that dogged the US presence in the country.

Schema theory would argue that rational decision-makers have the ability to identify the most efficient and inefficient knowledge structures out of which information is produced and policy made.[69] Mark Laffey and Jutta Weldes, on the other hand, would argue that it is impossible to separate the very construction of understanding from the units of analysis used to understand that knowledge.[70] It is clear that the enemy images used by both Bush Sr. to understand Iraq in 1990 and by Bush Jr. in 2003 played a central role in the failures they faced in the aftermath of the wars themselves. What is not open to debate is whether those wars could have been launched in the first place without the central role played by the demonization of Saddam.

Notes

1   Alexander L. George, *Bridging the Gap Theory and Practice in Foreign Policy* (Washington, DC: United States Institute of Peace Press, 1993), p. 34.

2   Richard N. Haass, *War of Necessity; War of Choice* (New York: Simon & Schuster, 2009).

3   Toby Dodge, 'The Sardinian, the Texan and the Tikriti: Gramsci, the Comparative Autonomy of the Middle Eastern State and Regime Change in Iraq', *International Politics*, Vol. 43, No. 4, (2006), pp. 453–73.

4   Vendulka Kubálková, 'Foreign Policy, International Politics and Constructivism', in Vendulka Kubálková (ed.) *Foreign Policy in a Constructed World* (Armonk, NY: M.E. Sharpe, 2001), p. 15.

5   Roxanne Lynn Doty, 'Foreign Policy as Social Construction: A Post-Positivist Analysis of U.S. Counter insurgency Policy in the Philippines', *International Studies Quarterly*, Vol. 37, No. 3, (September 1993), pp. 298–9.

6   David Patrick Houghton, 'Reinvigorating the Study of Foreign Policy Decision Making: Toward a Constructivist Approach', *Foreign Policy Analysis*, Vol. 3, No. 1, (2007), p. 28.

7   See e.g. Deborah Welch Larson, 'The Role of Belief Systems and Schemas in Foreign Policy Decision-Making', *Political Psychology*, Vol. 15, No. 1, (March 1994), p. 25. The partial exception to this is early work on operational codes, especially Alexander L. George, 'The "Operational Code": A Neglected Approach to the Study of Political Leaders and Decision-Making', *International Studies Quarterly*, Vol. 13, No. 2, (June 1969), pp. 190–222.

8   Most obviously in Alexander Wendt, *Social Theory of International Politics* (Cambridge: Cambridge University Press, 1999).

9   Jerel A. Rosati, 'The Power of Human Cognition in the Study of World Politics', *International Studies Review*, Vol. 2, No. 3, (autumn 2000), pp. 56, 59.

10   Robert Axelrod, 'Schema Theory: An Information Processing Model of Perception and Cognition', *American Political Science Review*, Vol. 67, No. 4, (December 1973), p. 1248.

11   Shannon Lindsey Blanton, 'Images in Conflict: The Case of Ronald Reagan and El Salvador', *International Studies Quarterly*, Vol. 40, No. 1, (March 1996), pp. 22–5.

12   Rosati (2000), p. 52.

13   Ibid., p. 56.

14   Jutta Weldes, 'Constructing National Interests', *European Journal of International Relations*, Vol. 2, No. 3, (1996), pp. 281–2.

15   Ibid., p. 285.

16   Blanton (1996), p. 25.

17   David J. Finlay, Ole R. Holsti and Richard R. Fagen, *Enemies in Politics* (Chicago, IL: Rand McNally, 1967), p. 7.

18   Brett Silverstein and Robert R. Holt, 'Research on Enemy Images: Present Status and Future Prospects', *Journal of Social Issues*, Vol. 45, No. 2, (1989), p. 171.

19   See Gerald N. Sande, George R. Goethals, Lisa Ferrari and Leila T. Worth, 'Value-Guided Attributions: Maintaining the Moral Self-Image and the Diabolical Enemy-Image', *Journal of Social Issues*, Vol. 45, No. 2, (1989), p. 93, and Blanton (1996), p. 26.

20   Brett Silverstein and Catherine Flamenbaum, 'Biases in the Perception and Cognition of the Actions of Enemies', *Journal of Social Issues*, Vol. 45, No. 2, (1989), p. 53.

21   Quoted in Bob Woodward, *The Commanders* (New York: Simon & Schuster, 1991), p. 223.

22 George Bush and Brent Scowcroft, *A World Transformed* (New York: Alfred A. Knopf, 1998), p. 308, and James A. Baker III with Thomas M. Defrank, *The Politics of Diplomacy: Revolution, War and Peace* (New York: G. P. Putnam's Sons, 1995), p. 274.

23 Quoted in Steven Hurst, *The United States and Iraq since 1979: Hegemony, Oil and War* (Edinburgh: Edinburgh University Press, 2009), p. 72.

24 Bush and Scowcroft (1998), p. 383.

25 H. Norman Schwarzkopf with Peter Petre, *The Autobiography; It Doesn't Take a Hero* (London: Bantham Press, 1992), p. 318.

26 Bush and Scowcroft (1998), pp. 400–1.

27 Woodward (1991), p. 204.

28 President George H. W. Bush, 'Remarks and an Exchange With Reporters on the Iraqi Invasion of Kuwait', 2 August 1990; and President George H. W. Bush, 'Remarks and a Question-and-Answer Session With Reporters in Aspen, Colorado, Following a Meeting With Prime Minister Margaret Thatcher of the United Kingdom', (2 August 1990). Available online at: http://bushlibrary.tamu.edu/research/public_papers.php?id=2123&year=1990&month=8; http://bushlibrary.tamu.edu/research/public_papers.php?id=2124&year=1990&month=8.

29 Scowcroft quoted in Woodward (1991), pp. 224–35.

30 Haass (2009), pp. 61–2.

31 Bush and Scowcroft (1998), p. 374.

32 President George H. W. Bush, 'Address to the Nation Announcing the Deployment of United States Armed Forces to Saudi Arabia', (8 August 1990). Available online at: http://bushlibrary.tamu.edu/research/public_papers.php?id=2147&year=1990&month=8.

33 President George H. W. Bush, 'Remarks to Department of Defense Employees', (15 August 1990). Available online at: http://bushlibrary.tamu.edu/research/public_papers.php?id=2165&year=1990&month=8.

34 Bush and Scowcroft (1998), p. 349.

35 Ibid., p. 375.

36 Yuen Foong Khong, *Analogies at War; Korea, Munich, Dien Bien Phu and the Vietnam Decisions of 1965* (Princeton, NJ: Princeton University Press, 1992), p. 10.

37 Bush, (8 August 1990).

38 Bush and Scowcroft (1998), pp. 375, 340.

39 See Steve A. Yetiv, *Explaining Foreign Policy; U.S. Decision-Making and the Persian Gulf War* (Baltimore, MD: Johns Hopkins University Press, 2004), pp. 61–9, and Schwarzkopf (1992), p. 378.

40 Khong (1992), p. 23.

41 Quoted in Woodward (1991), p. 261.

42 Colin L. Powell, *A Soldier's Way; an Autobiography* (London: Hutchinson, 1995), p. 491.

43 Toby Dodge, 'The Failure of Sanctions and the Evolution of International Policy Towards Iraq 1990–2003', *Contemporary Arab Affairs*, Vol. 3, No. 1, January, 2010, pp. 82–90; Yetiv (2004), pp. 68–9, 71–5 and Richard J. Payne, *The Clash with Distant Cultures; Values, Interests and Force in American Foreign Policy* (Albany, NY: State University of New York Press, 1995), pp. 95, 107–9.

44 Baker (1995), p. 399.

45 Quoted in ibid., p. 403.

46 See Chas W. Freeman Jr., *America's Misadventures in the Middle East* (Charlottesville, VI: Just World Books, 2010), pp. 33–4, and Schwarzkopf (1992), p. 354.

47 Baker (1995), p. 414.

48 'Bush Statement; Excerpts From 2 Statements by Bush on Iraq's Proposal for Ending Conflict', (16 February 1991). Available online at: http://query.nytimes.com/gst/fullpage.html?res=9D0CEFD91331F935A25751C0A967958260&scp=8&sq=Iraq&st=nyt.

49 Bush and Scowcroft (1998), p. 438.

50 Government of the United States of America, *The National Security Strategy of the United States of America September 2002*, p. 1. Available online at: http://www.whitehouse.gov/nsc/nss.pdf.

51 Dodge (2006).

52 Bob Woodward, *Plan of Attack* (New York: Simon & Schuster, 2004), p. 1.

53 George W. Bush, 'President Delivers State of the Union Address', The United States Capitol, Washington, DC, (29 January 2002). Available online at: http://georgewbush-whitehouse.archives.gov/news/releases/2002/01/20020129-11.html).

54 George W. Bush, *Decision Points* (London: Random House, 2010), p. 228.

55 Ibid., pp. 427–8.

56 Bob Woodward, *State of Denial* (New York: Simon & Schuster, 2006), pp. 90–1.

57 Donald Rumsfeld, *Known and Unknown: A Memoir* (New York: Sentinal, 2011), p. 514.

58 Quoted in Mark Perry, *How to Lose the War on Terror* (London: Hurst & Co, 2010), p. 13.

59 Douglas J. Feith, *War and Decision: Inside the Pentagon at the Dawn of the War on Terrorism* (New York: Harper, 2008), pp. 419, 430.

60 Bremer received specific assurance from President Bush on this. See L. Paul Bremer III with Malcolm McConnell, *My Year in Iraq: The Struggle to Build a Future of Hope* (New York: Simon & Schuster, 2006).

61 James Dobbins, Seth G. Jones, Benjamin Runkle and Siddharth Mohandas, *Occupying Iraq: A History of the Coalition Provisional Authority* (Santa Monica, CA: RAND Corporation, 2009), p. xiii.

62 Bremer (2006), pp. 38, 51, 53.

63 Ibid., p. 71.

64 Feith (2008), pp. 419, 430.

65 Astri Suhrke, 'Peace in Between', in Astri Suhrke and Mats Berdal (eds) *The Peace in Between: Post-War Violence and Peacebuilding* (Abingdon: Routledge, 2011), pp. 1–24.

66 Rajiv Chandrasekaran, *Imperial Life in the Emerald City: Inside Baghdad's Green Zone* (London: Bloomsbury, 2007), pp. 76–7.

67 Quoted in Bremer (2006), p. 39.

68 Quoted in Special Inspector General for Iraq Reconstruction, *Hard Lessons; The Iraq Reconstruction Experience*, p. 74. Available online at: http://www.sigir.mil/publications/hardLessons.html.

69 Larson (1994), p. 25.

70 Mark Laffey and Jutta Weldes, 'Beyond Belief: Ideas and Symbolic Technologies in the Study of International Relations', *European Journal of International Relations*, Vol. 3, No. 3, (1997), pp. 193–237.

CHAPTER NINE

Anglo-American perceptions of Osama bin Laden after 9/11

Peter R. Neumann and Fernande van Tets

Introduction

Following the terrorist attacks against the United States on 11 September 2001, many Western commentators portrayed Osama bin Laden, the leader of al Qaeda and mastermind of the 9/11 attacks, as the 'world's most dangerous man'. Yet, by the time of his death, bin Laden was widely regarded as a failure. The obituaries that were published in the wake of his death on 2 May 2011 described him as the 'icon' and 'poster boy'[1] of violent 'jihad', who had achieved 'cult status'[2] among his followers. But they also made it clear that nearly all of his aims and ambitions remained unfulfilled. According to the BBC's Frank Gardner, for example, bin Laden had 'failed to remove any Arab "apostate" regimes, nor [had he] instigated a transnational conflict between mainstream Muslims and the West'.[3] Indeed, his killing by American special forces seemed a fitting conclusion to the decade-long 'War on Terror', which had – just recently – been replaced by the peaceful revolutions of the Arab Spring as the principal paradigm for looking at the Middle East.

This chapter examines American and British elite views of bin Laden during the 'War on Terror'. It begins by offering an analysis of the opinions and statements of government leaders, especially President George Bush and Prime Minister Tony Blair. It then proceeds to take a broader and, arguably, more sophisticated look at the fluctuations and changes in elite perceptions throughout the decade, using the quality press in Britain and the United States as a proxy. Using both qualitative and quantitative methods, it analyses the bin Laden coverage, hoping to identify the major themes and ideas that have informed Anglo-American perceptions.

In doing so, it shows that Anglo-American elite views of bin Laden underwent a major transformation over the course of the decade. Initially perceived as an effective political and military leader who had managed to vent the frustrations of millions of Muslims across the world, bin Laden came to be seen as an 'isolated loner' who had lost influence and momentum and whose statements and actions were seen as increasingly irrational. For British and American commentators, bin Laden's leadership of al Qaeda was never in doubt, but there were questions of what exactly 'leadership' amounted to, given that Western forces were believed to be in hot pursuit and his physical condition was considered weak. The one area where their views differed substantially was bin Laden's character and 'humanity'. Whereas conservative elite publications did not hesitate to describe bin Laden as a 'monster', liberal sources were more likely to emphasize bin Laden's good character and intellectual pursuits. It is difficult, therefore, to speak of a single 'Western' view or perception, except for the overwhelming sense of military and political failure which emerged from the middle of the decade and represents the dominant theme of bin Laden coverage during the War on Terror.

Leaders' views

The portrayals of bin Laden by Western government leaders – especially of the countries at the heart of the 'Global War on Terrorism', the United States and the United Kingdom – are less instructive than one may think. Both Bush and Blair made numerous statements about bin Laden in the lead-up to and during the military conflict that led to the downfall of the Taliban government in late 2001. The political purpose was to establish both bin Laden's responsibility for the 11 September attacks and his close relationship with the Taliban, which – taken together – provided the rationale for military action. No doubt the two leaders 'picked' on bin Laden because he personified the adversary and could easily be portrayed as the 'evil mastermind' against which Western public opinion had to be mobilized. In addition, it must have seemed obvious that bin Laden's capture would provide Western publics with an immediate sense of 'justice being done' – a phrase used repeatedly by Bush (less so by Blair). Ironically, therefore, the two leaders portrayed the 'Global War on Terror' as a police action, whose principal purpose was to hold bin Laden responsible for the crime he had committed on 9/11.

Although Bush and Blair both paid close attention to bin Laden in the months following the 11 September attacks, their respective tone and emphasis was different. Blair, in the House of Commons and elsewhere, talked about bin Laden as a terrorist and mass murderer, and Foreign Secretary Jack Straw on one occasion accused him of being 'psychotic and paranoid'.[4] Yet, overall, the British government's rhetoric was sombre and restrained. Downing Street released documents that were meant to prove bin Laden's culpability,[5] while Blair 'made the case' against bin Laden in interviews and speeches, but he never resorted to using personal insults or overly emotive language.[6] By contrast, Bush struck a very different tone by declaring that bin Laden had to be captured 'dead or alive',[7] reflecting the mood of a nation that had just lost 3,000 of its citizens in a devastating terrorist attack. On numerous occasions, Bush described bin Laden and his organization, al Qaeda, as 'evil', which seemed to require no further explanation or elaboration.[8]

Importantly, though, both leaders made it clear that bin Laden's actions must not be equated with the religion of Islam. Bush and Blair were keen to deny bin Laden's religious legitimacy, and they went to great lengths to separate bin Laden's 'terror' from the views of Muslims across the world.[9] Blair, for example, argued that, far from being a religious figure in his own right, bin Laden was 'exploiting people's faith'.[10] Similarly, Bush claimed that, in spite of the war against al Qaeda, he and the American people were 'friends of almost a billion worldwide who practice the Islamic faith'.[11]

When it became obvious that bin Laden could not be captured quickly, Bush's emphasis shifted dramatically from bin Laden to al Qaeda. As early as March 2002 – barely six months after the 11 September attacks – the President told the White House press corps that bin Laden was no longer a priority. In his own words:

> Who knows if he's hiding in some cave or not. We haven't heard from him in a long time. The idea of focusing on one person really indicates to me [that] people don't understand the scope of the mission. Terror is bigger than one person. He's just a person who's been marginalized.[12]

Bush's comments reflected his government's failure to capture or kill bin Laden at the Battle of Tora Bora in December 2001,[13] but they also pointed towards changing priorities. After all, 2002 was the year in which the Bush administration shifted its attention from Afghanistan to Iraq. Given that bin Laden was certain to be hiding in Pakistan or Afghanistan – not Iraq – it made political sense to downplay bin Laden's continued significance. Indeed, four years later, when the United States had become bogged down in Iraq and the Taliban had not (yet) re-emerged, Bush went even further, suggesting that the American government was pulling away from hunting down bin Laden altogether. He told a conservative magazine editor that bin Laden 'doesn't fit with the administration's strategy for combating terrorism', and that getting bin Laden was 'not a top priority use of American resources'.[14]

In making the case for war against Iraq, Bush and his Vice-President, Dick Cheney, cited bin Laden as a justification, but never elaborated on his whereabouts or condition. Cheney in particular conveyed the impression that there existed a link between Saddam Hussein's regime, bin Laden and the 9/11 attacks,[15] which made the war against Saddam appear like an extension of a police action to capture and punish bin Laden. By contrast, Blair and the British government never claimed that bin Laden had any direct connection with Iraq.[16] Instead, they focused on Saddam's suspected stockpiles of weapons of mass destruction (WMD) and his record of sponsoring terrorist groups, arguing that – post 9/11 – any link between WMD and state sponsorship of terrorism could no longer be tolerated.[17] Hardly any statements by British government ministers dealt with bin Laden. By early 2002, even the mission in Afghanistan was framed more broadly: in late January, Blair affirmed his commitment to finding bin Laden and his remaining associates, but emphasized the need for humanitarian relief and reconstruction as a way of making sure that 'terrorists' – not bin Laden specifically – would never again look to Afghanistan as a safe haven.[18]

Neither Gordon Brown nor David Cameron, who succeeded Tony Blair as Prime Minister in 2007 and 2010 respectively, made any significant statements on bin Laden until his death in May 2011. By contrast, Bush's successor as President, Barack Obama, made a point of focusing American energies back on bin Laden. His argument – articulated numerous times during the 2008 presidential election campaign – was that Iraq had been a distraction and that the 'War on Terror' (a label he quietly abandoned) should always have been limited to finding bin Laden and making sure that Afghanistan would not re-emerge as a safe haven for al Qaeda fighters. In his own words,

> [W]e made a bad judgment going into Iraq in the first place when we hadn't finished the job of hunting down bin Laden and crushing al-Qaida. ... [I]f we have Osama bin Laden in our sights and the Pakistani government is unable or unwilling to take them out, then I think that we have to act, and we will take them out.[19]

Overall, therefore, Anglo-American leaders' public statements are not especially useful as a means of gauging Western perceptions of bin Laden. Throughout the 'War on Terror', mentions of bin Laden by those leaders served obvious political purposes, but they are devoid of the kind of intimate description that would provide a sense of what they really thought. As a result, the following sections will look at representations of bin Laden in the media, which seems to offer a better way of gauging the perceptions of elites on all sides of the political spectrum.

Media views

So many articles have been written about bin Laden in the Western press that it is almost impossible to provide a comprehensive survey of 'Western views'.[20] Rather than going through every publication about bin Laden over the past decade, we decided to pick a sample of (mostly) magazine-length pieces. The idea was to capture a broad representation of Western elite views, which could then be analysed in greater depth. In particular, we thought it was important to see if bin Laden's perception had changed over time, and if media sources from different parts of the political spectrum had come to similar conclusions. As a result, we selected three media sources each for the United Kingdom and the United States. Each media source had to represent a particular political orientation (left-wing/liberal, centrist or conservative), and they all had to have covered bin Laden throughout the post-9/11 period. For Britain, we picked the *Guardian* (left-wing), the BBC (centrist) and the *Telegraph* (conservative). Our American sources were the *New York Times* (liberal), the *Washington Post* (centrist) and the *Washington Times* (conservative).[21]

Overall, therefore, we looked at 54 articles, with one article per media source for each of the nine years between 2002 and 2010. Most of the bin Laden related coverage took place in the month of September, typically during the anniversaries of the 11 September attacks, which many publications saw as opportunities to 'take stock' of the 'War on Terror'. Similar clusters emerged whenever bin Laden decided to release a video or audio message which prompted Western media sources to speculate about his whereabouts and state of health. Despite the wealth of coverage, we are conscious that the sample has many flaws. For example, articles in the British media often drew on commentary from American experts – such as Steve Coll, Peter Bergen, Bruce Riedel, Michael Scheuer and Bruce Hoffman – which coloured their analysis and made it difficult, at times, to maintain the distinction between countries of origin. Furthermore, our media sources are all from what is often referred to as the 'quality press'. Popular newspapers, such as the *Sun* in Britain or *USA Today* in the United States, may have covered bin Laden in an entirely different way, but they were not considered for this study. The study, in that sense, is a review of elite opinions rather than popular sentiment in Britain and America more generally. Even so, we believe that the sample offers a reasonably good impression of the key themes and opinions that have dominated the Anglo-American bin Laden coverage since 2001, and that it was sufficiently representative to qualify for more rigorous forms of testing and analysis.

In terms of content, we were interested in three aspects of bin Laden's perception, all of which featured prominently in the Western literature on the al Qaeda leader.[22] The first related to commentators' views about bin Laden's political standing and relevance. This translated into three questions: (1) Are his actions believed to generate popular support? (2) Is he portrayed as a product of popular politics? (3) To what degree is he seen as a 'political' leader? A second area concerned Western views about bin Laden's relationship to the terrorist group al Qaeda and his political and military leadership of the 'jihadist' movement. The texts were interrogated for the following: (1) Is he portrayed as being fully in charge of al Qaeda? (2) To what extent is he viewed as a military leader? (3) Is he seen as successful? Finally, we looked for descriptions of bin Laden's personal traits and characteristics. We were interested in the following: (1) Is he described as weak and frail? (2) To what extent is his behaviour portrayed as 'rational'? (3) Is he regarded as 'human'? The principal findings that have resulted from this analysis are described in the following sections.

From mastermind to figure of ridicule

The main development in Anglo-American portrayals of bin Laden is his gradual transformation from being a voice of oppressed Muslims to an isolated loner, whose ideas and statements are of little consequence. In the years immediately following the 9/11 attacks, many newspapers treated bin Laden like a serious political leader who had captured the imagination of millions of Muslims across the world. They recognized that Muslims in places like Pakistan and Saudi Arabia did not necessarily buy into his entire political and religious agenda, but that bin Laden had become a symbol of defiance, who had managed to accomplish what generations of Muslim and Arab leaders had failed to do, that is, to stand up to America and vent ordinary Muslims' deeply felt frustrations and sense of humiliation. According to the *New York Times*, the al Qaeda leader had 'eloquently expressed [Muslims'] anger over the foreign policies of the United States and Israel'.[23] The *Guardian* argued that – through one act of violence – bin Laden had succeeded in 'elevating a distorted, twisted cause to the top of the global agenda'.[24] bin Laden, in other words, had 'acquired a poke them in the eye, Robin Hood legitimacy across the Islamic world, even among moderate Muslims'.[25]

Over the course of the decade, however, the perception of 'popular support' for bin Laden declined significantly. Although al Qaeda's Iraqi affiliate was pounding Western coalition forces, and even though the London attacks in July 2005 proved that al Qaeda could still hit Western civilians at home, many commentators felt that bin Laden had been sidelined by others in his own movement, and that organizations like Hamas and Hezbollah had overtaken bin Laden as chief avengers of the Muslim world. For the *Washington Post*, for example, the increasing frequency of audio and video messages from bin Laden no longer symbolized importance and vitality, but conveyed his 'fear [of] losing influence in the fragmented world of Islamic fundamentalism'.[26] Rather than *being* the 'champion of oppressed Muslims around the world', bin Laden was believed to be desperately '*trying*' to assert this role (emphasis added).[27] Simply put, by the end of the decade, Western commentators had concluded that bin Laden had lost popular support, and that the once powerful leader of al Qaeda had become irrelevant.

A similar development may be observed when considering how Western commentators have judged bin Laden's 'success'. In the years following 9/11, his 'not being caught' was sufficient for bin Laden to be seen as successful. The *New York Times*, for example, saw bin Laden as the Muslim world's David, who had 'defeated' the American Goliath by avoiding capture:

> His success in evading the toughest troops in the American forces – with every advantage of satellite technology and helicopters and other modern technical wizardry – has made him an irresistible icon to many in the Muslim world, especially among the alienated young.[28]

Bin Laden's every sign of life came to be seen as an assertion of his continuing appeal, and every terrorist attack anywhere in the world was treated as evidence of his inspirational powers. The *Telegraph*, for example, considered bin Laden's video message on the eve of the American presidential election in 2004 a 'stunning intervention'.[29] The *Washington Post*, by contrast, believed that suicide attacks in places like 'Iraq, Saudi-Arabia, Qatar, Spain, Egypt and now apparently London' had all been inspired by bin Laden.[30] In fact, only by the end of the decade did Western assessments of bin Laden become more grounded in political and military realities. In 2007, the *Telegraph* concluded that 'Bin Laden is probably as far away from achieving his strategic aims as he was before September 11 [2001]'.[31] In 2010, the *Washington Post* now considered him no more than an 'afterthought' in most of the important 'jihadist' battlefronts, including Afghanistan.[32]

One of the most compelling findings is how Western perceptions of success seemed to be correlated with perceptions of rationality. In the first years, many accounts of bin Laden highlighted his role as 'mastermind' of the 11 September attacks, stressing the careful planning and preparation that had gone into the attacks. By the middle of the decade, however, the sophistication of 9/11 seemed to have been forgotten. Rather than being conscious and cold-blooded, bin Laden was frequently portrayed as 'desperate and angry'.[33] His video statements were seen as 'rambling' and 'idiosyncratic'.[34] The *Telegraph* even compared bin Laden to Elvis Presley.[35] Despite repeated warnings that al Qaeda was not finished and that bin Laden still had a constituency in places like Pakistan, it seems very clear, therefore, that – by the end of the decade – Western commentators had 'lost faith' in bin Laden. A person whom they once portrayed as a voice of the oppressed with near magical powers to inspire terrorist attacks all over the world had turned into a figure of ridicule whose time had passed and who was successful and consistent only in 'his dedication to losing causes'.[36]

A different kind of leader?

Throughout the post-11 September period, Western commentators never questioned bin Laden's leadership of al Qaeda, although his leadership style and ability is seen as different from 'conventional' political and military leaders. Nearly all the items that we have looked at discuss bin Laden's relationship with al Qaeda, and – in particular – the extent to which he controlled the group's military campaign. None of the articles doubted bin Laden's direct involvement in 9/11, but many were not sure if his direction and direct involvement had survived the subsequent invasion of Afghanistan and the US-led 'Global War on Terror'. Typically, video messages from bin Laden and his deputy, Ayman Al Zawahiri, led to speculation that the two leaders were 'still alive and in control of the terror network',[37] whereas their absence fuelled suggestions that the two 'faces of Al Qaeda' were on the run and, therefore, unable to manage their group.[38] According to a 2006 article in the *New York Times*: 'The way you show leadership is to show yourself. So why haven't we had a videotape?'[39] By 2007, American intelligence sources appeared to suggest that bin Laden and 'Al Qaeda Central' in the tribal areas of Pakistan had reasserted some control over the organization, and this came to be reflected in many articles, which claimed that al Qaeda's 'leadership command and control is robust' after all.[40] By 2010, however, the idea of purely 'inspirational leadership' had once again come to dominate the bin Laden coverage, with most media sources agreeing that bin Laden had no involvement 'or even knew in advance' of terrorist plots that were hatched in the name of al Qaeda.[41]

One of the factors that influenced Western commentators' assessments of bin Laden's ability to direct al Qaeda was his state of health. Immediately after 9/11, there were numerous reports about bin Laden suffering from kidney failure, hepatitis and/or diabetes, in addition to being hit by Western or Northern Alliance forces in their assault on the Taliban. Accordingly, Western commentators looked at bin Laden's video or audio tapes as 'signs of life' that were analysed in great depth for any indications of his physical condition. Very rarely, though, was there any consensus. In 2002, for example, one of bin Laden's video messages was seen as an indication that 'he is alive and well'[42] and in 'good health'[43] by the *Washington Times* and the BBC respectively, whereas the *Washington Post* concluded – based on the same video message – that he 'is probably in very poor health and unable to travel extensively'.[44] Five years later, the *Washington Post* identified bin Laden's physical appearance and supposed good health as the 'most striking feature' of his half-hour-long video message, and deduced that his recuperation must be one of the reasons for the revival of 'Al Qaeda Central'.[45] Needless to say, none of the media sources – nor, as we now know, the American government – had any idea of bin Laden's whereabouts or his actual state of health for most of the decade, which shows that even lengthy assessments of bin Laden's leadership were often based on virtually no factual insight or evidence.

Our quantitative analysis revealed no significant differences between country of origin and political orientation when it came to commentators' assessment of bin Laden's leadership. The one exception is the framing of bin Laden's leadership style as 'businesslike', which seems to be a constant point of reference in the American media but significantly less so for British commentators. Accordingly, American articles often portray bin Laden as a 'CEO', whose management style and principles 'might be familiar to business executives the world over'.[46] This analogy, then, provides a powerful metaphor for explaining how bin Laden can still be the leader of al Qaeda without directing the organization on a day-to-day basis. According to the *Washington Times*, for example, bin Laden had at some point stopped being al Qaeda's 'CEO' and assumed the role of 'chairman of the board', putting others – 'the executive vice presidents, the operating officers, the people responsible for certain aspects of the organization' – in charge of running the campaign.[47] al Qaeda and bin Laden, in other words, had become a 'brand [rather] than a tight-knit group'.[48] The American media, therefore, succeeded in identifying a model of leadership that made sense of bin Laden and al Qaeda's purely 'inspirational' role while resonating with America's (capitalist) culture, whereas British commentators struggled to describe bin Laden's leadership, ranging from crude military analogies to the idea of bin Laden as a revolutionary or 'resistance' leader similar to those that had been prominent during the era of decolonization.[49] None of these, however, are as clearly and consistently developed and expressed as the uniquely American idea of 'terrorist as CEO'.[50]

Poet or monster?

The only variable for which 'political orientation' made a difference was bin Laden's perceived 'humanity'. Having coded all the articles in our sample, it became obvious that the right-wing media looked at bin Laden – the person – very differently, and that those differences transcended other 'dividers', such as time and country, in significance. No doubt negative portrayals and value judgments of bin Laden could be found in articles of every political hue, but very rarely would left-wing publications resort to describing bin Laden as 'evil'. For commentators on the political Left, bin Laden represented a 'mystery' precisely because neither his intelligence, character nor physical appearance seemed to confirm the popular idea of a mass murderer. Indeed, bin Laden's intellectual pursuits, especially his interest in books and poetry, were given much attention in left-wing and centrist publications. In a 2008 piece, for example, the *New York Times* pointed out that 'Bin Laden is noted as a stickler for Arabic grammar and rhetorical flourishes'.[51] That same year, the BBC described bin Laden as 'a skilled poet' who had managed to combine 'mystical references, jihadist imagery ... [and] 1,400-year old poetry' in his video and audio messages.[52]

The right-wing media painted a very different picture of the al Qaeda leader. The *Telegraph*, for example, described bin Laden as a 'hate-filled'[53] terrorist who had no compunctions about engaging in 'hideous' attacks and acts of 'mass murder'[54] and posed a truly 'apocalyptic' threat to the West.[55] Like their left-wing and centrist counterparts, right-wing media provided much space for stories about bin Laden's motivations, as well as his origins and upbringing. Furthermore, there is considerable discussion of bin Laden's political and religious ideas and some engagement with al Qaeda's political demands. In contrast to the left-wing media, however, none of the context serves to 'humanize' bin Laden. Rather, it is meant to explain how the al Qaeda leader has, in the words of the *Washington Times*, '[come to be] the revolutionary monster that the world now knows only too well'.[56] Even some of the centrist papers occasionally resorted to such language, portraying bin Laden as a 'cruel zealot' and 'tyrannical and selfish father'[57] who had little or no concern for human life. According to the *Washington Post*, for example, bin Laden 'lives to kill, the pursuit of violent jihad overpowering even the most basic human feelings and paternal concerns'.[58] It seems clear, therefore, that – as far as bin Laden's personality was concerned – no single Western 'take' existed.

Conclusion

Western elite views of bin Laden were more complex than one might have expected. Neither was he consistently portrayed as a 'religious crazy' nor was he used as a 'bogeyman' for asserting a sense of superiority over the Middle East, as Edward Said would have predicted.[59] Our overwhelming impression is that Western experts and journalists were trying hard to provide a balanced and, indeed, nuanced assessment of the al Qaeda leader. Jason Burke and Lawrence Joffe's obituary in the *Guardian* is a good example:

His life was one of extremes and of contradictions. Born to great wealth, he lived in relative poverty. A graduate of civil engineering, he assumed the mantle of a religious scholar. A gifted propagandist who had little real experience of battle, he projected himself as a mujahid, a holy warrior. ... One of the most notorious people on the planet, Bin Laden lived for years in obscurity, his public presence limited to intermittent appearances in videos on the internet. ... To his enemies ... he was a religious fanatic, a terrorist with the blood of thousands on his hands. ... To his supporters, whose numbers peaked in the few years after the attacks of 11 September 2001 in America that he masterminded, he was a visionary leader fighting both western aggression against Muslims and his co-religionists' lack of faith and rigour.[60]

No doubt, more simplistic views could have been found in the tabloids, and – as we saw in the previous section – there were exceptions to the pattern of nuance and sophistication even in the quality press. Even so, the dominant story about bin Laden was not his 'barbarism' or 'moral depravity', but – quite simply – the failure of his military campaign. Bin Laden came to be seen as 'irrational' and 'isolated' not because of commentators' (misguided) ideas about the Muslim character or the 'Arab personality', but – rather – because he had failed to sustain his terrorist campaign in the wake of 9/11. For Anglo-American elites, he was a 'loser' much more than he was a fanatic, and it is likely to be his failure, not the nature of his aims and aspirations, for which he will be remembered.

Notes

1 'Osama bin Laden', *Daily Telegraph*, (2 May 2011).

2 John Simpson, 'Obituary: Osama bin Laden', *BBC News*, (2 May 2011).

3 Frank Gardner, 'Analysis', *BBC News*, (2 May 2011).

4 Nicholas Watt, 'Bin Laden is Psychotic, Says Straw', *Guardian*, (6 November 2001).

5 'Full Text of Tony Blair's Speech to Parliament', *Guardian*, (4 October 2001).

6 See e.g. ibid.

7 Michael White and Lucy Ward, 'Blair Distances UK From "Dead or Alive" Claim', *Guardian*, (19 September 2001).

8 Alan Elsner, 'Bush Use of the Term "The Evil One" Raises Eyebrows', *Reuters*, (25 October 2001).

9 Bush quoted in Scott Lindlaw, 'Bush Says Islam is Peaceful Faith', *Newsday*, (15 November 2002).

10 'The Tragedy is that Bin Laden is Exploiting People's Faith', *Guardian*, (12 October 2001).

11   Cited in 'Address to the Nation Delivered by George W. Bush on 7 October 2001'; full text available online at the University of Chicago Library: http://fathom.lib.uchicago.edu/1/777777190152/3570_GWB.htm.

12   Bush quoted in Alex Seitz-Wald, 'Bush On Bin Laden: "I Really Just Don't Spend That Much Time On Him"', *Think Progress*, (2 May 2011).

13   'US ends Bin Laden hunt in Tora Bora', *Guardian*, (8 January 2002).

14   Ibid.

15   See e.g. 'Cheney Blasts Media on al Qaeda–Iraq Link', *CNN*, (18 June 2004).

16   Matthew Tempest, 'Blair Makes no Promises over Iraq', *Guardian*, 16 July 2002; Patrick Wintour, 'Blair Denies that Iraq Focus is Misguided', *Guardian*, (15 October 2002).

17   Ibid.

18   See Simon Left and Sarah Jeffery, 'Blair Reaffirms Commitment to Afghanistan', *Guardian*, (31 January 2002).

19   Obama quoted in Bill Adair, 'In 2008, Obama Vowed to Kill Bin Laden', *Tampa Bay Times*, (1 May 2011).

20   For example, there are nearly 8,000 references to articles about Bin Laden in the British *Guardian* newspaper alone; see search for Osama Bin Laden in the online archives of the *Guardian;* available online at: http://www.guardian.co.uk/search?q=osama+bin+laden&section=.

21   Needless to say, such classifications are somewhat subjective. The BBC, for example, has been accused of bias by conservatives and left-wingers alike. See, for instance, Toby Helm, 'Labour Turns on BBC over Pro-Coalition Coverage', *Guardian*, (31 December 2011). Conservatives in the United States suspect media bias everywhere and tend to rate every media source, including press agencies such as the Associated Press, as 'liberal' unless they are explicitly conservative, making the classification of any media source as 'centrist' near impossible. See Tim Groseclose, *Left Turn: How Liberal Media Bias Distorts the American Mind* (London and New York: St Martin's Press, 2012). To make matters worse, the political spectra in both countries are different, which means that what would be considered left-wing in the United States (say, for instance, support for a National Health Service) is mainstream and centrist in the United Kingdom. Based on the idea that newspapers generally attract readers who hold views similar to their paper, the classification of US newspapers is based on a study by University of Chicago economists Matthew Gentzkow and Jesse Shapiro. See Matthew Gentzkow and Jesse Shapiro, 'What Drives Media Slant? Evidence from U.S. Daily Newspapers', *University of Chicago Working Paper*, (13 November 2006); available online at: http://papers.ssrn.com/sol3/papers.cfm?abstract_id=947640. In the UK's case, the assessment is based on newspapers' support for political parties in past general elections, which included both Conservative and Labour in *The Times*' case (hence, its classification as centrist) and Labour and the Liberal Democrats for the *Guardian* (resulting in its classification as left-wing). The BBC's legal commitment to non-bias, though disputed by partisans on both sides of the political spectrum, makes it centrist.

22 See e.g. Peter Bergen, *The Osama Bin Laden I Know: An Oral History of al Qaeda's Leader* (New York: Free Press, 2006); Thomas Mockaitis, *Osama bin Laden: A Biography* (London: Greenwood, 2009); Michael Scheuer, *Osama bin Laden* (New York: Oxford University Press USA, 2011); Lawrence Wright, *The Looming Tower: Al Qaeda and the Road to 9/11* (New York: Vintage, 2007).

23 Don Van Natta, 'Sizing Up the New Toned-down Bin Laden', *New York Times*, (19 December 2004).

24 'A World and its Losses: One Year On, Lessons Remain Unlearned', *Guardian*, (11 September 2002).

25 'The War of Unintended Consequences: Four Years after 9/11', *Guardian*, (12 September 2005).

26 Craig Whitlock, 'On Tape, Bin Laden Warns of Long War; He Accuses the West of Acting as "Crusader"', *Washington Post*, (24 April 2006).

27 Ibid.

28 John F. Burns, 'Threats and Responses: The Manhunt', *New York Times*, (30 September 2002).

29 Anton La Guardia, 'Bin Laden aide's tape taunts American analysis', *Daily Telegraph*, (11 September 2004).

30 Peter Bergen, 'The Jihadists Export their Tage to Book Pages and Web Pages', *Washington Post*, (11 September 2005).

31 David Blair, 'Al-Qa'eda Prepares for New Wave Of Terror', *Daily Telegraph*, (31 May 2007).

32 Craig Whitlock, 'Al-Qaeda Presence Limited in War', *Washington Post*, (23 August 2010).

33 Sara Carter, 'Bin Laden Slams U.S. Role in Pakistan', *Washington Times*, (4 June 2009).

34 Scott Shane, 'Bin Laden, Resurfacing in Audio Recordings, Urges Aid for Pakistan Flood Victims', *New York Times*, (3 October 2010).

35 Alex Russell, 'Bin Laden's Trail "Has Gone Stone Cold"', *Daily Telegraph*, (11 September 2006).

36 'Bin Laden Goes Green', *Washington Times*, (4 October 2010).

37 James Risen and David Johnston, 'Two Years Later: Bin Laden is Seen with Aide on Tape', *New York Times*, (11 September 2003).

38 See e.g. Gordon Corera, 'Al-Qaeda Resurgent Six Years On', BBC News, (11 September 2007).

39 Michael Slackman, 'Bin Laden Says West is Waging War Against Islam, and Urges Supporters to Go to Sudan', *New York Times*, (24 April 2006).

40 Mark Mazzetti and David Rohde, 'Terror Officials See Qaeda Chiefs Regaining Power', *New York Times*, (19 February 2007).

41 Henry Samuel, 'Bin Laden Wanted a Satellite TV Dish to Watch 9/11 Attacks from Afghan Hideout', *Daily Telegraph*, (16 April 2010).

42 Rowan Scarborough, 'Message Seen as Warning of Terror', *Washington Times,* (14 November 2002).

43 'Pinning Down Al-Qaeda's Loose Alliance', BBC News, (14 October 2002).

44 Susan Schmidt and Dana Priest, 'U.S. Fears Low-Level Al Qaeda Attacks', *Washington Post,* (9 September 2002).

45 Craig Whitlock, 'The New Al Qaeda Central', *Washington Post,* (9 September 2007).

46 David von Drehle, 'Bin Laden Portrayed as a Hands-On Leader', *Washington Post,* (17 June 2004).

47 Joseph Curl, 'Stopping Bin Laden is "Greatest Challenge"', *Washington Times,* (4 March 2005).

48 Bergen (September 2005).

49 See e.g. 'Through the Mist, US Forces Catch Glimpses of their Elusive Quarry', *Guardian,* (26 July 2010).

50 Drehlen, 'Bin Laden'.

51 Neil McFarquhar, 'Tapes Offer a Look Beneath the Surface of Bin Laden and Al Qaeda', *New York Times,* (11 September 2008).

52 Michael Hirst, 'Analysing Bin Laden's Jihadi Poetry', BBC News, (24 September 2008).

53 Patrick Bishop, 'A Cowboy Fan Who Grew to Hate America', *Daily Telegraph,* (11 September 2002).

54 Simon Scott Plummer, 'The Islamic World is Turning its Back on Al-Qaeda and Bin Laden', *Daily Telegraph,* (26 September 2008).

55 'How the West is Winning', *Daily Telegraph,* (11 September 2003).

56 Martin Sieff, 'A Dynasty's Story', *Washington Times,* (30 March 2008).

57 Thomas Lippman, 'My Father, the Terrorist', *Washington Post,* (15 November 2009).

58 Ibid.

59 See Edward Said, *Orientalism* (New York: Vintage, 1979).

60 Jason Burke and Lawrence Joffe, 'Osama bin Laden Obituary', *Guardian,* (2 May 2011).

CHAPTER TEN

Reliable enemy?
Bashar al-Asad and the United States

David W. Lesch

Introduction

Syrian President Bashar al-Asad officially took the constitutional oath of office and delivered his inaugural speech on 17 July 2000, in Damascus. By Syrian standards, it was a remarkably enlightened speech replete with criticisms of certain policies in the past, even those of his predecessor and father Hafiz al-Asad, who ruled Syria from 1970 until his death in June 2000. The frankness of the speech confirmed the hopes among many in and outside of Syria that indeed Bashar was a breath of fresh air who would lead the country in a new direction.[1]

His speech conveyed clear ideas on how Syria could move forward in terms of economic reform and technological modernization, although it was ambiguous, even evasive, on the extent of political reform along a more democratic model. Despite this, however, there was a genuine air of exuberance among many who had longed for change in Syria. Bashar was a licensed ophthalmologist who had studied in London. He had nurtured a collaborative relationship with elements of the intelligentsia after returning from London in 1994 upon the death of his older brother Basil, who had been the putative heir being groomed to succeed the father. Bashar was chairman of the Syrian Computer Society (SCS), something of a computer nerd himself who revelled in the technological toys of the West. It was hoped as well that the new president would improve Syria's relationship with the West.

Relations between the United States and Syria have had their ups and (mostly) downs since Bashar al-Asad came to power. US–Syrian relations, however, were not always strained. Syrian troops were stationed alongside US forces in the 1990–1 Persian Gulf crisis and War. Syria was a key participant in the convening of the Madrid peace process sponsored by the United States and the Soviet Union, which led to the Oslo Accords, a Jordanian–Israeli treaty, and almost a decade of on-again, off-again US-brokered Israeli–Syrian peace negotiations. For years, Syria was also the only one of the original seven charter members of the US-designated list of 'states that sponsor terrorism' that maintained full diplomatic relations with the United States.

Even during the heyday of the superpowers' Cold War, when Syria was considered a client state of the Soviet Union, there were important moments of US–Syrian cooperation, such as the US-brokered 1974 disengagement agreement between Israel and Syria regarding the Golan Heights following the 1973 Arab–Israeli war. Such was the importance of Syria in the Middle East from the point of view of Washington that the man who negotiated that disengagement agreement, former Secretary of State Henry Kissinger, commented that while there could be no war in the Arab–Israeli arena without Egypt, there could also be no peace without Syria.

Contrary to popular belief, Hafiz al-Asad's assumption of power in 1970 signalled the departure of an ideologically based foreign and domestic policy to a more pragmatic one prepared to diplomatically resolve the Arab–Israeli conflict but nonetheless whole-heartedly committed to a full return of the Golan Heights. Domestically, Asad developed an authoritarian-based regime with a pervasive clientelist network in and outside of the government. It was also a regime that became 'bonapartist', i.e. regime maintenance became the most important objective, whereas domestic policy and much of Syria's foreign policy was but a means to this end. Asad constructed an alliance of sorts between Alawites and the Sunni business class that some have called the 'military-merchant complex', and the Alawites, who came to dominate the military-security apparatus, were not about to relinquish their hold on power and all of the political, social and economic benefits that accrued from this; in fact, it may be surmised that they were not about to accept even a dilution of that power, which certainly factored into the equation when Hafiz's son, Bashar, was chosen as president in 2000. Yet despite the hopes for a more constructive rather than confrontational posture between the United States and Syria, moments of cooperation between Washington and Damascus became for the most part a thing of the past soon after Bashar al-Asad came to power.

Downgrading Bashar

Iterations emanating from Washington and beyond early on in Bashar's tenure in power regularly derided, even mocked, the Syrian president as incompetent, naive and weak. US congressional testimony in 2002 and 2003 surrounding the passage of the sanction-lined Syrian Accountability Act (SAA, signed into law by President George W. Bush in 2004) helped establish this negative view of Bashar by overtly attacking Syria and its president, oftentimes in an insulting fashion.[2] These diatribes emerged out of the post-9/11 environment when Congress was on anti-terrorist 'steroids', each member trying to outdo the other in building up his or her anti-terrorist credentials.

Syria was an easy target, as was its president. It was, in the jargon of the time, low-hanging fruit. It could be easily attacked verbally – and even militarily in targeted strikes – without serious repercussions. In testimony before the House Committee on International Relations in September 2002 on the SAA, Dick Armey (R-TX) proclaimed,

> Our inaction on holding Syria accountable for its dangerous activities could seriously diminish our efforts on the war on terrorism and brokering a viable peace in the Middle East ... Syria should be held accountable for its record of harboring and supporting terrorist groups; stockpiling illegal weapons in an effort to develop weapons of mass destruction; and transferring weapons and oil back and forth through Iraq.

The co-sponsor of the SAA, Eliot Engel (D-NY), asserted, 'We will not tolerate Syrian support for terrorism. We will not tolerate Syrian occupation of Lebanon ... I do not want to witness horrors worse than 9/11. I urge the Administration to get tough on Syria.' His cohort, Gary Ackerman (D-NY), said, 'This is not too big a nut to crack. Syria is a small, decrepit, little terror state that has been yanking our diplomatic chain for years.' Alluding to President Bashar being a licensed ophthalmologist, Shelly Berkley (D-NY) stated the following:

> I don't care if he's a doctor, a lawyer, a plumber, a carpenter – this is not a kinder and gentler leader. This is a kinder and gentler terrorist, and we don't need another one of those. He is no different from his father; perhaps, even worse because he should know better. This is a disgrace that this country isn't standing up to this terrorist and making sure that this type of behavior is not only condemned, but eliminated.[3]

Bashar had been in power for a little over two years when these comments were made. They were based on a lack of knowledge in Congress of how

Syria works – or in many cases, doesn't work. For instance, Bashar had announced in the early days of his regime that he intended to authorize the opening of private banks in Syria, a novelty for a public sector-dominated country where most of the fluid capital found its way to Lebanese banks. When the private banks did not materialize by 2003, Bashar was taken to task by some members of Congress and officials in the Bush Administration for not following through what he had promised, thus a further indication of his ineptitude and prevarication. In other words, he could not be trusted.

The fact of the matter is that Syria is practically immune to innovation and short-term change because of an almost institutionalized convulsive reaction against it from the low-level bureaucrat to the head of a ministry. Change in Syria just does not happen quickly. It is incremental at best. This is the Syrian way, but in the sound-byte, four-year term American socio-political system, it did not happen fast enough.

But raised expectations were Bashar's main problem from the beginning. I half-jokingly mentioned to him the first time we met in May 2004 that he made a mistake in letting it be known to the media, which widely disseminated it, that he liked Phil Collins' music. This tended to feed into an emerging profile that he was a pro-West modernizing reformer not cut from the same mould as his taciturn father. Bashar was the ophthalmologist, not the heir to the throne as had been his more flamboyant and charismatic elder brother. He was the forward-looking head of the SCS, not the inert dictator.

Bashar is partially to blame for these raised expectations. But mostly, officials and commentators in the West failed to comprehend that he spent all of 18 months in London, and they weren't during the formative years of his life. He is the son of Hafiz al-Asad. He is a child of the Arab–Israeli conflict. He grew up amidst the Cold War. He lived through the tumult in Lebanon. These are the relationships and historical events that shaped his *weltanschauung*, not his sojourn in the United Kingdom. Israel is Syria's primary competitor. He is suspicious of the United States. Lebanon should be non-threatening at all costs and preferably within Syria's sphere of influence. And he is the keeper of the Alawite flame. Sony camcorders and listening to Phil Collins' music are his hobbies. Maintaining Syria's traditional interests is his obligation.

US–Syrian relations deteriorate

Syria is one of the few countries in the Arab world that can play both sides of the fence. Its Arab nationalist credentials are intact because it served as the cradle of modern Arab nationalism and because it has not signed a peace treaty with Israel. It still confronts Israel indirectly through its support of

Hizbullah and Palestinian groups such as Hamas and Islamic Jihad. Despite the Islamic extremism that threatens the Syrian regime, support for these groups is painted as resistance against Israel and placed within a clear Arab–Israeli paradigm. Syria has historically been at the vanguard of the so-called steadfastness front in the Arab world arrayed against Israel in the 1970s and 1980s. Thus it can legitimately adopt, at least rhetorically, a radical position vis-à-vis Israel when it is advantageous to do so. On the other hand, owing to its track record of serious involvement in the Madrid peace process and its participation in the US-led Gulf War coalition in 1991, Syria has been able to hop over to the other side of the fence when necessary and re-enter peace negotiations with Israel and/or adopt a more cooperative stance with the United States when the environment dictates it.

The tragic events of 11 September 2001 afforded the United States and Syria an opportunity to improve their relationship. Following 9/11, there seemed to be a brief period for a dramatic reversal in the Bush Administration's position in the Middle East. It understood that it needed as many allies as possible, especially in the Muslim world, to go after the Taliban and al Qaeda in Afghanistan and fight what was now a global war against terrorism. The Bush Administration appeared at first to distance itself from Israel and draw closer to the Arab states, including Syria. Bashar sent a letter of condolence to Bush after 9/11 expressing Syrian officials' sympathy for the United States by describing how their country had itself experienced death and destruction from Islamic extremism in the late 1970s and early 1980s. At a more practical level, Syria began to cooperate by sharing intelligence information with its US counterparts regarding al Qaeda, to the point where State Department officials were commenting that Syria had helped save American lives.[4]

But certain political appointees in the Pentagon were becoming more vociferous in their complaints about Syria, and pressure groups, including Christian Lebanese, Syrian exiles, American evangelicals and neocon-servative think-tanks in Washington heightened their anti-Syrian rhetoric while trying to convince the administration that Syria belonged with Iran, Iraq and North Korea in the 'axis of evil' that was announced in President Bush's State of the Union address in January 2002.[5]

Asad may have grown a little too complacent, imagining that the mantra that Syria had saved American lives would insulate the country from the Bush Administration's post-9/11 interventionist policy of pre-emptive military action encapsulated in the Bush Doctrine. Essentially, the Syrians did not adequately adjust to the important underlying changes in American foreign policy as a result of 9/11, which heightened Syria's exposure to US regime change rhetoric. Damascus thought the old rules of the game were still in place, and State Department and other administration officials led them to believe that such was the case. Therefore, the Syrians may have been guilty of selectively hearing what they wanted to hear. But at the same time, the new rules of the game were being written in Washington in the corridors of Congress, the Pentagon and influential conservative think-tanks by those who saw Bashar and his regime as part of the problem rather than the solution. The focus of foreign policy power in the Bush Administration had shifted to the Pentagon with the wars in Afghanistan and then Iraq, which led to a more bellicose posture towards Syria.

Thus Bashar's continued verbal assaults on Israel and support for groups such as Hizbullah and Hamas well into 2003 played right into the hands of the ascendant group of American foreign policy ideologues. Apparently, Bashar was relatively unaware that he and his regime were becoming more of a target. President Bush said in a speech on 4 April 2002 that 'Syria has spoken out against al-Qaida. We expect it to act against Hamas and Hizbullah as well', and on 24 June Bush added, 'Syria must choose the right side in the war on terror by closing terrorist camps and expelling terrorist organizations'.[6] Syria perhaps assumed that the clear differences between al Qaeda on the one hand and Hamas/Hizbullah on the other were self-evident, as they were understood by most in the region. But these distinctions were not recognized by the Bush Administration.

No longer could the differences between Washington and Damascus be resolved as part of a Syrian–Israeli peace process, which had been the putative arrangement under Hafiz al-Asad; Syria now had to meet all of Washington's concerns before negotiations could even begin with Israel. From the point of view of Bashar al-Asad this was a nonstarter, since it would entail relinquishing Syria's few remaining 'assets', such as its ties with Hizbullah, Hamas and Iran before the initiation of peace talks. Furthermore, the Bush Administration's increasing focus on Iraq rather than on the Arab–Israeli arena diminished Syria's utility in the eyes of many in the administration who had been deeply suspicious anyway of Syrian motives during the peace negotiations in the 1990s. Syria's participation in the 1991 Gulf War coalition and its involvement in the Madrid peace process tended to be glossed over or trivialized.

The deterioration in US–Syrian relations accelerated with the March 2003 US-led invasion of Iraq. A range of US accusations against Syria appeared soon after the invasion began, from harbouring Saddam regime members and hiding Iraq's WMD to supplying military equipment to Iraqi fighters. On 14 April 2003, White House spokesman Ari Fleischer stated bluntly that Syria is a 'rogue nation'.[7] President Bashar, in response to accusations such as this, stated:

> some see me as bad, some see me as good – we don't actually care what terms they use. It is not right to apply this term to Syria – I mean, look at the relationship that Syria has with the rest of the world; if you have good relations with the rest of the world, you are not a rogue state just because the United States says you are.[8]

The most pointed accusation of all, however, would only gain momentum as the Iraqi insurgency took shape: that the Syrian regime was actively assisting the insurgents with financial and logistical assistance. In short, US officials insisted that Syria's stance was now costing American lives. Syria had crossed the line. With the Bush Doctrine, Syria could no longer play on both sides of the fence – it had to choose one side. And as the Bush Administration shifted its emphasis towards promoting democracy in the region, Syria's authoritarian regime became a natural target. By early 2005, while the Bush Administration officially pushed for a change in behaviour on the part of Damascus, particularly in demanding that it do more to stop the flow of insurgents crossing into Iraq, it was widely believed that its unofficial policy towards Syria was one of regime change through regional and international pressure combined with support of anti-Asad Syrian exile groups and potential disaffected members of the regime itself.

Of course, as seen from Damascus, the invasion of Iraq implanted 150,000 US troops in a country on its eastern border, armed with the Bush Doctrine and fresh off a swift, and to the Syrians shockingly easy, military removal of the only other Ba'thist regime in the world. To the north was Turkey; and while Syria had markedly improved its relationship with Ankara (and Turkey's parliament refused to allow US troops access through its country on the way to Iraq), Turkey was still a member of NATO. To the south were Israel and Jordan, both US allies. Bashar looked out from his perch in Damascus and saw that his country was virtually surrounded by actual and potential hostile forces. The only friendly neighbour was Lebanon, and even there various domestic factions were agitating more assertively for a Syrian troop withdrawal and less Syrian interference in their country's affairs.

In the fresh glow of the Bush Administration's 'mission accomplished', several implicit threats were hurled at Damascus that Syrian officials took very seriously. As a result, the Syrian regime at the very least cast a blind eye towards Arab insurgents crossing over into Iraq. Damascus wanted the Bush Doctrine to fail, and it hoped that Iraq would be the first and last time it was applied. Anything it could do to ensure this outcome, short of incurring the direct military wrath of the United States, was considered fair game. It was a delicate – and dangerous – balancing act.

While certainly under pressure from the United States to do more on the border, Bashar also had to face a domestic constituency that identified strongly with the Iraqi insurgency. The Syrian regime was caught a bit off guard by the popular reaction in the country, particularly among Sunni Muslim *salafist* groups. Because Bashar had yet to solidify his hold on power, he could not afford to be seen doing Bush's bidding – nor did he want to. In fact, the more the United States pressured Syria, the more it compelled Asad to appeal to a combination of Arab, Syrian and Islamic nationalism to strengthen its base of support.

The Lebanon wedge and Asad's survival

The deterioration in US–Syrian relations went from serious to grave, however, on 14 February 2005, when Rafiq Hariri, the billionaire businessman and former Lebanese prime minister, was assassinated in a massive car bombing in Beirut. Syria was immediately held at least indirectly responsible for the killing, with many in the region and in the international community – certainly in Washington – suspecting that it was ordered by Damascus. The US ambassador to Syria was recalled the day after the assassination. The United States, Europe (particularly France, whose president at the time, Jacques Chirac, had close ties to Hariri), and most of the Arab world (especially Saudi Arabia, whose royal family also had close ties to Hariri) were united in calling on Syria to withdraw its 14,000 to 16,000 remaining troops from Lebanon.

This development was Bashar al-Asad's severest test to date, and it gave additional ammunition to those who wanted to contain Syria, if not to generate regime change. Although Bashar had reduced Syria's troop presence in Lebanon by over 50 per cent since he came to power, he had to succumb fully to regional and international pressure and implement a complete withdrawal in April 2005.

Syria cooperated to a minimal extent with the UN investigation. However, UN Security Council members such as Russia, China and Algeria were opposed to expanding the breadth of the investigation as well as the imposition of a tougher sanctions regime against Syria. By early 2006, the focus of the Bush Administration seemed to shift more towards concerns regarding Iran's alleged attempts to develop a nuclear weapons capability. From the perspective of Damascus, the threat environment had receded somewhat with the United States sinking deeper into a quagmire in Iraq. Even the UN investigation process slowed considerably, thus causing a little less angst in Damascus, which naturally viewed the whole affair as a political instrument used by the Bush Administration to pressure the Syrian regime.[9]

Bashar adeptly survived 2005. He was no longer the inexperienced, untested ruler. No one survives as president of Syria for any length of time without political cunning and resolve. He used the internal fall-out of 'losing' Lebanon to push aside internal foes, manifest in the forced resignation of Vice-President 'Abd al-Halim Khaddam at a Ba'th party congress meeting in June 2005. He also deflected the increased international pressure by drumming up a nationalistic response that strengthened domestic support for the regime and facilitated the portrayal of internal critics as being accomplices of the West. In addition, the external threat environment allowed the regime to heighten political repression in the country, particularly against civil society and democracy activists.[10] With chaos reigning in Iraq, it was not hard to remind the Syrian populace that US-inspired democracy promotion could likewise rip the fabric of its own society apart.

The summer 2006 Israeli–Hizbullah war also improved Bashar's regional position. Israel was unable to 'defeat' Hizbullah. As Robert Malley stated, 'A war waged to reassert Israel's power of deterrence and to spoil Hezbollah's image has significantly eroded the former while unintentionally improving the latter'.[11] A 'victory' for Hizbullah was a victory for Syria. As Syria is weak militarily and now isolated in the international community, Bashar had very few strategic assets left as of early 2006 other than non-state actors such as Hizbullah and Hamas, and Syrian foreign policy under the Asads is all about having leverage for quid pro quos, particularly regarding a return of the Golan Heights.

The Bush Administration had been basically saying to Bashar: there is nothing you can do to hurt us, and you have nothing to offer us. The actions by both Hamas and Hizbullah in summer 2006, however, showed that these quasi-state and sub-state actors can make a significant difference in the Middle East political and strategic landscape, thus providing Syria with more regional diplomatic leverage. Bashar rode Hizbullah leader Hassan Nasrallah's popularity to boost his own on the home front as well as his regime's popular legitimacy in the region. Maybe now Syria could regain a seat at the diplomatic table and use its new-found leverage to restart Syrian–Israeli negotiations and engage the United States in a dialogue on more equal terms.

Common ground?

There was no shortage of signals emanating from Damascus after the 2006 war that Syria was prepared to resume negotiations with Israel.[12] A debate ensued inside and outside of the Israeli government on whether to explore Syrian intentions. But Prime Minister Ehud Olmert remained steadfast in rejecting Bashar's peace overtures, in part because he did not want to negotiate from a position of perceived weakness following the debacle in Lebanon. It was also widely believed that the Bush Administration was pressuring Israel not to re-engage with Syria in order to maintain the US-led isolation of Damascus.

Then came the Democratic victory in both houses of Congress in the November 2006 mid-term elections, widely seen as a repudiation of Bush's foreign policy, followed by the publication in early December of the bipartisan Iraq Study Group report. The commission was chartered to produce recommendations regarding Iraq, but commissioners soon saw that Iraq's problems were so tightly interwoven with its neighbours that they concluded that the question of improving the US position in the Middle East overall would have to be addressed. Accordingly, they advocated a broader regional diplomatic offensive, including a call for the United States to re-engage Syria.

Syrian officials, however, were both crestfallen and angry over the lack of a positive response from the Bush Administration to their overtures in late 2006. They met with Iraq Study Group representatives, and several US senators visited Damascus and met with Bashar in December 2006. Syrian officials truly believed a corner had been turned with the United States. Disappointed, Bashar concluded that he must wait until another administration came to power in Washington, which, regardless of political party, could only be better than Bush.

In lieu of a US role, regional players began to enter Middle East negotiations as arbiters and brokers, from Qatar to Turkey; indeed, many were surprised by the announcement in May 2008 that Turkey had been brokering indirect Syrian–Israeli peace negotiations. This not only revealed the diplomatic vacuum in the region that the United States should have filled, but it also indicated, contrary to Bush Administration lamentations that Damascus only wanted the benefits of involving itself in a peace process without ever making the commensurate sacrifices, that, indeed, Syria was serious about peace with Israel. Unfortunately, the Israeli offensive in Gaza in December 2008 and January 2009 forced all sides to cancel the negotiations.

Syria showed it could play a positive role when necessary. Syria apparently gave the green light to Hamas leader Khalid Meshaal's participation in the Saudi-brokered meetings in Mecca in February 2007 between Hamas officials and Palestinian Authority President Mahmoud Abbas, which resulted in a Palestinian Authority power-sharing agreement (that completely broke down shortly thereafter). Nonetheless, this, along with Syria's role in the 2008 Doha agreement over Lebanon, showed the contributions Syria could make to peace and stability in the region. This is exactly how Bashar tried to position Syria. He preferred not to sever relations with Iran, Hizbullah and Hamas; instead, he preferred to use Syria's unique capacity to play both sides of the fence in order to facilitate Iranian, Hizbullah and Hamas engagement with the West. Bashar was confident that he had placed the country on the right side of the strategic equation in the inter-Arab arena, especially following Israel's heavy-handed military action against Hamas in Gaza. He consistently refused to give into what in the region has been called the 'American project'. It is almost as if the Arab world moved closer to his consistently held position rather than the other way around.

The walls of isolation of Syria were fast crumbling in 2008. In April, the new speaker of the House of Representatives, Nancy Pelosi, led a bipartisan delegation of congresspersons, including the chairman of the House International Relations Committee Tom Lantos, and the chairman of the

Committee on Oversight and Government Reform Henry Waxman – both of whom are close to Israel – for a high-profile visit to Syria and meeting with Bashar al-Asad. This was certainly a far cry from the antagonistic attitude Congress had towards Syria in the period surrounding the passage of the SAA. High-level diplomats from a host of European countries found their way to Damascus. Even the Israelis deemed Bashar's peace overtures worth exploring, as he continued to maintain the strategic choice for peace with Israel.[13] This despite a September 2007 Israeli attack on a suspected Syrian nuclear facility, launching an IAEA investigation into the matter, as well as a US cross-border raid into Syria from Iraq in October 2008 to kill an alleged key figure in the Iraqi insurgency.[14] These incidents did not alter Bashar's overall course. He responded in a relatively limited fashion, understanding that he could not do much more, but also realizing that he did not want to sour the relationship with the United States at a time when an anticipated Obama presidential victory might usher in a whole new diplomatic environment.

The legacy of the Bush Administration resulted in tremendous distrust on both sides of the equation, as well as a web of UN resolutions, a UN tribunal, an IAEA investigation and the SAA. All of these things have found their way into the US–Syrian dynamic, and they could not be easily disentangled, especially as the Obama Administration was compelled to deal with other important domestic and foreign policy matters soon after it came to office in 2009. What should have been a sagacious foreign policy of dialogue and cooperation with Syria on Islamic terrorism, peace with Israel and political space in Lebanon fell victim to a neoconservative ideological strait-jacket that continued to dominate the American approach to the Middle East.

Obama and Asad

Barack Obama's victory in the 2008 presidential election seemed to create another opportunity to improve the US–Syrian relationship; indeed, in 2009 and 2010 high-level US and Syrian officials met on a regular basis. In June 2009, the Obama Administration announced that it would return the US ambassador to Damascus, and in early 2010 an ambassador-designate was chosen and a recess appointment was made later in the year, a situation indicative of lingering US–Syrian tensions as well as the partisan nature of US domestic politics. However, Obama was not able to wave a magic wand and immediately build a productive relationship with Syria. He still had to contend with the anti-Syrian ideology and institutional inertia prevailing in Washington DC. The bureaucratic and cultural momentum arrayed against normal relations with Syria was too difficult to overcome in the short term, and it hampered the attempts of Obama to establish a dialogue with the Syrian regime. Due to the lack of movement on the Palestinian issue, the appearance of a right-wing government in Israel shortly after Obama came to power, and the domestic economic priorities of the Obama Administration, progress on Syria was halting at best.

Then came the Arab Spring in late 2010 and early 2011, first in Tunisia and Egypt, soon thereafter in Bahrain, Yemen and Libya. Many thought Syria would be the exception to the wave of opposition movements, but this would not be the case, as it, too, became engulfed in serious uprisings by March 2011.[15]

The perfect storm in the Arab world of higher commodity prices that made basic items more expensive, a youth bulge that created a gap between mobilization (education and expectations) and assimilation (adequate jobs and a living), and even Wikileaks, which revealed the profligate lifestyles of the ruling elite, bared for all to see the widespread socio-economic problems, corruption and political repression. In this Syria was no different. After the popular uprisings in Tunisia and Egypt led to the removal of the *ancien régime* in each country, the barrier of fear of the repressive apparatus of the state had been broken across the Arab world.

But Asad thought Syria was, indeed, different. In January and February amid the uprisings in Tunisia, Egypt, Libya, Bahrain and Yemen, Asad portrayed his country as almost immune from such domestic unrest.[16] The mouthpieces of the Syrian regime consistently echoed this view, even to the point of expressing support for the protesters in other Arab states.[17] It was pointed out that the septuagenarian and octogenarian leaders of these countries were out of touch with their populations. They were also corrupt lackeys of the US and Israel. The implication, of course, was that Asad, a relatively young 45-year-old, was in touch with the Arab youth. He had also consistently confronted the US and Israel in the region and supported the resistance forces of Hamas and Hizbullah, thus brandishing credentials that played well in the Arab street. Bashar al-Asad himself was generally well liked in the country – or at least not reviled. All this may have bought him some time, but it was a misreading of the situation – or a denial of it. Syria was suffering from the same socio-economic underlying factors that existed in other non-oil-producing Arab countries that created the well of disenfranchisement and disempowerment, especially among an energized and increasingly frustrated youth.

Syrian paranoia

Syria is a crossroads of history. However, this often means that a country has been conquered by more powerful enemies throughout its history, contributing to an almost pathological paranoia that frames the nature of threat. As a result, convulsive chauvinism often trumps opportunity.

This was put on full display in Asad's first public speech before the Syrian Parliament on 30 March 2011 in reaction to the growing anti-regime protests.[18] Rather than focus on the socio-economic problems behind the unrest and offer ways to address them, he blamed terrorists, conspirators and external enemies for instigating the protests. Most outside of Syria were left scratching their heads after the speech, but anyone who has spent time in the country would understand that for the most part Asad was preaching to the converted. It is a national psyche that generally believes in conspiracy. The problem is that there has been just enough real conspiracy perpetrated by outside powers in Syria over the years to lend credence to such notions.

One of the results is that the *mukhabarat,* the security forces in Syria, have been given a tremendous amount of leeway to ensure domestic stability and protect the regime. In what is almost always a threatening environment in the heart of the Middle East, this is not unexpected. But the *mukhabarat's* accumulation of power over the years, overseen if not sanctioned by the government, led to systemic recklessness that obviously backfired against the regime.[19] After all, it was their collective hubris in arresting and roughly handling schoolchildren who had written anti-regime graffiti in the Syrian southern town of Deraa early in February 2011 that launched the uprising.

By incrementally ratcheting up the pressure in April and May short of calling for regime change, the Obama Administration tried to give Bashar every opportunity to end the violence and implement real political reform. Obama's leaving a crack in the window open for Bashar reflected Washington's continuing concern regarding a breakdown of order in Syria, hoping against hope that Asad would finally understand the gravity of his situation, end the violence, and engage in dialogue with opposition elements towards real reform. As distasteful as Asad has been to some countries, many believed that it was better for him to stay in power and maintain stability in a very strategic part of the Middle East rather than press for the precipitous fall of central authority that might lead to political instability. Since Syria is ethnically and religiously diverse, it could implode into sectarian civil war if the Asad regime was removed, as happened in Iraq when Saddam Hussein fell from power in 2003. The prospect of this has the potential of destabilizing not just Syria but the entire region. With considerable doubt as to who or what would replace Bashar al-Asad, as well as the potential negative regional security repercussions, many shared the viewpoint of 'better the devil you know'. But the continuing violent crackdown by the Syrian regime (killing over 2,600 protesters by September 2011 according to UN and human rights organizations) made it harder for the international community to cast a blind eye, and eventually the Obama

Administration declared Bashar illegitimate and called for him to step down.

A conceptual gap

Early on in Bashar's presidency he decreed the elimination of military uniforms in primary and secondary schools. At the time, US media and analysts dismissed, even ridiculed, the change as virtually worthless and emblematic of how little Bashar was actually reforming his country. However, when examined more closely, there was more to the decree than meets the eye. Where Bashar could, in a system almost immune to change and at a time when his authority was less than what it would soon become, he tried to redirect Syria's operational philosophy away from the symbols and trappings of martial indoctrination to a more normal educational environment that focused on developing skill sets. The conceptual gap on the utility and effectiveness of this decree between the US and Syria was indeed wide. This was also the case with the creation of private banks in Syria. While the US saw it as dilatory and of little significance, Bashar believed it was a transformational moment and harbinger of things to come in terms of economic liberalization.

On one of my visits with Bashar al-Asad, this one soon after the withdrawal of Syrian troops from Lebanon in April 2005, he expressed anger that the United States did not appreciate the 'enormous' concession he made by agreeing to withdraw. The implication, of course, was that he could have made a lot more trouble had he wanted to or even have kept the Syrian forces ensconced in Lebanon. He felt he received no credit for his supposed magnanimity.

These are but a few examples of the conceptual gap between Syria and the United States. Most of those outside of Syria scoffed at Bashar's 30 March 2011 speech, dismissing such blatant misdirection from the real socio-economic and political problems that brought the Arab Spring to Syria. But many Syrians, maybe even Asad himself, readily believe such exhortations. Their perception of the nature of threat is vastly different from what we see outside of Syria. Blame it on Syrian paranoia bred by 'imperialist conspiracies' of the past, Arab–Israeli conflict and/or regime brainwashing to consecrate the necessity for the security state, but it is in large measure a function of living in a dangerous neighbourhood where real threats are indeed often just around the corner.

It is this conceptual and perceptual gap that is often at the root of the impasse between what the United States and much of the international community demand of the Syrian regime and what Bashar is actually doing (or feels he should do). I am sure that if I met with Bashar at the time of writing (autumn 2011) he would point out to me that he has made extensive concessions and enacted dramatic reforms in response to the protests. He would again complain that he is not receiving any recognition or credit for this, and as such, he would conclude, as he has done in the past, that the United States has it in for him, that no matter what he does it will not be enough.

Bashar al-Asad is the product of an authoritarian system, one that is a paradigm of stagnation and control. The Syrian system is not geared to respond to people's demands – it controls people's demands. It is not geared up to implement dramatic reform. It is constructed to maintain the status quo and survive. At any other time the reforms announced by Bashar in 2011 – lifting the emergency law, providing for Kurdish citizenship, creating political parties, etc. – would indeed be significant. During the protests, however, they were seen as self-serving, after-the-fact and insufficient. In any event, to reform more deeply and rapidly is anathema to the Syrian system under the Asads simply because it would spell the end of the regime itself. They are counterintuitive to the basic instincts of an authoritarian, neopatriarchal system.

What this means is that the ability of the Syrian regime to meet the demands of the protesters and the international community in the requisite time frame is slim or none. If the protests miraculously stopped, maybe the reforms would have developed into something meaningful. Then again, without internal and external pressure, the regime might dilute the reforms to insignificance or revoke them altogether. After all, Asad has not inspired confidence in terms of his ability – or even his willingness – to actually implement political reforms beyond their mere announcement. Some of this is him, some the inert Syrian system.

Thus, there was not much that the Obama Administration could do. The United States tried to squeeze blood from a turnip by pushing for dramatic political reform from a system that simply isn't built for it mechanically or intellectually. The United States had to be careful about intervening more energetically to help the Syrian opposition for fear of discrediting them by attaching a made-in-USA label to it in addition to providing the regime the narrative of threat it has been propagandizing to legitimate the use of force. In the end, then, it must be a Syrian solution to a Syrian problem. The United States has very little direct leverage on Syria in the short term.

Conclusion

Those making policy decisions in Washington, at the UN or in European capitals regarding Syria are from a decidedly different world and conceptual paradigm than the leadership in Damascus. The *weltanschauung* prisms are anchored in vastly different experiences, preconceptions, local politics and ideologies, and they have a very hard time seeing – and understanding – each other.

Bashar's initial strategic vision for an internationally respected and integrated Syria has been consumed by a Syrian paradigm of political survival. He was either unwilling or powerless to stop what in Syria is a reflexive response to perceived threat. He retrenched into a typically Syrian authoritarian mode of survival, an Alawite fortress to protect the sect's stranglehold on power. In the end, when the pressure was greatest, Asad was not the enlightened, Western-educated ophthalmologist. He returned to his roots as a child of the Arab–Israeli conflict, the superpower Cold War and Hafiz al-Asad, which appears to have shaped the nature of his response more so than anything else.

He desperately needed to break out of the stifling, anachronistic box of Syrian politics as usual and embrace a transformational role in his country. No one denies the difficulty of doing so, especially with powerful pockets of resistance to any significant change to the status quo arrayed against him. But he was not up to the task. Unfortunately, unless there is a dramatic turnaround, this means that he and his regime will either be overthrown at some point amid more bloodshed or he will be president of a country that has become the North Korea of the Middle East.

From the perspective of the United States, perhaps both the Bush and Obama administrations put too many eggs in the Bashar basket, one in a more negative and the other in a more positive direction, when it was the Syrian system that should have been more accurately assessed in terms of what it could or could not do depending upon the circumstances at a given time. As early as the 1950s US administrations placed increasing emphasis on individual leaders, especially in countries deemed strategically crucial as the Cold War heated up. Dictators in strategically located countries were candidates for overthrow or viewed as transitional authoritarian leaders who would eventually lead their respective countries towards democracy. In the latter, authoritarianism was a necessary temporary condition to fight the Cold War because evolutionary transitions to democracy took too long and were too messy, thus opening up windows of opportunity for the Soviets. It turned out that the transitional authoritarian leaders did not want to transition, and they constructed apparatuses that would keep them in power. Bashar al-Asad did not change the system as many had hoped; instead the system changed him, which is all too often the case with even the most well-intentioned authoritarian leaders. As such, the United States did not accurately perceive the limitations of and opportunities presented by Bashar based on Syria's dependency on regional and international actors to acquire strategic relevance. Indeed, most of the time Washington and Damascus were on completely different wavelengths, leading to mistrust, suspicion, and ultimately to antagonism.

Notes

1 For text of speech see www.al-bab.com/arab/countries/syria/bashar00a.htm.

2 For text of Syrian Accountability Act see www.treasury.gov/resourcecenter/ sanctions/Documents/13338.pdf.

3 For these quotes, see David W. Lesch, *The New Lion of Damascus: Bashar al-Asad and Modern Syria* (New Haven, CT: Yale University Press, 2005), pp. 99–100.

4 On Syrian–US intelligence cooperation, see James Risen and Tim Weiner, 'CIA is Said to Have Sought Help from Syria', *New York Times*, (30 October 2001). I was informed by a high-level US source that this article was extremely accurate.

5 For more on this, see Lesch (2005), pp. 103–110.

6 Speeches by President George W. Bush, 4 April 2002, see www.whitehouse. gov/ news/releases/2002/04/20020404-3.html, and (24 June 2002), www. whitehouse.gov/news/ releases/2002/06/20020624-3.html.

7 Cited in David Stout, 'U.S. Sharply Scolds Syria and Threatens Sanctions', *New York Times*, (15 April 2003). In June 2003, Under-Secretary of State John Bolton placed Syria on a 'second tier axis of evil' along with Cuba and Libya (Iran, Iraq and North Korea were on the first tier). Syria was termed by administration officials as a member of the 'junior varsity of evil', the 'ladies auxiliary of the axis of evil', and an 'axis of evil aspirant'. Quoted in Ross Leonard Fisher, 'There's Something About Syria: US Foreign Policy Toward Syria During the Clinton and George W. Bush Administrations, 1994–2004', Ph:D diss., (Dunedin, New Zealand, University of Otago 2004), pp. 122–3.

8 Interview with the author, Damascus, Syria, 27 May 2004. Then-foreign minister of Syria Farouk al-Shar'a had a more biting response: 'You happened to have different teachers in school. One you respect and one you do not respect just because the style or conduct of that person is not attractive to you. But the one that you respect, if he just winks at you angrily, you spend the whole day upset because you respect him; but if you do not respect him, even if he says "go to hell," you do not accept it. You say to a friend that this man I do not respect, so whatever he says to me I am not going to respect. It would have been very harsh if it [calling Syria a rogue state] was directed at us by a respectable nation. How dare they put us in accountability, especially now with what is going on in Iraq?' (Interview with the author, Damascus, Syria, 3 June 2004).

9 By 2010 the focus of the investigation had shifted towards Hizbullah, with members of Hizbullah actually indicted in June 2011.

10 For a delineation of actions against civil society and democracy activists in Syria during this time, see David W. Lesch, 'Syria', in *Countries at the Crossroads* (New York: Freedom House, 2007).

11 Robert Malley, 'A New Middle East', *New York Review of Books*, Vol. 53, No. 14, (21 September 2006), pp. 10–15.

12   For instance, Syrian Deputy Foreign Minister Faysal Maqdad stated on 27 August on a visit to Oman that 'when Israel, supported by the US, is ready to resume the peace process on the basis of international resolutions, Syria will be constantly ready to achieve results that restore the Arabs' legitimate rights, notably a just peace. ... We will continue our efforts to bring about a just peace.' Quoted in *Times of Oman*, (27 August 2006). Can be accessed at www.timesofoman.com/ print/asp?newsid=34652.

13   See an especially positive-toned interview Bashar gave to the British paper the *Guardian* on 17 February 2009. This may be found in Ian Black, 'Assad Urges US to Rebuild Diplomatic Road to Damascus'.

14   Eric Schmitt and Thom Shanker, 'Officials Say U.S. Killed an Iraqi in Raid in Syria', *New York Times*, (27 October 2008).

15   Having met with President Asad a number of times from 2004 through 2009, I can almost guarantee that he was absolutely shocked when the uprisings in the Arab world started to seep into his own country. I believe he truly thought he was safe and secure and popular in the country and beyond condemnation, but not in the Middle East of 2011.

16   See in particular an interview Asad gave to the *Wall Street Journal*. Jay Solomon and Bill Spindle, 'Syrian Strongman: Time for Reform', (31 January 2011).

17   For instance, see an essay written by Bouthaina Sha`ban, the Media and Political Adviser to the Office of the President and one of Asad's closet advisers: 'The Real Evils Plaguing the Region', *Forward Magazine* (Damascus), No. 48, (February 2011), p. 16. In the same issue, see also an essay by Sami Moubayed, a leading commentator and analyst in Syria who often reflects regime exhortations, entitled 'Lesson from Egypt: West is not Best', p. 4.

18   For text of Asad speech, see syriacomment.com blog at http://www.joshualandis.com/blog/?p=8917&print=true.

19   I have seen this phenomenon up close and personal a number of times in Syria – and several times with President Asad himself. On one occasion in late 2007, when I was travelling to Syria for a scheduled meeting with President Asad, I was detained at the airport, my passport confiscated, and I was interrogated in a threatening manner for three hours. I was released only after I convinced the Syrian security officer to call the president's office to confirm the meeting. The right hand did not know what the left hand was doing; nor did they seem to care about being on the same page, a disconnect that is at one and the same time both an abdication of authority and dangerous. When I met with Bashar, I expressed my anger at being detained. I told him that upon my return to the United States a few days later I was scheduled to give testimony promoting a US–Syrian dialogue in front of the Senate Foreign Relations Committee. I asked him what would have happened had I not convinced the officer to make the call. What if I had been incarcerated or even tortured? It could have instantly turned a friend of Syria into an enemy. I strongly suggested to him that he needed to rein in the security forces because the freedom he allowed them could come back to haunt him.

CHAPTER ELEVEN

Mubarak: The embodiment of 'moderate Arab leadership'?

Rosemary Hollis

Introduction

Throughout his nearly 30 years in power, President Hosni Mubarak of Egypt was depicted as a 'cautious' man, a 'moderate' Arab leader and a dependable ally by American and British diplomats, politicians and commentators. What singled him out for such endorsements and to what extent he earned them, either by default or design, is discussed below. Be that as it may, however, Mubarak did not enjoy consistently high approval ratings in Washington. As of the late 1990s he was increasingly subject to criticism, particularly among US policy analysts and Congressmen, for the way he exercised his power, both at home and in regional affairs. Yet it was only when the Egyptian people rose up and demanded he step down that the United States (and Britain) finally abandoned him.

In keeping with the central theme of this volume, the main purpose here is to ascertain how US-UK perceptions of Mubarak changed from positive to lukewarm to negative. On the face of it, it would be quite easy to argue that what changed was the circumstances, such that, whereas initially Mubarak was judged simply on the basis of his capacity to survive in the immediate aftermath of the assassination of President Anwar el Sadat, subsequently he was found to be incapable of managing a transition to democracy in Egypt, held on to power for too long and turned a blind eye to corruption in high places. Alternatively, the case can be made that Mubarak did not change but US and British expectations of him did, from feasible to impractical, in terms of what any Egyptian president could hope to deliver. Neither theory presumably holds to the exclusion of the other, of course, and other factors warrant consideration.

The task here therefore is to present and weigh the evidence and thence identify the factors which emerge as the most decisive. To do so, various sources have been consulted, including the commentaries of journalists based in Cairo, diplomatic cables, policy analysis and academic works. The following account also offers insights gleaned from interviews with a number of former US and UK officials whose responsibility it was to lead on US or UK bilateral relations with Egypt, among them ambassadors who had direct access to Mubarak.[1]

In structuring this chapter a deliberate attempt has been made to try to avoid reaching conclusions too early or arranging the material to fit with any one explanation for changes in perceptions of Mubarak. Thus, a summary of what some of the interviewees believe the explanation to be is left to the end and the bulk of the chapter is devoted to a step-by-step account of how Mubarak the man was described and understood in Washington and London during the three decades of his presidency. This account also covers US and UK references to the government presided over by Mubarak and their assessments of elite and public opinion in Egypt. As confirmed by Dan Kurtzer, US Ambassador to Egypt from November 1997 to June 2001, it is fair to assume that when policy analysts in Washington referred to the Egyptian leadership as a collective, they meant Mubarak and his immediate circle, including the top military and security officials.

Having traced the evolution of US-UK depictions of Mubarak, the analysis then shifts to a review of successive strategic plans or doctrines for the Middle East writ large between 1980 and 2010 – to give a sense of the broader canvas or context within which both Washington and London viewed the place of Egypt and the role of Mubarak. By reading across from what the United States and Britain wanted of the Egyptian leadership, their 'strategic scripts' if you will, to what they saw in Mubarak personally, it is possible to reach some tentative conclusions on the process by which Mubarak transited from favoured ally to dispensable liability.

Two points do warrant mention from the outset. One is that, in comparison to the Americans, on the whole the British appear to have been more sanguine about Mubarak's qualities and leadership style, i.e. they basically took him as they found him. The probable explanations for this difference are posited later, but as will become clear, this variance in views has proved instructive to this inquiry. The second point is that among both the Americans and the British, differences are apparent between professional diplomats and intelligence operatives on the one hand and politicians and political analysts on the other. While the former are, no doubt necessarily, 'on message' in terms of the national narrative as set by their political masters, they show pragmatism in their acceptance of, and adaptation to, what they find 'on the ground'. By contrast, politicians, and in particular the more ideological among them, such as the neoconservatives, are more wedded to a particular view of the world rather than reflective about the situation and personalities as they find them.

Early assessments of Mubarak

US and UK portrayals of Hosni Mubarak when he was still vice-president of Egypt (1975–81) compared him favourably with the flamboyant President Anwar el Sadat, essentially on the grounds that he was 'modest', dull even, by comparison. In a short profile of Mubarak published in 1980, the *Financial Times* noted that he had been the butt of popular jokes when he was first selected as vice-president,[2] but had increasingly won respect.[3] He had distinguished himself as an air-force pilot and officer, particularly in the 1973 Arab–Israeli War, and was credited with having worked his way up to high office from humble beginnings by hard work, a 'penchant for discipline' and without resort to corruption or self-aggrandisement. Furthermore, he was described by those who knew him as 'a serious man, cautiously ambitious and with a hard cutting edge when the occasion requires', though some apparently suggested he was 'too dour, too much the "good soldier" and too little the charismatic actor-manqué that to some extent has characterised both Nasser and Sadat' to be suitable for the presidency.[4]

As described by Thomas Lippman, who was *Washington Post* bureau chief in Cairo from 1975 to 1979:

> As Vice President, Mubarak was widely understood to be strong where Sadat was weak. He is unpretentious, he works hard, he is apparently incorruptible, he keeps his family out of public view and he has a very thick skin.

Also according to Lippman:

> If there were doubts about Mubarak's qualifications for the presidency, they centred on his intellectual capacity, not his integrity or dedication. Students called him 'La Vache Qui Rit' the laughing cow, because of his supposed resemblance to the trade mark animal on French cheese.[5]

A former British official who was serving in Jordan in the 1970s said that he heard a senior Jordanian politician joke that the Egyptians had chosen 'a donkey' as vice-president. Yet this and other former officials interviewed did point out that if they had to choose they would prefer a practical man to an intellectual one.[6] As for his image as 'Mr Clean', apparently there were rumours from the start that his wife's cousin might not be so scrupulous.

Whatever the theories about Mubarak's stolid soldierly qualities and lack of intellect, observers noted that he had been masterful in manoeuvring himself into the vice presidency and making Sadat believe he was both dependable – a 'fall-guy' even – and that he posed no threat to his boss. As vice-president he was not only deputy to Sadat, but also Secretary-General of the National Democratic Party, with effective control of Egypt's military procurement programme. He also coordinated the intelligence services, ran the presidential office and was party to most of Sadat's discussions with US officials and other foreign visitors on Middle East issues. In addition, he made official visits to the United States and Britain, among other countries, and represented Egypt in discussions with the US about military aid and joint military ventures for the production of arms.

In effect, Mubarak was not an unknown quantity to either the US or Britain in the period immediately preceding his assumption of the presidency. Yet the American press were reporting in March 1980 that Washington was becoming increasingly invested in the survival of the regime of Anwar el Sadat, as protector of US interests in the region.[7] This was only a year after the Iranian revolution had toppled the Shah of Iran, Washington's proxy policeman in the Persian Gulf region, and the media (as too the State Department) were particularly conscious of the dangers of relying too heavily on the fate of one key ally.[8] When Sadat was assassinated on 6 October 1981 there was thus no shortage of speculation that Washington might have repeated the same mistake with Egypt that it had made with Iran. Eight months on, however, the *Financial Times* considered it not entirely fair to judge Mubarak harshly for the 'cautious and conservative' approach he had adopted upon assuming the presidency, since:

> He kept cool and kept the country together during the extremely tense period after the assassination ... when Moslem extremists, in spite of the round-up of more than 1,000 of them last September, were still on the loose and notably, caused an uprising in the city of Asyut in Upper Egypt in which 87 people died.[9]

For much of the 1980s, US and British press coverage of Egypt frequently made reference to Mubarak's maintenance of the peace treaty with Israel brokered by his predecessor while also noting his cautious resistance to building closer ties with the Jewish state. The press implied that such caution made sense in the context of general Arab hostility to Israel (and Sadat's decision to end the state of war with Israel). US Congressmen apparently tried to urge Mubarak to develop a warmer relationship with Israel, but the sense prevailed that the Egyptian president was right to move slowly while still consolidating his power and managing security threats at home.[10]

Economic issues

Where there was criticism of Mubarak in the 1980s it was for his economic policies, or lack of them. Throughout the 1980s, reportage on Egypt repeatedly drew attention to the high unemployment levels, the overweening size of the public sector, the growing gap between the rich few and the poor masses, corruption and the urgent need for bold structural changes. Yet blame for inertia at the top was frequently directed more at the senior figures in the cabinet and around the president than at Mubarak himself and he was urged to make better appointments.[11]

What is striking in reviewing descriptions of Egypt in the 1980s is the prevalence of the very same problems that were still being identified not only in the 1990s but right up until the revolution of 2011, including in US diplomatic cables.[12] However, in Kurtzer's view, the condition of the Egyptian economy improved exponentially during Mubarak's three decades. When Kurtzer was posted in Cairo as a political officer in 1979: 'Egypt was broke and its infrastructure was in a parlous state. You couldn't make a telephone call; there was sewerage in the streets; and electricity was in short supply.'[13] With US assistance, in the 1980s the Egyptian infrastructure was rebuilt and by the late 1990s Egypt was exporting electricity, had a new sewerage system and could boast an advanced telecoms industry – but, according to Kurtzer, such gains did not feature in the perceptions of the populace.

Some American and British diplomats also considered that Egypt entered a new and promising phase from 2004, when Mubarak appointed ministers capable of leading an economic and fiscal reform programme that produced unprecedented growth. According to several sources, however, those same ministers presided over changes which the Egyptian populace perceived as benefiting the corrupt few rather than the whole population.[14] In addition, whereas the State Department tended to the view that over time the progress made in reforming the Egyptian economy was broadly positive, British commentators were not convinced that increased prosperity for the few would eventually 'trickle down' to the poor masses.

Military relations

By making peace with Israel, Egypt secured the return of the Sinai Peninsula occupied by Israel in the 1967 war and only partially retrieved by Egypt in the 1973 war. As president after Sadat's assassination, it was Mubarak who managed the arrangements for the transfer of territory and thereafter adhered to the agreed terms for limited Egyptian force levels near the border with Israel. From shortly after the treaty was signed, the United States made

Egypt the second largest recipient (after Israel) of US overseas aid, largely in the form of military assistance.[15] Thus began a US programme to re-equip the Egyptian armed forces (previously supplied by the Soviet Union), which included the transfer of relatively sophisticated armaments, joint production agreements and military training.

By the mid-1980s the US was providing military grants averaging $1.2 billion a year and a further $1.7 billion per year in support for military training. From 1983, the US and Egyptian armed forces began a regular programme of joint military exercises entitled BRIGHT STAR. As noted by a former British official, military cooperation featured only minimally in UK–Egyptian relations, not least because the British could not afford to supply the Egyptian forces without charging for the equipment transferred.

In the opinion of Chas Freeman, former US Ambassador to Saudi Arabia and Assistant Secretary of Defence for International Security Affairs, 'the motivations for this [US] assistance effort were political rather than military' and Israel and 'its American partisans', rather than the defence establishment, were its chief advocates in Washington.[16] The centrality of military cooperation and aid in the bilateral relationship is nonetheless an important factor for understanding the value placed on Mubarak's leadership by the Americans, including the US military establishment. A military man with near dictatorial powers and himself eager to extract maximum benefit from military cooperation and support was clearly ideal for the development of this aspect of the relationship. As Phebe Marr reflected in the early 1990s, good relations with Egypt (among other strategically placed regional powers, including Israel, Turkey and the Arab Gulf states) were beneficial to the United States in part because 'they are governed by a pragmatic leadership that helps set the tone of discourse and cooperation with the West in the region'.[17]

Mubarak became identified with a broader 'moderate' Arab camp in the region as of the mid-1980s, linking Egypt not only with Jordan (whose King Hussein was the first Arab leader to break the isolation of Egypt – in place since the signing of the Egypt–Israel Treaty) but also the rulers of Saudi Arabia.[18] The high point in Mubarak's reputation in Washington came in 1990–1 in the context of the Iraqi occupation of Kuwait and the US-led campaign that drove Iraq out. Mubarak opted not only to support the US-led coalition but was instrumental in garnering support from other Arab states, committed over 30,000 Egyptian troops to the campaign and facilitated the US operations out of Egypt.[19] According to hearsay at the time, especially around the Arab world, George H.W. Bush personally had to pressure Mubarak to cooperate, but General Norman Schwarzkopf, Commander of US Central Command (CENTCOM) at the time, as well as the Saudi commander General Khaled Bin Sultan, claimed that the Egyptian president took little persuading.[20]

In any case, US recognition of Egypt's contribution to the war effort was manifested in Washington's cancellation of Egypt's $6.7 billion military debt. Beginning in 1992, Egypt started assembling M1A1 tank components imported from the United States and manufactured about 40 per cent of the components of 555 tanks subsequently produced.[21] The BRIGHT STAR exercises continued and by the late 1990s were expanded to include troops from some of the Gulf Cooperation Council (GCC) states. US military assistance to Egypt continued at an average of just over $2 billion a year for the remainder of the decade, even though, with the end of the Cold War, US military aid to all countries other than Egypt and Israel was phased out.[22]

The Security Agenda

Following the 1990–1 Gulf War, Egypt was accorded a central role in the new US-led quest for a comprehensive settlement of the Arab–Israeli conflict, launched in Madrid in November 1991, and became a leading voice in the multilateral talks on arms control and disarmament. In this context, however, the Egyptians clashed with Israel over the nuclear issue and whether or not to include the Gulf in calculations about the regional military balance. In addition, all was not well on the Egyptian home front and the Mubarak regime was challenged by a series of violent attacks perpetrated by Islamist militants. Mubarak's response was to deploy the state's emergency powers to round up and incarcerate would-be and potential opponents. Neither the Americans nor the British offered much complaint about the methods used, though the reflections of former diplomats suggests they drew certain conclusions on the nature of power and risks of political reform in Egypt.

The perpetrators of the violent attacks on representatives of authority, Copts and tourists in Egypt in the 1990s included breakaway elements of the Muslim Brotherhood who had become radicalized in Afghanistan or jail, or both. The violent campaign of Gamaa Islamiya and others killed over 1,000 people before the group's leaders called off the armed struggle (following the slaughter of 58 tourists in Luxor in 1997).[23] The attacks of Islamist extremists were not limited to Egypt and the Arab world of course – witness the bombings of the World Trade Center in 1993, the Paris underground and the US embassies in Kenya and Tanzania. At the same time the practice of intelligence sharing between US, British and other Western agencies and their Arab counterparts was an established practice. In the circumstances, Mubarak and the Egyptian security forces were allies in counter-terrorism long before 9/11 triggered the US declaration of a 'war on terror'.

According to one British source familiar with intelligence (and confirmed by Kurtzer), the Egyptian strategy under Mubarak's leadership included rounding up and jailing or killing the main suspects; using the Islamic establishment to portray the *jihadists* as deviants; and investing heavily in trying to persuade militants to reform – a tactic also adopted in Saudi Arabia. In any case, when either the British or the Americans attempted to advise the Egyptians on what to do they were told to mind their own business and deal with their own terrorist threats. A US source intimated that among the senior US figures in the first and second Bush administrations, both Dick Cheney and Donald Rumsfeld were of the opinion that, in terms of counter-terrorism, Mubarak was 'our man' and would torture whomever the US 'rendered' to him. They reportedly thought more highly of the Egyptian techniques than those of the Saudis who allegedly thought they could 'make friends of the extremists'.[24]

Signs of fracture

In contrast to his amenability in the 1990–1 US-led war with Iraq, when Washington proposed invading Iraq in 2003 Mubarak was not enthusiastic. Apparently his main concern was the US approach – inclusive of disbanding the Iraqi armed forces and Ba'ath Party – and thought a much better strategy would have been decapitation of the regime in a military putsch. In public, Mubarak warned that the invasion would 'open a Pandora's box' of instability and antagonism in the region and on one occasion said it would produce 'a hundred bin Ladens'.[25]

However, the Bush Administration was not inclined to heed Mubarak on this issue. In fact, signs of frustration with Mubarak and his closest aides and advisers had already surfaced in Washington in the late 1990s. One cause of irritation was the way in which Egypt continued to enjoy almost unparalleled US military assistance, yet still maintained an oversized, lumbering military machine incapable of conducting the sort of rapid reaction or intervention operations that the United States believed were most useful in the context of the late twentieth century.[26] In the late 1990s the US Congress was looking for ways to reduce the federal budget and members were beginning to question the value of so much aid to Egypt.

A Congressional Research Service (CRS) briefing paper on Egypt–United States relations updated in April 2003 noted several problems in the relationship along with the benefits over the years.[27] Among the points of contention were: Egyptian resistance to US involvement in the inquiry into the crash of Egypt Air Flight 990 off New York in 1999; failure to persuade the Palestinians to accept Israeli terms for their redeployment in Hebron; withdrawal of the Egyptian ambassador to Israel and curtailment of cooperation with Israel on all issues except the Palestinian issue in protest at Israeli measures to counter the second Intifada; human rights abuses by the security forces, including torture and detention without trial; the imprisonment of human rights activist Saad al-Din Ibrahim; discrimination against the Copts; and the slow pace of democratization and economic restructuring.

In an article published in *The Middle East Quarterly* in Summer 2005 Samuel Spector identified a list of concerns with the Egyptian leadership similar to those documented in the CRS report and added various other grievances.[28] Spector accused the Egyptian government of having actively sought to isolate Israel in the context of the Middle East Peace Process in the 1990s; undermining the sanctions regime on Iraq; opposing the invasion of Iraq, and developing relations with Sudan and Libya despite US objections. In his conclusion Spector stated:

> Egypt has consistently sought to quash any challenge to its role as the Arab world's paramount broker of moderation and stability. To Cairo's decision-makers, such goals take a back seat to preventing the emergence of any new order – including democratisation – that Egypt cannot dominate.[29]

In marked contrast to this stinging assessment, former British diplomats interviewed for this study offered a much more nuanced appraisal of the Egyptian leadership and its policies.[30] The British had lower expectations of the Mubarak regime's capacity to democratize and were themselves much more invested in the maintenance of stability. They thought Egypt's strategy of winning over the Islamists was delivering gains, though they thought the Egyptian security services in need of modernization. Some British diplomats shared US frustration with the group of advisers close to the president, deeming them too complacent and out of touch with the new generation. Several regretted that Mubarak did not attempt to 'win hearts and minds' among the population, but kept aloof – even though, according to one source, he could be engaging and entertaining.[31]

All those consulted for this study thought that Mubarak 'dropped the ball' when it came to his son Gamal's quest to succeed his father. Allegedly it was Gamal's mother Suzanne who most encouraged her son in his ambitions and Mubarak simply paid little attention. Since his resignation, claims have come to light that the senior military warned Mubarak that they would not tolerate Gamal as his successor, but the president ignored that warning and allowed popular disillusionment as well as military antipathy to fester.[32]

In any case, the assessment in Washington was that another military man would most likely succeed Mubarak and did not push for any particular candidate. Of all the facets of US–Egyptian relations, political reform was not high on the list until George W. Bush became US president. Even then, it was the neoconservatives in the Bush Administration who were most wedded to the idea of democratization in the Arab world and as of the invasion of Iraq in 2003 this goal rose up the US agenda for Egypt. By then, as described by one US source, Mubarak had grown bored with his job, had seen it all, several times over, and was simply hanging on as the head of a sclerotic regime. He resisted US demands for democratization as far as he could and when the Muslim Brotherhood made a strong showing in the 2005 elections, Mubarak claimed vindication – warning that it was either him (and the ruling National Democratic Party) or the Islamists. In light of this and US experience of resistance and sectarian violence in Iraq, when Mubarak told the Bush Administration to 'back off', as of 2006 it did.[445]

In 2008 Mubarak was invited to become co-president of the Union for the Mediterranean, alongside President Nicolas Sarkozy of France, who had initiated this new scheme for relations between Europe and the Mediterranean littoral states outside the EU. Egypt having by then lost much of its influence in the Arab world, and Mubarak's role in the near moribund Middle East Peace Process having been reduced to managing the border with Gaza and mediating between the Palestinian factions, this invitation must have given the ageing Egyptian leader a fillip. So too the choice of Cairo for US President Barack Obama's first visit to the Middle East and the platform for his speech about restoring more cooperative relations with the Arab world.

A diplomatic cable of May 2009 from the US Embassy in Cairo to Washington, preparing the ground for a visit by Mubarak, stated:

> President Mubarak last visited Washington in April 2004, breaking a twenty year tradition of annual visits to the White House. Egyptians view President Mubarak's upcoming meeting with the President as a new beginning to the U.S.–Egyptian relationship that will restore a sense of mutual respect that they believe diminished in recent years.

The cable also said of Mubarak:

> *He is a tried and true realist, innately cautious and conservative, and has little time for idealistic goals. Mubarak viewed President Bush as Naïve, controlled by subordinates, and totally unprepared for dealing with post-Saddam Iraq, especially the rise of Iran's regional influence.*

And that:

> Peace with Israel has cemented Egypt's moderate role in Middle East peace efforts and provided a political basis for continued U.S. military and economic assistance ($1.3 billion and $250 million, respectively). However, broader elements of peace with Israel, e.g. economic and cultural exchange, remain essentially undeveloped.[34]

In sum, Mubarak and his regime retained a reputation for moderation and caution through three decades. The value of the US alliance with Mubarak's Egypt to the pursuit of US interests in the region was reiterated in language used repeatedly from the beginning of the Mubarak presidency. As discussed below, it was the Egyptian uprising and the way the president reacted to it, rather than a fundamental reassessment in either Washington or London, that eventually convinced the United States and Britain to drop their reliance on Mubarak and call for him to go.

The US policy agenda over the decades

Between 1981 and 2011 successive US administrations framed their aspirations for the Middle East in terms of strategic plans or doctrines, identifying US interests and how they were to be advanced. In the final decade of the Cold War the Reagan administration was preoccupied with countering any extension of Soviet influence in the region. The Soviet invasion of Afghanistan and the Iranian revolution in 1979 had clearly raised alarm in Washington that the Soviets were advancing towards the Persian Gulf and the fall of the Shah meant that Iran no longer served as a US ally that could be relied upon to block that advance. In this context Washington identified Israel as the only reliable ally in the region, the defence of which should be a priority 'as a bulwark against Soviet penetration and domination of the Middle East and against radical Arab expansionism'.[35]

The Reagan Administration's formula for protecting the Middle East from Soviet expansion was to build a 'Strategic Consensus' among the regional states considered friendly to Washington, namely: Turkey, Jordan, Saudi Arabia and Egypt (Sadat having switched from the Soviet to the US camp in the early 1970s) together with Israel. However, Jordan and Saudi Arabia professed to be more worried about Zionism than Communism and proved unwilling, at least initially, to cooperate with Egypt because of its peace treaty with Israel.[36] The Strategic Consensus idea was therefore quietly dropped and the United States entered a phase of what one US academic termed 'episodic diplomacy'.[37] Two regional conflicts dominated the scene: the Iran–Iraq War (1980–8) and the war in Lebanon (1975–90) which Israel invaded in 1982. As of 1983 apparently, the idea of a 'Cairo–Baghdad axis was seen as a counterweight to Syrian influence in the region'.[38]

Reagan also hoped to use US intervention in Lebanon and an Israeli–Lebanese peace deal to engender a wider process, floating 'the idea of us continuing to help, as we did at Camp David, in furthering that process bringing more nations into the kind of peaceful arrangement that occurred between Egypt and Israel, producing more Egypts, if you will'.[39] However, such hopes did not bear fruit, though Egyptian, Saudi and Jordanian assistance to Iraq, encouraged by the United States (and Britain), did help Iraq avoid defeat by Iran and Washington investigated developing closer relations with Iraq, only to have that possibility dashed when Iraq invaded Kuwait in August 1990.

Egypt's role in the US-led campaign to oust the Iraqis from Kuwait in 1991 was noted above. In the aftermath of that war, President George H. W. Bush launched the idea of 'a new world order'. In the Middle East this was to entail: a new push for resolution of the Arab–Israeli conflict; the disarmament and rehabilitation of Iraq; a new defence arrangement for the defence of the GCC states with US support; and economic prosperity for people in the region. When Bill Clinton became US president in 1993 he inherited 'the most promising environment for Arab–Israeli peacemaking in the history of America's involvement in the issue'.[40] Resolution of the conflict, through US mediation, became a central focus of US diplomacy for the next eight years. On the premise of 'making the region safe' for Israel to reach peace with its Arab neighbours and the Palestinians the Clinton Administration also pursued a policy of 'Dual Containment' of Iraq and Iran.[41]

By the end of the Clinton Administration, Jordan had signed a peace treaty with Israel (1994) and the Palestinians had attained autonomous control of their internal affairs in the Gaza Strip and their main population centres in the West Bank. However, the make-or-break summit at Camp David in July 2000 had failed to resolve the final status issues at stake in the Israeli–Palestinian dimension of the conflict and the second Palestinian Intifada erupted in September 2000. Israeli–Syrian talks collapsed earlier the same year. Meanwhile, containment of Iraq was not accompanied by a conclusive outcome to the UN-led disarmament programme there, and the US and Britain stood almost alone in their rigorous enforcement of the sanctions regime on Iraq. The British did not join the US in imposing sanctions on Iran and for a while EU efforts to develop a rapport with Tehran, inclusive of the British, enabled trade between Iran and Europe to expand.

The arrival of George W. Bush in the White House in 2001 opened a fundamentally new era in US foreign policy, particularly with respect to the Middle East. The ascendance of the neoconservatives in the administration presaged a new agenda even before 9/11 led to the declaration of the 'war on terror', the invasion of Afghanistan and then Iraq.[42] As indicated above, Mubarak's Egypt did not measure up to US expectations of its long-standing ally during the Bush Administration, especially as the view of those pushing the democratization agenda gained momentum in 2004 and was set out in the Broader Middle East and North Africa Initiative, launched at the G8 Sea Island summit that June.[43] However, as also noted above, as of 2006 the US Administration desisted from calls for more democracy in Egypt for fear of the Islamists. On the Israeli–Palestinian front President Bush broke new ground by calling specifically for a 'two-state' solution to the conflict, but no such agreement was forthcoming.

Many analysts and officials in the United States, as too in Britain, looked to President Obama to succeed in the Middle East Peace Process where his predecessor had failed. Yet, despite a concerted attempt to bring about a 'two-state' solution, this ran up against Israel's opposition to halting the expansion of Jewish settlements. Mediation between the Palestinian Islamist movement Hamas – which had seized control of the Gaza Strip from its Fatah rivals in 2007 – was effectively delegated to Egypt. Yet Washington remained opposed to the idea of a Palestinian unity government inclusive of Hamas, and Egypt gave precedence to containing the movement in Gaza while trying to avoid ending up as Israel's proxy policeman there.

British views

British policy in the Middle East in the 1980s and 1990s was less the product of strategic doctrines akin to those of the Americans than of a more modest understanding of the limits of British power and reach. The British Empire was no more and the last vestiges of Britain's imperial presence in the region had been wound up by the beginning of the 1970s.[44] During the last decade of the Cold War the British were clearly supportive of the US worldview and agenda to contain Soviet expansionism. In addition, they essentially looked to the United States to take on roles in the region that they could no longer assume. Retaining a close alliance with the United States was in itself a UK priority and Prime Minister Margaret Thatcher established a close rapport with President Reagan. She is also credited with having galvanized George Bush senior to take a tough stance with Iraq over Kuwait in 1990, just as the Cold War was ending.

Within this broader context, the British were nonetheless rivals as well as partners to the Americans in the competition to sell arms to the GCC states. As noted above, however, since the British had no armaments to give away as opposed to sell, they did not even attempt to rival the Americans in terms of military assistance to Egypt. On the Arab–Israeli front, British Arabists in the Foreign Office did not always share the US perspective on how best to resolve the conflict, but they conceded that Washington had much more influence with Israel than Britain and British policy was effectively tailored to persuading successive American administrations to drive the peace process in ways that the British could not.

During the period that Tony Blair led the British government (1997–2007), aligning British policy with that of Washington became a central objective. Blair himself tried to carve a niche for Britain in the Middle East Peace Process that was designed to make Britain America's partner and help US diplomacy in every way possible.[45] Yet according to former British diplomats who served in Egypt, Britain was not privileged with access to US dealings with Mubarak on the Arab–Israeli issue and sometimes relied more on the Egyptians than the Americans in Cairo to tell them what was going on.

Blair and his family enjoyed the hospitality of Mubarak on a number of occasions, yet according to one former British ambassador the friendship between Blair and Mubarak was not as close as Blair appeared, or wished, to believe.[46] Another British source was more dismissive, suggesting that Blair courted Mubarak in part in order to enjoy the benefits of holidays in Sharm el-Sheikh.[47] Be that as it may, among Egyptian intellectuals, Blair's reputation nose-dived following his decision to support the US invasion of Iraq in 2003.[48] In such circles there was no enthusiasm for the invasion of Iraq in any case, and Blair was criticized for acting like a junior lieutenant in Bush's war. The Egyptians thought that the British, with their decades of involvement in the region, ought to have known better.

In fact, British diplomats who served in Cairo said that they personally did not feel handicapped by association with Blair, because the Egyptian leadership did not hold against them the failings they attributed to the British Prime Minister. Blair himself, meanwhile, hung on to his reading of Mubarak and his presumed rapport with the man to the point of sounding out of touch with the import of events in 2011. Shortly before Mubarak was obliged to step down, Blair called him 'immensely courageous and a force for good'; said he did not think there was majority support for the Muslim Brotherhood in Egypt; and identified a need to 'manage' transition in Egypt.[49]

With or without Blair, British access in Egypt was consistently good during the Mubarak presidency and British diplomats found their Egyptian counterparts highly professional and engaging. Meanwhile, as noted above, the British had a fairly close rapport with the Egyptians on intelligence matters, though cooperation in counter-terrorism did not extend to any involvement in or discussion about Egyptian internal security. British businessmen and officials who dealt with the Egyptians in connection with commercial projects did have reservations though, and described their frustrations when dealing with Egyptian bureaucracy.[50]

Abandoning Mubarak

Between late January and mid-February 2011 the US position on Mubarak progressed through three phases: from assuming he could hold the situation, to wishing to see him step down gracefully, to seeking his immediate departure. By all accounts Washington was taken by surprise by the size and import of the Egyptian uprising and initially the Obama Administration downplayed the crisis. As noted in the *New York Times*:

> When the first protesters appeared in Tahrir Square, [Secretary of State Hillary] Clinton, working off the traditional American script that portrays Mr. Mubarak as a reliable ally in need of quiet, sustained pressure on human rights and political reform, said, 'Our assessment is that the Egyptian government is stable and is looking for ways to respond to the legitimate needs and interests of the Egyptian people'.[51]

However, by the end of January 2011 President Obama (and British Prime Minister David Cameron) were calling for 'an orderly transition of power',[52] and in the words of Clinton, it was time for Mubarak to 'move out of the way'.

Yet, according to several commentators, including Nathan Brown, an authority on Egyptian constitutional law, Washington was not the sole or even the lead arbiter of events.[53] Mubarak's departure required a consensus in the senior Egyptian military establishment and in the event their resolve proved more forthcoming than some in Washington and London initially dared hope, especially since Mubarak himself was resistant. Seemingly intending to smooth the path and find a way to protect Mubarak's dignity, Washington called on former ambassador to Egypt Frank Wisner to intercede. Wisner was known to have a close rapport with the Egyptian president, yet his handling of the situation turned out to be more conciliatory than the Obama Administration apparently intended. After visiting Cairo on 30 January 2011, Wisner subsequently told the media that: 'President Mubarak's continued leadership is critical – it's his opportunity to write his own legacy.'[54]

Clinton distanced the administration from Wisner's remarks.[55] Crucially, meanwhile, Mubarak himself sacrificed what remaining sympathy he retained in Washington when, on 1 February 2011, he made a defiant speech asserting that he would remain in place until the next presidential elections – scheduled for September 2011 – and claimed that he had never intended to stand again then anyway.[56] No sooner had he finished the speech then Obama telephoned him and had what was reportedly a testy 30-minute conversation. Thus began the third and decisive phase in Washington's position on Mubarak, wherein his swift departure became imperative. Yet there were complications. Washington apparently assumed that Omar Suleiman, Mubarak's newly appointed deputy, could take over, but according to the Egyptian Constitution it was the speaker of the Parliament, not the vice-president, who was bound to replace him.[57]

Thus it was that the Egyptian military, rather than the United States, proved the decisive player in the drama, even though Washington accommodated without apparent difficulty the assumption of the president's powers by the Supreme Council of the Armed Forces (SCAF).[58] The long-established channel of communication between the US military and their Egyptian counterparts was used to convey messages and keep in touch during this critical period, but not to call the shots. Washington's priority was for order and stability to be maintained while preparations for parliamentary and presidential elections were managed by SCAF. Where Washington did draw the line, however, was with respect to the use of force against unarmed civilian demonstrators, as was made clear to Cairo when violence was unleashed against the crowds on 4 February 2011.[59]

In comparison with the Americans, the British were less involved in the detail of Mubarak's exit, but also seemingly more enthusiastic about his departure. Their attitude may be attributed to what one Foreign Office source described as a policy shift that pre-dated the Arab revolutions.[60] Whereas the Americans had backed away from pressing for democratization after 2006 (as discussed above), the Foreign Office had come to regard dictatorships as a threat to stability. The Conservative-led coalition also inclined to this view. Their priority, they said, was trade promotion. Thus, when the Egyptian revolution erupted, Foreign Secretary William Hague revealed that he had previously warned the Egyptian government over the need for openness and reform.[61] Cameron not only called for Mubarak to go sooner rather than later, but also criticized the EU for failing to condemn 'state-sponsored' violence.[62]

David Cameron took the opportunity, afforded by a previously scheduled trip to the region, to visit Cairo ten days after Mubarak left office. He was the first Western leader to do so. The fact that his trip was overshadowed by his intention to promote British military sales in the region, and the inclusion in his entourage of British businessmen including arms manufacturers, did not present a problem as far as Cameron was concerned. He asserted that British policy went beyond simply promoting trade and said: 'Our message, as it has been throughout this [government], [is] that the response to the aspirations that people are showing on the streets of these countries must be one of reform and not repression.'[63] Cameron's stance was no doubt made easier by virtue of the fact that he had not had time to establish a personal relationship with Mubarak before the Egyptian president suffered his political demise.

Conclusion

What emerges from the foregoing review of US and British attitudes towards Mubarak and how these may or may not have been dictated by their broader objectives suggests that the Americans had more cause for frustration and disappointment than the British. One explanation for this appears to be that the British did not have the same expectations of the Egyptian president simply because their regional ambitions and capacities were more modest. Even if the British had wanted to, they were no longer in a position to try to make Egypt a model of modernity, democracy and stability. However, because the British had, for the most part, prioritized stability over democratization, they took Mubarak as he presented himself, namely as a leader whose style was best suited to delivering stability. Their professed change of heart in the recent past, wherein they now espouse democracy as the preferred route to stability, came rather too late to exonerate them from the charge that they remained largely blinkered by their 'strategic script' for three decades.

The Americans, by contrast, appear to have hoped for more than their British counterparts, insofar as they wanted Mubarak to be everything that he was – solidly committed to containing the 'threats' posed to himself and the United States by both Islamists and terrorists – while also wanting him to gradually introduce a democratization process that would surely have led to his own political demise. Those least able to see the logical contradiction in their own aspirations were the proponents of democratization across the Arab world, and as of the administration of George W. Bush they became more vocal. Yet the US leadership did back off when they saw the mayhem that followed regime change in Iraq and the success of the Muslim Brotherhood in the 2005 Egyptian elections. Those Americans who sensed there had to be a trade-off between stability and democratization, meanwhile, preferred the former all along.

In retrospect – with Mubarak gone and new elections in Egypt delivering strong results not only for the Muslim Brotherhood but also for Islamists of a much more radical character – it appears that both camps in Washington had unrealistic expectations. Suppression of democratic rights cannot endure indefinitely and when the masses get their choice, they opt for the very elements the Americans fear. In the face of the revolutions of 2011, in Egypt and elsewhere, the Americans are back in the dilemma they faced in Iraq (after 2003), Egypt (in the 2005 elections), Palestine (in the 2006 elections) and Lebanon (in the 2011 elections), namely how serious are they when they say they stand for freedom, democracy and the pursuit of happiness as core American values?

Thus the conclusion to be drawn here would seem to be that the Americans (as too the British in their way) were operating with a strategic script that parted company with reality. For a period, the British actually claimed that: 'values and interests merge' and Britain could be 'a force for good' in the world by 'projecting British values' through its foreign policy.[64] That thesis took Britain into the ill-fated Iraq adventure, though it seems not to have fundamentally affected British dealings with Egypt, especially since the Egyptians themselves, Mubarak included, never took the Blair rhetoric very seriously.

In the US case, Egypt had a special place in Washington's strategic script for the Middle East, and according to Kurtzer, the tenets were well known to every US diplomat from 1980 onward.[65] There could be no question of making policy 'ad hoc'. The goals were to (1) anchor the Middle East Peace Process, and particularly the Israel–Egypt Treaty, by helping Mubarak to contain domestic and regional antipathy to the treaty; (2) turn the Egyptian armed forces into a US-trained and equipped fighting force that could contribute to a pro-US regional agenda; (3) turn around the failing Egyptian economy such that it could be viable and sustainable in the face of a large and rapidly rising population; and, to a lesser extent, (4) promote democratization of the Egyptian polity.

From Kurtzer's perspective, the first three of these goals were achieved, though having proved its worth in the 1991 Gulf War, the Egyptian military failed to modernize thereafter. The quest to save the Egyptian economy made great strides, but, he believes, Mubarak's ouster has derailed that progress. In sum, it could be said that the US strategic script for Egypt not only guided policy but delivered, for at least two decades. Certainly the record seems to show that US disenchantment with Mubarak increased insofar as he proved uncooperative in playing the role assigned to him. The charge that could therefore be levelled at the United States was its unwillingness to grant that no Arab leader could realistically be expected to fulfil the role assigned to the President of Egypt in the US policy agenda and remain a champion of his people.

Over time, not only was the president supposed to contain Islamist extremism and democratize the Egyptian political system, he was also expected to downsize the armed forces and curtail the role of the military in Egyptian commercial activities. At the regional level the role required of Egypt in the US script progressed from one of helping Iraq to deny victory to the Islamic Republic of Iran in the Iran–Iraq war of the 1980s; to joining the US-led coalition that reversed the Iraqi occupation of Kuwait in 1990–1; then to uphold sanctions on both Iraq and Iran throughout the 1990s; support the US invasion of Iraq and ouster of Saddam Hussein in 2003; and finally line up with the United States, Jordan and Saudi Arabia against an emboldened Iran. On the Arab–Israeli front, meanwhile, Egypt was expected to keep the peace with Israel and bring other Arab states, plus the Palestinians, into a broader peace deal, inclusive of regional economic normalization with Israel, but, as it transpired, absent an Israeli government convinced of the need for a 'viable' Palestinian state.

To conclude, the task here was to establish whether US-UK perspectives on Mubarak were dictated by their adherence to a script rather than an understanding of the man. The verdict is yes, on three counts. First, what they valued in Mubarak as a leader on the Egyptian domestic front in the 1980s proved over time to be the very attributes that would turn his people against him in the long run. While Mubarak and his understanding of his leadership role stayed more or less static, the circumstances of ordinary people in Egypt worsened. Albeit reluctantly, Mubarak was persuaded to adopt economic reform measures that pleased the IMF, but failed to deliver a better standard of living to ordinary people, and corruption increased. Since they had no say in the composition of their government, the Egyptian people could not 'own' the policies that made their circumstances more difficult to endure. When they revolted in 2011, 'dignity' was one of their key demands, along with jobs and an end to corruption.

Second, the role played by Mubarak in countering Islamist-inspired terrorist groups and violence on the Egyptian home front in the 1990s was greeted by Washington and tolerated in London as a necessary evil. After 9/11 and the declaration of the 'war on terror', some of Mubarak's methods were even emulated by the United States and Britain. If not actually deploying such methods directly themselves, they sought the cooperation of Mubarak and other Arab dictators in dealing with the threat of al Qaeda, its affiliates and emulators – including 'rendering' suspects for interrogation and torture by Arab security forces. Over time, the qualities attributed to Mubarak which inclined Washington (and London) to regard him as an ally in the war on terror – his toughness, intolerance and hold on power – proved over time to be the very same attributes that turned the United States (and Britain) against him. Whereas once he was 'our man', he became an embarrassment.

Third, the US strategic script for the region (to which the British broadly acquiesced), and thence the expectations of Mubarak, changed significantly between the 1980s, when the Cold War still endured, and the 2000s, when the Americans and British decided to invade Iraq and believed they could bring democracy to the Arab world by intervention. Whereas in the 1980s Egypt's strategic interests, as understood by Mubarak, were in harmony with those of the United States, by 2003 they were not, and thence he could not be expected to put US interests and requests ahead of his own. In Washington he was criticized, as detailed above, for being insufficiently supportive of the US agenda. Not least, Mubarak was faulted for his handling of Israeli–Palestinian issues. Yet, whereas in the 1990s the Middle East peace process looked as if it would deliver, by the following decade it was going nowhere. Mubarak needed it to work, not content himself with managing Palestinian factional politics and policing the Gaza Strip.

In sum, the context and the US-UK agendas changed fundamentally between 1981 and 2011, though Mubarak largely did not. And, to paraphrase one former US official consulted for this study: he lasted as long as he was useful.

Notes

1 I am indebted to several such sources for providing me with insights, which they did mostly on the basis of non-attribution. In certain specific instances, however, key individuals have agreed to be quoted directly, for which I am most grateful.

2 As also attested to by former US and British diplomats.

3 'Men who have made their mark', *Financial Times* feature, (23 July 1980).

4 Ibid.

5 Thomas W. Lippman, *Egypt after Nasser* (New York: Paragon House, 1989), p. 220.

6 Former Egyptian Ambassador to Washington Nabil Fahmi also reminded me that Sadat had tasked Mubarak with presiding over a clean-up of corruption at the top of the Egyptian government, in part because Mubarak himself was deemed uncorrupt.

7 Youssef Ibrahim, 'U.S. Stake in Egypt Rests On One Man – Anwar el-Sadat', *New York Times*, (30 March 1980); Eddy Cody, 'U.S. is seen increasing its stake in stability of Sadat Regime', *International Herald Tribune*, (31 March 1980).

8 For discussion of the fall-out within the State Department following the 'loss' of the Shah, see Robert D. Kaplan, *The Arabists: The Romance of the American Elite* (New York: Macmillan, 1993).

9 Anthony McDermott, 'Waiting For Some Firm Policies', *Financial Times Feature on Egypt*, (28 May 1982).

10 Alan Mackie, 'A Cautious Approach Begins To Work for Mubarak as Vote Consolidates Party's Power', *International Herald Tribune*, (14 June 1984).

11 Tony Walker, 'Country at the Crossroads', *Financial Times Survey on Egypt*, 5 June 1985; Julian Nundy, 'Mubarak Scores Points for Foreign Policy, but Economic Woes Remain', *International Herald Tribune*, (15 June 1985).

12 Secret Cairo 000874, 19 May 2009, 'Scenesetter: President Mubarak's Visit to Washington'. Available online at: http://www.guardian.co.uk/world/us-embassy-cables-documents/207723 (accessed 31 December 2011).

13 Author interview with Dan Kurtzer, (28 December 2011).

14 See e.g. Galal Amin, *Egypt in the Era of Hosni Mubarak 1981–2011* (Cairo: The American University in Cairo Press, 2011), ch. 13; John Bradley, *Inside Egypt: The Road to Revolution in the Land of the Pharaohs* (New York: Palgrave Macmillan, 2011), Ch. 6. In an interview with Egyptian economist Samir Radwan by the author in January 2006, Radwan attributed some of the problems to the fact that the reformist ministers did not have a free hand and were constrained by others fearful of losing their privileges.

15 Clyde R. Mark, 'Egypt–United States Relations', *Congressional Research Service*, 2 April 2003, pp. 10–13. Available online at: http://fpc.state.gov/documents/organization/19440.pdf (accessed 28 December 2011).

16 Chas. W. Freeman, 'US–Egyptian Defense Relations', in Phebe Marr (ed.) *Egypt at the Crossroads: Domestic Stability and Regional Role* (Washington, DC: National Defense University Press, 1999), p. 204.

17 Phebe Marr, 'Strategies for an Era of Uncertainty: The U.S. Policy Agenda', in Phebe Marr and William Lewis (eds) *Riding the Tiger: The Middle East Challenge After the Cold War* (Boulder, CO: Westview Press, 1993), p. 230.

18 Julian Nundy, 'Mubarak, Hussein Take Lead in New Bloc of Moderates', *International Herald Tribune*, (15 June 1985).

19 General H. Norman Schwarzkopf, *It Doesn't Take a Hero: The Autobiography*, written by Peter Petre (London: Bantam Press, 1992), p. 381; and Mark (2003), p. 11.

20 Ibid., and HRH General Khaled Bin Sultan with Patrick Seale, *Desert Warrior: A Personal View of the Gulf War by the Joint Forces Commander* (London: HarperCollins, 1995), pp. 178–9.

21 Mark (2003), p.10.

22 Freeman (1999), p. 204.

23 Gilles Keppel, *The War for Muslim Minds* (Cambridge, MA: Harvard University Press, 2004), p. 82.

24 This somewhat sarcastic depiction was offered by a US official who did not wish to be named. His remarks reflected US scepticism about Saudi faith in their ability to change the attitude of anti-Western radicals in the Kingdom, which contrasted with the lower expectations of Egyptian intelligence about the long-term effects of incarceration and pressure, not to say torture, of such radicals in Egypt.

25 See Samuel J. Spector, 'Washington and Cairo – Near the Breaking Point?', *Middle East Quarterly*, (summer 2005), pp. 45–55, p. 49.

26 Freeman (1999), pp. 204–210.

27 Mark (2003).

28 Samuel J. Spector, 'Washington and Cairo – Near the Breaking Point?', *Middle East Quarterly*, Vol. XII, No. 3, (Summer 2005), pp. 45–55.

29 Ibid., p. 52.

30 Consultations with former British diplomats including former ambassadors, who chose to be 'off the record'.

31 Former diplomat consulted for this study on a non-attributable basis.

32 Author interview with Dan Kurtzer, (28 December 2011).

33 In an article she wrote in response to the uprising that overtook Egypt in early 2011, former US Secretary of State Condoleeza Rice laid the blame on Mubarak himself for reneging on the democracy agenda that she had been advocating: 'The Future of a Democratic Egypt' *Washington Post*, (16 February 2011). However, as of 2008 the USAID budget for democracy promotion in Egypt was cut; see Mark P. Lagon, 'Egypt's Challenge for U.S. Rights Policy', *Council on Foreign Relations*, (11 February 2011). Available online at: http://www.cfr.org/egypt/egypts-challenge-us-rights-policy/p24080 (accessed 19 February 2012).

34 Secret Cairo 000874, 19 May 2009, 'Scenesetter: President Mubarak's Visit to Washington'. Available online at: http://www.guardian.co.uk/world/us-embassy-cables-documents/207723 (accessed 31 December 2011).

35 Gershon Kieval and Bernard Reich, 'The United States', in Bernard Reich (ed.) *The Powers in the Middle East: The Ultimate Strategic Arena* (New York: Praeger, 1987), p. 63.

36 Ibid., p. 84.

37 Ibid., p. 85.

38 Ibid., p. 91.

39 Reagan's comments to visiting journalists. Transcript in *Washington Post*, 25 October 1983, quoted in Reich (2003), p. 95.

40 Aaron David Miller, *The Much Too Promised Land: America's Elusive Search for Arab–Israeli Peace* (New York: Bantam Books, 2008), p. 237.

41 Martin Indyk's address to the Washington Institute for Near East Policy, 18 May 1993; see transcript in *Middle East International*, No. 452, (11 June 1993), pp. 3–4.

42 Michael Hudson, 'The United States in the Middle East', in Louise Fawcett (ed) *International Relations of the Middle East* (Oxford: Oxford University Press, 2009), pp. 308–29.

43 http://bmena.state.gov/ (accessed 16 December 2011).

44 For a more detailed discussion see Rosemary Hollis, *Britain and the Middle East in the 9/11 Era* (London: Wiley-Blackwell and Chatham House, 2010).

45 Ibid., Chs 4 and 7.

46 Author interview with former diplomat on a non-attributable basis.

47 Again the former diplomat concerned only agreed to be interviewed on a non-attributable basis.

48 Author interviews with Egyptian 'intellectuals' in Cairo, (January 2006).

49 Chris McGreal, 'Tony Blair: Mubarak is Immensely Courageous and a Force for Good', *Guardian*, (2 February 2011).

50 Ongoing conversations with British businessmen dealing with the Middle East in the 1980s, 1990s and 2000s.

51 David E. Sanger, 'As Mubarak Digs In, U.S. Policy in Egypt is Complicated', *New York Times*, (5 February 2011).

52 John R Bradley, 'The Tyrant Must Go, But Beware What Comes Next', *MailOnline*, (31 January 2011). Available online at: http://www.dailymail.co.uk/debate/article-1352090/EGYPT-RIOTS-Hosni-Mubarak-beware-comes-next.html (accessed 28 February 2012).

53 Author interview with Nathan Brown on 19 January 2012 and with a British Foreign Office official, who declined to be named, on 16 February 2012.

54 Quoted in Sanger (2011).

55 'Obama Administration Distances Self From Own Envoy to Mubarak', ABC News, (5 February 2011).

56 Sanger (2011).

57 Author interview with Nathan Brown, 19 January 2012 and 'Obama Administration Distances Self From Own Envoy to Mubarak', ABC News, (5 February 2011).

58 For a discussion of the constitutional parameters and enduring confusion about the powers adopted by SCAF see Nathan J. Brown and Mara Revkin, 'Court Decision on Presidential Election Law: Road Block or Minor Speed Bump for the Military', *Carnegie Endowment for International Peace*, (19 January 2012). Available online at: http://carnegieendowment.org/2012/01/19/court-decision-on-presidential-election-law-road-block-or-minor-speed-bump-for-military/950f.

59 Interview with Nathan Brown, 19 January 2012; Richard Spencer, 'Egypt Protests: Camel and Horse Riders Who Invaded Tahrir Square Say They Are "Good Men"', *Daily Telegraph*, (5 February 2011).

60 Interviewed, off the record, on (16 February 2012).

61 'William Hague: Repression Is Not the Answer, *Daily Telegraph*, (28 January 2011). Available online at: http://www.telegraph.co.uk/news/worldnews/africaandindianocean/egypt/8289331/William-Hague-repression-is-not-the-answer.html (accessed 28 February 2012).

62 'Britain's Foreign Policy Needs to be Made Clear on Egypt', *Telegraph View*, (4 February 2011). Available online at: http://www.telegraph.co.uk/comment/telegraph-view/8304463/Britains-foreign-policy-needs-to-be-made-clear-on-Egypt.html (accessed 28 February 2012).

63 Nicholas Watt, 'David Cameron Arrives in Egypt to Meet Military Rulers', *Guardian*, (21 February 2011).

64 An attitude discussed in detail in Hollis (2010).

65 Author interview with Dan Kurtzer, (28 December 2011).

CHAPTER TWELVE

British official perceptions of Muammar Gaddafi, 1969–2011

Christopher Andrew

Introduction

British official perceptions of Muammar Gaddafi were powerfully influenced by a remarkable combination of open sources and secret intelligence. For most of his 42 years in power, he devoted more energy to the public exposition of what he claimed was his political philosophy and to the cultivation of what became a strikingly flamboyant image of leadership than perhaps any other leader of his time. Secret intelligence, however, revealed another side to Gaddafi: his active involvement for 30 years in a considerable range of terrorist operations, some of which directly threatened British interests. Eventually, however, the UK government, along with the US, chose to 'rehabilitate' Gaddafi in exchange for the dismantlement of his WMD programmes. The UK and US also developed close 'counter-terrorist' links with Tripoli, thus making Gaddafi an 'ally' in the 'War on Terrorism'. And yet, as a result of the uprisings that occurred in Libya in 2011, and his harsh response to them, Gaddafi again became a 'rogue', this time to be toppled from power.

Early impressions of Gaddafi

When a group of junior officers, led by Gaddafi, overthrew the monarchy in a bloodless coup on 1 September 1969, there was little sign either of his future political pretentiousness or of his later fascination with terrorism. Gaddafi was probably the best-looking leader in the world. He was also unpretentiously dressed. An Egyptian businessman who was in Tripoli at the time of the Libyan Revolution recalls seeing him dressed in flip-flops. A photograph of Gaddafi at an informal buffet with visiting British students in 1973 shows him squatting on a carpet, casually dressed in a short-sleeved shirt and a cheap cotton hat set slightly askew.[1] Even on state occasions, for some years he wore only his khaki colonel's uniform; out of respect for his hero, Colonel Nasser, he refused promotion to a higher rank. Though Gaddafi had no liking for Western officials, the British chief pilot of Libya's VIP 'Special Flight', Neville Atkinson, a former member of the Royal Navy Fleet Air Arm, found him friendly and unpretentious; he would often abandon the comfort of his passenger seat for a jump-seat in the cockpit to talk to Atkinson.[2] There was no hint yet of Gaddafi's later transformation into the most eccentrically dressed autocrat in modern history, obsessed with his personal image.

Though Gaddafi closed US and UK military bases soon after taking power and expelled most Italian settlers in 1970, he did not appear to be a major potential threat to Western security. A British intelligence asset posted to Libya six months after the revolution found the atmosphere tedious rather than intimidating:

> Gaddafi was still busy 'Islamifying' everything and removing any trace of Italian and other European influence. Depressing too – evenings spent in the hotel bar, chatting and solemnly drinking water! And not much on the menu except lamb couscous. Not even a decent spaghetti.[3]

Secret intelligence was not required to plot the course of Gaddafi's programme of Islamicization and campaign to eradicate all trace of Libya's colonial past. The evidence was even more graphically displayed on the streets of Tripoli than on restaurant menus. White paint obliterated all Italian street names and Roman letters on car number-plates, leaving only the Arabic versions. But the most striking visual symbol of the rejection of Western values was the decision to turn Tripoli's Catholic cathedral into a mosque – a unique event in the modern history of North Africa (though Algiers Cathedral had experienced the same transformation, it had originally been a mosque, unlike its counterpart in Tripoli).

The main challenge to British interests during Gaddafi's early years in power was over oil. As some (perhaps most) privately recognized in Whitehall, Gaddafi had a good case for demanding the renegotiation of contracts signed by King Idris' government, which left the oil business in the hands of foreign petroleum companies and gave them half the revenue. Gaddafi's determination to end the unequal oil treaties was so vociferously stated that secret intelligence on his demands was scarcely needed. He achieved a dramatic public victory. Despite the complex disputes which followed the nationalization of BP's share of Libyan oil production late in 1971, Libya became the first developing country to secure a majority of the revenues from its own oilfields. In 1973, it took a controlling interest in all other petroleum companies operating in Libya. The boom in oil prices following the embargo declared in October 1973 by the members of the Organisation of Arab Petroleum Exporting Countries enabled Libya to finance a major expansion of education, healthcare and housing. A *Special Report* in the *Guardian* concluded in April 1976: 'Libya's policy on oil prices, unlike many of its other enterprises, has been both successful and beneficial.'[4]

The general Whitehall view of Gaddafi himself, however, was that his dictatorial personal power combined with oil wealth had turned him into a pretentious self-centred autocrat. Peter Tripp, in his valedictory despatch to the Foreign and Commonwealth Office (FCO) as ambassador in Tripoli in March 1974, thought it possible that Gaddafi had 'started out with good intentions', but 'Virtue itself turns vice, being misapplied':

Had his policies at home made Libya a happier place for Libyans themselves, he might be excused some of his excesses. But the plain fact is that Qadhafi is indifferent to and contemptuous of Libyans as a whole. He uses them for his own ends and to further his own ambitions. ... The power which vastly increased oil revenues confers has – quite apart from Libyan xenophobic arrogance and egocentricity – made the regime indifferent to the admonitions and criticisms of the rest of the world. ... All major decisions are made by Qadhafi or by the R[evolutionary] C[ommand] C[ouncil]. Ministers are rarely consulted on policy, only on execution. The Ministry of Foreign Affairs, the only Ministry with which foreign missions are allowed to deal direct, has been without a Minister for all but seven months of my three years here. The job is now passed round from hand to hand – Qadhafi continuing to make his own foreign policy without advice ... and often without informing his colleagues. ... He is too egocentric and erratic ever to make a benevolent dictator.[5]

On his last day as ambassador, while waiting for the plane for London in the VIP suite at Tripoli airport, Tripp encountered Atkinson, who he knew sometimes had cockpit conversations with Libyan leaders. On discovering that the VIP on the Special Flight that day would probably be the Prime Minister, Major Abdusalem Jalloud, he asked Atkinson, as 'a great favour', to raise with Jalloud the still unresolved issue of the compensation due to BP after the nationalization of its Libyan assets. 'I will let you into a secret,' Tripp told Atkinson. 'In the three years that I have been here, I have never spoken to a single member of the Libyan Government.' In the course of the day Atkinson succeeded in having friendly, but probably inconsequential, conversations about the compensation due to BP with both Jalloud and Gaddafi.[6]

Atkinson's friendly relations with the VIPs he flew with on the Special Flight, combined with his privileged lifestyle, seem to have blinded him to the repressive nature of the Gaddafi regime.[7] Despite Gaddafi's high-blown rhetoric about Libya's creation of a new form of direct democracy, his main administrative achievement was to set up a police state. The 'revolutionary committees', supposedly the instruments of direct democracy, organized large networks of informants to monitor and intimidate opponents of the regime. A law of 1972 banned political parties, condemned by Gaddafi as undemocratic. In a speech at Tripoli in November 1974, he warned the 'politically sick' against any attempt to organize political opposition: 'I could at any moment send them to the People's Court ... and the People's Court will issue a sentence of death based on this law, because execution is the fate of anyone who forms a political party.'[8] The creation of the police state imposed serious limitations on diplomatic reporting from the British and other embassies in Tripoli. Tripp wrote in his valedictory despatch: 'Personal contacts are excluded because people are too frightened by the secret police to respond to one's friendly overtures.'[9] Secret Intelligence Service (SIS) reports from its Libyan contacts as well as sources elsewhere in the Middle East with Libyan connections thus acquired an enhanced importance.

A hard man to deal with

Though recognizing that Gaddafi's posturing was combined with considerable political skill in maintaining his personal dictatorship and fragmenting potential internal opposition, the FCO seems to have shown limited curiosity in exploring the roots of his antagonism to the West, and the United Kingdom in particular. When Gaddafi's future intelligence chief and foreign minister Musa Kusa, then in his early thirties, was appointed head of the London People's Bureau (the renamed Libyan Embassy) in 1979, it was known that in the previous year he had been awarded an MA by Michigan State University for a thesis on Gaddafi's political leadership,[10] but no attempt was made to obtain a copy.[11] The thesis (of which, 20 years later, Kusa gave copies to several British official contacts) contains important insights into Gaddafi's views of the outside world. Though a strong supporter of Gaddafi, Kusa emphasized the xenophobia of his family background:

> His family and his society were highly religious and hated all non-Moslems. Therefore, Qadafi's background engendered in him a

hatred of foreigners. ... Although Qadafi did not see any Italian soldiers in his childhood, family influences made him view the [foreigners] as the enemy of the people.[12]

Kusa's thesis also records some of the lingering resentments Gaddafi had acquired during ten months on a training course at the British Army signals HQ at Beaconsfield in 1966:

> We met a British major of Norwegian origin. He represented to us the typical ugly British colonialist. He asked many questions concerning our national feelings. It was obvious that he hated the Arabs and wanted to know our reactions.

Gaddafi also implied that he was shocked by London nightlife and the Swinging Sixties: 'I put on my Al-Jird [Arab robes] and went to Piccadilly. I was prompted by a feeling of challenge and a desire to assert myself.'[13]

Gaddafi's most widely publicized political initiative in the later 1970s was the publication between 1976 and 1979, in the three slim volumes of the *Green Book*, of his supposedly ground-breaking political philosophy. Gaddafi claimed to have resolved the contradictions inherent in capitalism and communism by setting up a proliferation of committees which would replace all existing forms of government – 'authoritarian, family, tribal, factional, class, parliamentary, partisan or party coalition' – with 'direct democracy' and 'people's power'. In 1977 he announced Libya's transformation into the Great Jamahiriyah or 'State of the Masses', the most advanced form of government in human history. Gaddafi himself ceased to occupy any official position, and held only the honorific titles 'Guide of the First of September Great Revolution of the Socialist People's Libyan Jamahiriyah' and 'Brotherly Leader and Guide of the Revolution'.

Instead of persuading most Western opinion-makers that he was a serious political thinker, the *Green Book* was interpreted as a pretentiously unconvincing attempt to portray Gaddafi's personal dictatorship as a revolutionary form of direct democracy.[14] Gaddafi told the Italian journalist and author, Oriana Fallaci, in a widely ridiculed interview in 1979:

> The Green Book is the new Gospel! The Gospel of the future, the new age! The Green Book is the world! In the beginning there was the word, say the Gospels. The Green Book is the word, my word! A word from my book can destroy the world, it can make the world explode! A word from my book can redeem the world and change the value of things. Their weight. Their volume. Everywhere and always! Because I am the Gospel. I am the Gospel.[15]

The precise authorship of the *Green Book* has yet to be clearly established. The probability is that most of it was drafted by some of Gaddafi's better-educated aides. But some passages are so eccentric and so open to ridicule that they probably stem directly from Gaddafi himself. The *Green Book* declares, for example, that 'Bedouin peoples show no interest in theatres and shows because they are very serious and industrious. As they have created a serious life, they ridicule acting'. In reality, for the remainder of his political career, Gaddafi was to spend more time acting and posturing than any other political leader of his time. The posturing included erecting monuments around Libya to the greatness of the *Green Book* (historically a very rare form of literary narcissism) as well as Centres for Recitation and Study of the Green Book. The Centre in Benghazi became one of the first buildings to be attacked during the uprising that began in February 2011.

Gaddafi's growing pretentiousness was exemplified by his increasingly flamboyant wardrobe; he was capable of changing, in the same day, from white naval uniform heavily adorned with gold braid and medals of dubious origin, to Arab dress with exotic Bedouin headgear, and then into a gold cape over a red shirt. Intelligence from SIS's leading agent in the KGB, Oleg Gordievsky, revealed that Moscow shared the common Western view of Gaddafi's narcissism. Gordievsky reported that Gaddafi's state visit to Moscow in 1981 left much Soviet resentment in its wake. The view in KGB headquarters was that Gaddafi was an affected dandy (*khlyshch*) whose posturing and extravagant uniforms were deliberately designed to emphasize the contrast between his own virility and the growing decrepitude of the Soviet leader, Leonid Brezhnev, who died in 1982.[16]

It is noteworthy that after 2003, when the 'rehabilitated' Gaddafi returned to the international stage, he was accompanied by an even more flamboyant wardrobe than before, which drew inspiration from what sometimes seemed to be Walt Disney versions of African regal robes, Arab tunics and heavily bemedalled Western military uniforms (among others). Academic research has yet to take adequate account of the priority which Gaddafi attached to his appearance and the impression he expected it to make on friend and foe. Unlike political and cultural historians who understand the central role of the visual image in election campaigns and leadership style, international relations specialists often seem relatively uninterested. The images easily available on the internet show, unsurprisingly, that some Western leaders were more disconcerted than others. A sequence of photographs taken at the 2009 G8 summit show President Obama first giving an obligatory handshake to Gaddafi, then appealing mutely but eloquently over Gaddafi's shoulder for an aide to come and rescue him.

Gaddafi and international terrorism

By far the most important intelligence obtained on Gaddafi from human and signals intelligence (HUMINT and SIGINT) concerned his growing addiction to international terrorism, which from the early 1970s to the early twenty-first century represented the main Libyan threat to British interests. Gaddafi's interest in terrorism seems to have been inspired by the extraordinary global media publicity given to the new wave of aircraft hijackings and terrorist attacks by the Popular Front for the Liberation of Palestine (PFLP) against Jewish and Western targets, which began at the end of the 1960s. Gaddafi was not, of course, the only opponent of the West to be impressed by the early exploits of the PFLP. KGB files show that in 1970 it recruited the head of PFLP foreign operations, Wadi Haddad, as Agent NATSIONALIST.[17]

Gaddafi was also enthused by Provisional IRA (PIRA) attacks on British targets during the Northern Irish 'Troubles', which began at about the same time as the PFLP hijacks. The visual images displayed by the world media of 'Bloody Sunday' in Derry on 30 January 1972, when 14 demonstrators were killed by the Parachute Regiment, followed by the burning down of the British Embassy in Dublin a few days later, probably made at least as great an impression on Gaddafi as the press reports. British Intelligence interest in Gaddafi dramatically increased during 1972 when he was discovered to be in contact with PIRA. An elaborate surveillance operation tracked the PIRA chief of staff, Joe Cahill, to a meeting with Gaddafi in Libya in early 1973. Cahill found Gaddafi possessed of 'an awful hatred of England': '[He] said he did not understand why we did not speak in Irish, and why did we speak in English, the language of our enemies?' PIRA chartered the freighter *Claudia* to transport a first arms shipment from Tripoli to Ireland in March 1973. The *Claudia*, with Cahill on board, was kept under surveillance throughout its voyage.

On 23 March the Foreign Secretary, Sir Alec Douglas-Home, sent an urgent telegram to the British ambassador in Dublin, informing him that, according to intelligence reports:

> [T]he *Claudia* left North Africa a few days ago carrying up to 100 tons of small arms and explosives reported to have been provided free by the Libyans for delivery to the IRA in the Republic. At least one senior member of the IRA is believed to be on board. The ship is due to rendezvous with two Irish fishing trawlers off the coast between Dungarvan and Waterford. ... We consider that interception of this arms shipment should be a matter for the Irish government.

When the Irish Navy intercepted the *Claudia* off the coast of County Waterford on 28 March, five tons of arms, ammunition and explosives were discovered in the hold – far less than had been expected. Intelligence reports that the Libyans had originally intended to supply much more were, however, correct. Gaddafi had been deterred by poor PIRA security and had scaled down the shipment. If the five tons had got through safely, they would no doubt have been quickly followed by more and larger consignments.[18] Gaddafi confided (accurately) in Atkinson, who informed the British Embassy, that, in the aftermath of the *Claudia* fiasco, he had stopped supplying arms to PIRA who, he nonetheless maintained, were freedom fighters.[19] When large-scale arms smuggling from Libya began in 1985, it was to transform the Provisionals' operational capability.[20]

The most dramatic public evidence of Gaddafi's involvement in planned terrorist attacks against British targets came in a BBC interview in July 1974 with Nasser's successor, Anwar el Sadat. Once a supporter of Gaddafi, Sadat had come to believe that he was '100 per cent sick and possessed of the devil'. Sadat claimed that Gaddafi had planned to instruct the Libyan commander of an Egyptian submarine in the Mediterranean to torpedo the British cruise liner, the *QE2*, while it was sailing with 590 Jewish passengers on board to celebrate the twenty-fifth anniversary of the state of Israel. Sadat claimed personal credit for preventing the attack from going ahead. Whether or not Gaddafi did more than fantasize about an attack on the *QE2*, the extraordinary denunciation of him by a neighbouring Arab head of state added to his growing public reputation as a reckless practitioner of state terrorism.[21]

By 1975, there was intelligence, as well as media rumours, that Gaddafi was bankrolling the most publicized terrorist of the decade, Ilich Ramírez Sánchez (better known as 'Carlos the Jackal').[22] MI5 had not been impressed by Carlos' bungled PFLP operations against London targets in 1973. Two years later, however, in a far better organized operation, Carlos took OPEC oil ministers hostage at their 1975 meeting in Vienna and loaded them onto a DC-10, which took them to Algiers, where they were eventually released after large ransoms had been paid for the Saudi Arabian and Iranian ministers. Gaddafi sent Atkinson to fly Carlos and four other hijackers on board the DC-10 from Algiers to Mogadishu via a roundabout route. Atkinson found Wadi Haddad and three other PFLP militants waiting for him at Mogadishu; at the request of the Libyan ambassador, who was doubtless fulfilling instructions from Gaddafi, he flew them to Baghdad.[23] Over the years Carlos formed a strong bond with Gaddafi. At the end of his second trial for terrorist murders in Paris in December 2011, at which he received a second life sentence, Carlos read a tearful tribute to Gaddafi: 'This man did more than all the revolutionaries. Long live the Revolution!'[24]

Negative impressions of Gaddafi were further bolstered by his campaign to kill Libyan dissidents living in the UK; a campaign in which Britain's future intermediary with Gaddafi, Musa Kusa, played a central role. Those

British diplomats and officials who met Kusa in 1979–1980 formed a positive impression of his intelligence and knowledge of the West. However, by the spring of 1980, MI5 possessed 'conclusive evidence' that the People's Bureau was 'directing operational and intelligence gathering activities against Libyan dissidents'. The first dissident to be killed was Muhammad Ramadan, who was shot dead outside the Regent's Park Mosque in April 1980. The gunman, Ben Hassan Muhammad El Masri, and his accomplice, Nagib Mufta Gasmi, were arrested near the scene of the killing and later sentenced to life imprisonment. A fortnight later another Libyan assassin, Mabrook Ali Mohammed Al Gidal, murdered the dissident Libyan lawyer Mahmoud Abbu Nafa in his Kensington office. Al Gidal had formerly shared a flat with El Masri and Gasmi; like them he was caught and sentenced to life imprisonment.

The assassinations were intended as a warning to other Libyan dissidents to obey Gaddafi's demand for them to cease their opposition and return to Libya. The deadline for their return on 11 June 1980 was marked by a dissident demonstration outside the London People's Bureau which caused predictable outrage in Tripoli. Reliable intelligence revealed that the Libyan Foreign Liaison Bureau (Foreign Ministry) reprimanded Kusa for failing to use force to disrupt the demonstration. He was told that, in order to demonstrate that all opposition would be mercilessly crushed, at least one of the demonstrators should have been killed. Probably in response to this reprimand, Kusa gave an interview to *The Times* declaring that Libya was prepared to support the Provisional IRA and approving a decision by the Libyan 'Revolutionary Committee' in the UK to sentence two further dissidents to death.

Following the publication of Kusa's interview on 13 June, he was given 48 hours to leave the country. That night there was a petrol-bomb attack on the British Embassy in Tripoli which must have required Gaddafi's approval. After Kusa's expulsion, reliable intelligence continued to indicate that the People's Bureau was engaged in the surveillance of dissidents in the UK and planning assassinations. MI5 passed intelligence on likely Libyan assassins to the Special Branch, who warned possible targets. No leading dissident was killed or wounded by People's Bureau hitmen in the remainder of the year.[25] The final victim of Gaddafi's assassins in Britain during 1980 was Ahmed Mustafa, a Libyan student at Manchester University, who was found murdered on 29 November. MI5 believed his killers were Libyan language students carrying out instructions received not from the Bureau but directly from Tripoli; they returned to Libya immediately after the killing. It was thought likely that they may have chosen the wrong target. After Mustafa's murder there was an unexpected lull in Gaddafi's assassination campaign in Britain, perhaps reflecting irritation that his hitmen during 1980 had either been caught or had killed the wrong man.[26]

Early in 1984, Gaddafi ordered a new campaign against dissident émigrés – or, as he preferred to call them, 'stray dogs'. From 10-12

March there were bomb attacks against Libyan dissidents in London and Manchester. The People's Bureau, MI5 reported, 'has strenuously denied complicity. It is quite clear, however, that they both directed and planned the bombing campaign'. On 16 April, the Special Branch discovered that an anti-Gaddafi group planned a demonstration outside the People's Bureau on the following day. It was not until after the demonstration on 17 April that MI5 learned that on the previous evening the People's Bureau had been authorized by Tripoli to fire on the demonstrators. What began as a peaceful demonstration on 17 April ended in tragedy. While policing the demonstration, WPC Yvonne Fletcher was killed by machine-gunfire from a first-floor window of the People's Bureau. Her killer was no doubt influenced by the knowledge that the Bureau had been heavily criticized by Tripoli for not firing on a similar demonstration four years earlier.[27]

Next day, 18 April, the KGB residency in London was informed that its Moscow HQ had reliable intelligence showing that the shooting had been personally ordered by Gaddafi. The residency's head of political intelligence, Oleg Gordievsky, passed on the information to his SIS case officer.[28] The Thatcher government broke off diplomatic relations with Libya and, after a siege of the People's Bureau, expelled more than 60 of Gaddafi's officials and supporters. The expulsions effectively brought to an end the Libyan terrorist campaign in mainland Britain.

Gaddafi took his revenge for the humiliations of 1984 by publicly announcing, and dramatically increasing, his support for the Provisional IRA: 'We do not consider the IRA a terrorist army; they have a just cause, the independence of their country. ... We are not ashamed of supporting it with all the means we have.' Gaddafi's emergence in the mid-1980s as the main arms supplier to PIRA posed a far greater threat to UK national security than his homicidal campaign against Libyan dissidents in Britain. Failure to detect and prevent Libyan arms shipments until 1987 was a major weakness in British counter-terrorist strategy that enabled PIRA to continue the 'Long War' for another decade.[29]

The important role of the allied British and US SIGINT agencies, GCHQ and NSA, in monitoring Gaddafi's involvement in terrorism, has never been officially acknowledged. In 1986, however, President Ronald Reagan gave away the secret in a broadcast to the American people after SIGINT revealed that an attack on a West Berlin night-club frequented by American servicemen was personally ordered by Gaddafi. Reagan horrified NSA (and doubtless GCHQ) by publicly citing intercepted communications between Tripoli and the People's Bureau in East Berlin in order to demonstrate that 'the terrorist bombing was planned and executed under the direct orders of the Libyan regime', and so justify a retaliatory airstrike on Tripoli.[30] Margaret Thatcher rarely made any public comment on intelligence, but on this occasion she acknowledged that 'I was always more reluctant to reveal intelligence than were the Americans. ... It is certainly true that a fair

amount of intelligence [SIGINT] dried up.'[31] A few months later Reagan
tried to mend his fences with NSA by becoming the first US President to
visit its HQ at Fort Meade. He told its staff: 'The simple truth is: Without
you I could not do my job, nor could Secretary [of State] Shultz conduct
diplomacy.' No world leader had ever paid such a public tribute to the
work of peacetime cryptanalysts.[32]

The peak of Gaddafi's reputation in Britain as the leading practitioner of
state terrorism came after the most homicidal terrorist attack ever to take
place in Britain. On the evening of 21 December 1988 a PanAm Boeing
747, en route to New York, crashed on the Scottish town of Lockerbie,
killing all 259 passengers and crew as well as 11 people on the ground.
Once again, intelligence was crucial in pinning responsibility on Libya.
No hard evidence pointed towards Libya until fragments of clothing from
inside the suitcase containing the bomb were traced to an outlet in Malta,
where the shopkeeper recalled selling the clothing to a man resembling
a suspected Libyan intelligence officer, Abdelbaset Al Megrahi. Other
evidence implicated Libyan intelligence and a Libyan Airlines representative
in the operation to put the suitcase containing the bomb on a connecting
flight from Malta.[33]

Gaddafi 'rehabilitated'

Though no one could have predicted it at the time, the Lockerbie tragedy
marked the climax of Libyan terrorism against Western targets rather than
the beginning of a new and particularly lethal campaign. Tired of his status
as an international pariah, punished by diplomatic isolation and economic
sanctions, Gaddafi began to show signs of a desire to distance himself from
his terrorist past. By the late 1990s he was attempting a *rapprochement*
with the West, which included an attempt to resolve the Lockerbie issue
by agreeing to the trial of Al Megrahi and another alleged Libyan intelligence officer, Lamen Khalifa Fhimah, by a Scottish court sitting in the
Netherlands. In January 2001, Al Megrahi was convicted and sentenced
to life imprisonment, while Fhimah was acquitted. The Joint Intelligence
Committee (JIC) concluded that Gaddafi's main motive for agreeing to the
trial was economic – Libya's need for Western, especially US, investment. A
rapprochement with Britain, Gaddafi was thought to believe, was the best
route to a *rapprochement* with the United States.

From 1998 to 2003 the JIC also reported increasing intelligence
on Libyan attempts to develop nuclear weapons and ballistic missiles
programmes. Until the summer of 2000, these programmes were judged to
be making little headway. Thereafter, however, Libya was identified as one
of the prime customers of the A.Q. Khan proliferation network. By 2003,

the JIC was reporting that Gaddafi had received nuclear material from the Khan network and was actively pursuing the acquisition and development of 'weapons of mass destruction'. The 2004 Butler 'Review of Intelligence on Weapons of Mass Destruction' later concluded that Gaddafi 'may well have thought that he could achieve rapprochement with the West while retaining nuclear, chemical and ballistic missile programmes. If so, it took some time for him to recognise the incompatibility between these two objectives.'[34]

The first evidence that Gaddafi had begun to 'recognise the incompatibility' came in the aftermath of the invasion of Iraq in March 2003 by coalition forces led by the United States and Britain. Following the rapid overthrow of Saddam Hussein, Gaddafi was thought to fear that his own WMD programme might provoke a US/UK-led invasion of Libya.[35] An approach to SIS from Gaddafi via a Palestinian intermediary indicated that he was willing to discuss the possible end to his WMD programme. Tony Blair, who seemed visibly excited by the approach, authorized a high-level SIS team to fly to Libya. Arriving by private jet at a former US Air Force base near Tripoli, they initially found no one there to receive them. After a brief interval, however, Gaddafi's intelligence chief, Musa Kusa (who, over 20 years earlier, had been expelled from London while head of the People's Bureau), arrived in a black Mercedes. A confused series of phone calls then established that Gaddafi was not in Tripoli as expected, but near his home town of Sirte, to which the SIS team flew with Kusa in a Libyan aircraft. On arrival they were taken by Mercedes to a large tent 'in the middle of nowhere' with, in one corner, armchairs and a television, where they were joined by Gaddafi's British-educated interpreter. It was more than an hour before Gaddafi himself turned up. He began with a monologue denouncing Saudi Arabia, which, he declared, ought to be divided into several independent states. Then he moved into a rambling discussion of WMD and the possibility of disarmament, during which he denied that Libya had a nuclear weapons programme.[36]

After Gaddafi had concluded his opening monologue, the SIS team made it clear that there could be no deal on WMD disarmament which did not include Libya's nuclear programme. Gaddafi then embarked on another monologue that ignored what his visitors had said. 'There was no dialogue,' one of them recalls. 'He spoke; then we spoke; then he spoke.' By the time the meeting ended, the SIS team felt frozen. Expecting to meet in Tripoli, they were wearing light suits in temperatures inside the tent which seemed barely above freezing point. Gaddafi, by contrast, had a large camel blanket wrapped around him. Though the meeting yielded no immediate result, there were some grounds for future optimism. Gaddafi's invitation to SIS was unprecedented. Musa Kusa, with whom further negotiations seemed possible, appeared to have Gaddafi's confidence as a future interlocutor. SIS was also confident that, in contrast to the inadequacies of its intelligence in Iraq, it possessed accurate and detailed intelligence on the location of 27 sites used in Libya's WMD programmes.[37]

Talks with Kusa during the remainder of 2003 were jointly conducted by Steve Kappes, then the CIA's deputy head of operations (later head of operations), and one of the SIS team who had taken part in the meeting with Gaddafi. The first breakthrough came at a meeting in a European hotel, where the three men were initially disconcerted over dinner to notice the former Israeli prime minister Ehud Barak at another table in the same restaurant. Director of Central Intelligence George Tenet wrote later:

> After some discussion, Musa Kusa essentially admitted that his country had violated just about every international arms control treaty it had ever signed. Then he said that they wanted to relinquish their weapons programs, that we should trust them to do so, and he asked for a sign of good faith from us.

In September 2003, Kusa invited Kappes and his SIS colleague to a meeting in Libya with Gaddafi.[38] A month later, an SIS combined operation with German and Italian intelligence led to the interception of the *BBC China*, a German-registered ship carrying centrifuge parts from the A.Q. Khan network to Libya, thus increasing the pressure on Gaddafi by providing incontrovertible evidence of his nuclear weapons programme.[39]

Before their meeting with Gaddafi, Kusa warned Kappes and his SIS colleague that, to begin with, they might find the meeting a 'little rough'. According to Tenet:

> After brief introductions, the visitors took seats and Musa Kusa put his head down, as if he knew what was coming, and the interpreter pulled out his pad. Gadhafi immediately launched into a loud and colorful diatribe, slamming the West, and the United States in particular, for every misdeed imaginable. The interpreter had great difficulty keeping up with the Arabic words as they flew off Gadhafi's tongue.
>
> Then, at about the seventeen-minute mark in the tirade, Musa Kusa's head came up as if he could tell that the rant was about to end. Sure enough, Gadhafi ran out of steam, took a breath for the first time, and smiled. 'Nice to see you. Thanks for coming,' he said. And then he got down to business. We want to 'clean the file,' he kept saying.
>
> Two hours later, Gadhafi ended the meeting by saying, 'Work things out with Musa Kusa.'

On 19 December 2003 the Libyan Foreign Ministry officially renounced the country's WMD programmes and agreed to international inspection to monitor compliance. Tenet wrote later of Musa Kusa's role in brokering this agreement: 'Illustrative of the surreal world in which we had to operate,

CIA officers found themselves exchanging pleasantries with the man who, by some accounts, was the mastermind behind the Pan Am 103 bombing' (a charge denied by Kusa).[40]

Despite Musa Kusa's past reputation, Britain had for the first time found a trusted Libyan interlocutor with, it appeared, the confidence of Gaddafi, with whom direct negotiations were believed to be almost impossible. Once a serious terrorist threat, Libya, chiefly through Musa Kusa, now provided valuable intelligence on al Qaeda in North Africa. Though Kusa became Foreign Minister in 2009 (remaining in that post until his defection from the Gaddafi regime in February 2011), he continued to play a central role in intelligence cooperation.

As far back as 1998 Libya had been the first state to seek an Interpol warrant ('Red Notice') against Osama bin Laden, who had encouraged Libyan Islamists to form the Libyan Islamic Fighting Group with the optimistic aim of overthrowing the Gaddafi regime. A decade later, Britain's views on the value of Libyan intelligence on Islamist terrorists appear to have mirrored those in this 2008 cable to the State Department from the US embassy in Tripoli:

> Libya has been a strong partner in the war against terrorism and cooperation in liaison channels is excellent. ... Worried that fighters returning from Afghanistan and Iraq could destabilize the regime, the G[overnment]o[f]L[ibya] has aggressively pursued operations to disrupt foreign fighter flows, including more stringent monitoring of air/land ports of entry, and blunt the ideological appeal of radical Islam.[41]

After Gaddafi's overthrow and death in 2011, British intelligence cooperation with his regime gave rise to claims by some of his Libyan opponents (which at the time of writing are the subject of litigation) that Britain had colluded in their mistreatment.

Eight years earlier, however, Gaddafi's abandonment of WMD and his cooperation in counter-terrorism had produced a dramatic rehabilitation on the international stage. During negotiations with senior UK and US intelligence officers late in 2003, he had emphasized his desire for a visit by Tony Blair to Tripoli. Blair duly arrived in 2004 and commended Gaddafi as an ally in the War on Terror. Though in subsequent years Gaddafi paid official visits to, among other countries, France, Russia (where he was allowed to pitch his tent in the Kremlin) and Italy, he was never invited to Britain. Musa Kusa, however, made a number of unpublicized visits to London. Having given up trying to unite the Arab world, Gaddafi concentrated on Africa instead. In 2008, he was named Africa's 'King of Kings' by a gathering of traditional rulers. In May 2010, despite an abysmal human rights record, Libya was elected by a large majority (155 votes out of a maximum 192) to serve a three-year term on the United Nations Human Rights Council.

Conclusion

During the many twists and turns of Britain's relations with the Gaddafi regime from 1969 to 2011, one constant remained. Direct negotiation with him appeared at best frustratingly difficult, more frequently virtually impossible. Hence the importance in the early twenty-first century of Musa Kusa as an intermediary who had Gaddafi's confidence until the early weeks of the Libyan revolt against the regime which began in February 2011. The British Foreign Secretary, William Hague, said after Kusa's defection a month later: 'Musa Kusa … has been my channel of communication to the regime in recent weeks and I've spoken to him several times on the telephone.'[42] The other great continuity in British perceptions of Gaddafi during most of his 42 years in power (the longest dictatorship in recent history), despite his eccentric narcissism, was a recognition of his shrewdness as a political operator. In 2009 the US ambassador in Tripoli cabled the State Department: 'While it is tempting to dismiss his many eccentricities as signs of instability, Gaddafi is a complicated individual who has managed to stay in power for 40 years through a skillful balancing of interests and realpolitik methods.'[43] Most Western commentators were so impressed by Gaddafi's success in maintaining his regime for so many years that, by the time the revolt against him began, they tended to exaggerate the strength of his hold on power and to underestimate the impact of the Arab Spring. Despite Gaddafi's claim to represent a new form of political leadership and his extraordinary personal flamboyance, the increasing corruption of his regime had much in common with other autocracies (including his neighbours in Tunisia and Egypt) which cultivated quite different international images. As one commentator put it after his death:

> In the end, for all Qaddafi's pretensions of ideological revolution and professed commitment to ruling on behalf of a people who loved him, his regime had become an old-fashioned family dictatorship, with key security posts doled out to his sons and trusted loyalists.[44]

Notes

1 The often prohibitive copyright cost of reproducing photographs and the additional publishing costs involved in using colour illustrations make it impossible to include a representative selection of photos in this chapter. All photos referred to in the text are, however, easily accessible on the internet.

2 Neville Atkinson, *Death on Small Wings: Memoirs of a Presidential Pilot* (Kinloss, Moray: Librario Publishing, 2006).

3 Unattributable communication to Christopher Andrew, (April 2011).

4   Anthony McDermott, 'Libya: A Special Report. Revolution Blessed with Oil and Identity', *Guardian*, (15 April 1976).

5   Most of the text of Peter Tripp's valedictory despatch is published in Matthew Parris and Andrew Bryson, *Parting Shots* (London: Viking, 2010).

6   Atkinson (2006), Ch. 8. Tripp knew that Gaddafi had previously confided in Atkinson that he had stopped arms supplies to PIRA. Atkinson persuaded himself that the subsequent compensation given to BP was due largely to his influence and later attempted unsuccessfully to obtain payment for his services from BP after his own financial fortunes collapsed.

7   Atkinson's good-natured naivety is evident from his belief that his conversations on the 'Special Flight' with Yasser Arafat helped to cause 'a marked decrease in aircraft hijackings and other violence emanating from Paslestinian sources. Although it could probably never be proved, I am happy to claim some of the credit for this decrease' (Atkinson (2006), Ch 6).

8   *Al-Inqad*, No. 37, 1993 (special issue on human rights in Libya); cited by Mohamed Eljami, 'Libya and the U.S.: Qadhafi Unrepentant', *Middle East Quarterly*, (winter 2006).

9   See n. 5.

10 Musa Kusa, 'The Political Leader and His Social Background: Muammar Qadafi, the Libyan Leader', MA thesis, (Michigan State University, 1978).

11 Senior British diplomat speaking at KCL Strategic Scripts conference, (May 2011).

12 I am grateful to Jason Pack for this reference from Kusa's thesis.

13 Kusa's MA thesis cited by Sharon Churcher and Robert Verkaik, 'Portrait of the Young Gaddafi', *Daily Mail*, (13 April 2011).

14 The minority view, that Gaddafi was a serious political thinker influenced by Rousseau, has been perhaps most eloquently argued by Jason Pack, who claims that 'most of Gadhafi's substantive pronouncements – as opposed to his frequent off-message rants – actually form a cohesive utopian economic and theological paradigm: ... Although some have dismissed the Green Book as nonsense, the fault with Gadhafi's ideology is that, like Marxism, it is unimplementable and false, not that it is incoherent' (Jason Pack, 'Gadhafi's Utopian Ideology', *Wall Street Journal*, 2 March 2011).

15 The interview is reprinted in Oriana Fallaci, *Interviews with History and Power*, revised edn (Milan: Rizzoli, 2011).

16 Intelligence provided by Gordievsky quoted in Christopher Andrew and Oleg Gordievsky, *KGB: The Inside Story of its Foreign Operations from Lenin to Gorbachev*, paperback edn (London: Sceptre, 1991), p. 553. Gordievsky was stationed at the London KGB residency from 1982 to 1985. Very few, even within the intelligence agencies, were aware that Gordievsky was the source of this and other intelligence until his defection in 1985 following a dramatic escape from Moscow, assisted by SIS.

17 The contents of the KGB foreign intelligence file on Haddad, smuggled out of its archives by Vasili Mitrokhin, were among the material exfiltrated from

Russia, along with the Mitrokhin family, by SIS in 1992. Christopher Andrew and Vasili Mitrokhin, *The Mitrokhin Archive II: The KGB and the World* (London: Penguin, 2005), pp. 246–50.

18 MI5 files cited by Christopher Andrew, *The Defence of the Realm: The Authorized History of MI5* (London: Allen Lane, 2009), pp. 620–3.

19 Atkinson (2006), Ch. 10.

20 MI5 files cited by Andrew (2009), pp. 737–8.

21 'Middle East: Sink the QE2', *Time*, (29 July 1974).

22 John Follain, *Jackal: The Secret Wars of Carlos the Jackal* (London: Weidenfeld & Nicolson, 1998), pp. 102–3.

23 Atkinson (2009), Ch. 9.

24 'Carlos the Jackal Given Another Life Sentence for 1980s Terror Attack', *Guardian*, (15 December 2011).

25 An attempt to poison members of a Libyan family in the Portsmouth area, however, almost succeeded in killing the two children. The family, however, contained no member of any dissident group and may have been chosen simply as a soft target. The failed assassin was caught and sentenced to life imprisonment.

26 MI5 files cited by Andrew (2009), pp. 688–90.

27 Ibid., pp. 700–3.

28 Intelligence provided by Gordievsky quoted in Andrew and Gordievsky (1991), pp. 632–3.

29 Andrew (2009), p. 703.

30 Christopher Andrew, *For The President's Eyes Only: Secret Intelligence and the American Presidency from Washington to Bush* (London: HarperCollins, 1995), pp. 482–4.

31 Margaret Thatcher, *The Downing Street Years* (London: HarperCollins, 1993), pp. 445–6. Unusually, however, Thatcher acknowledged that, on this occasion, it was vital to release some intelligence 'if the general public were to be convinced of the truth of the allegations we were making against Gaddafi'.

32 Andrew (1995), pp. 482–4.

33 MI5 files cited by Andrew (2009), pp. 746–8.

34 *Review of Intelligence on Weapons of Mass Destruction. Report of a Committee of Privy Councillors* (HC 898) [hereafter Butler Report], (14 July 2004), Ch. 2.

35 Hans Blix, then UN chief weapons inspector, commented: 'I can only speculate, but I would imagine that Gaddafi could have been scared by what he saw happen in Iraq.'

36 Private information.

37 Private information.

38 George Tenet, *At the Center of the Storm: My Years in the CIA* (New York: HarperCollins, 2007).

39 Butler Report, Ch. 2.

40 Tenet (2007).

41 'US Embassy Cables [Wikileaks]: Profile of "Intellectually Curious" but "Notoriously Mercurial" Gaddafi', *Guardian*, (7 December 2010).

42 Statement by William Hague, (31 March 2011); text on FCO website.

43 Cable from US Ambassador to Libya, Gene Cretz, 29 September 2009; quoted in David Leigh, 'WikiLeaks Cables: Muammar Gaddafi and the "Voluptuous Blonde"', *Guardian*, (7 December 2010).

44 Jason Pack, 'Qaddafi's Legacy', *Foreign Policy*, (7 February 2012).

CHAPTER THIRTEEN

The US and Iran: Turning Mahmoud Ahmadinejad into a cipher

Scott Lucas

Introduction

Many people in the 'West' have claimed to know Mahmoud Ahmadinejad, Iranian president from 2005 to (possibly) 2013. For some, he is first and foremost a denier of the Holocaust, a 9/11 'truther' declaring the US government's responsibility for the attacks on the World Trade Center and the Pentagon, an executive dedicated to a militarized programme, a supporter of terrorism in the Middle East, a man driven by an apocalyptic view of Shi'a Islam's Hidden Imam returning to Earth. For others – a distinct minority – he is a man with whom the US and Europe can do business, reaching a deal on the nuclear issue and, possibly, regional approaches from Lebanon to Iraq to Afghanistan. And for others, he is a cipher and a place-holder in a system in which the Supreme Leader, Ayatollah Khamenei, wields absolute power.[1]

The sobering truth, especially if one is considering how conceptions of a leader of the 'Other' can shape the foreign policy of US, Britain, or France, is that virtually none of these people 'know' Mahmoud. For it is no longer an evaluation of an Ahmadinejad that matters, at least for the US government. Instead, what matters is the projection of an 'Ahmadinejad', who may or may not match up to the flesh-and-blood president, in the service of a determined policy. The factors that offer complexity of analysis

– the gap between intelligence gathered in the field and that considered in Washington, the bureaucratic intricacies in Tehran – are now merely of academic value, not only for this chapter but in the political arena.

Projecting Ahmadinejad: discourses of inclusion and exclusion

By way of introduction, it is worth considering the display of 'Ahmadinejad' in September 2011, at the mid-point of his second term as President, when he made his annual visit to the United Nations in New York. The staging for his speech to the General Assembly was similar to that of the previous year: the President called for an international order rejecting centuries of domination and impoverishment by the 'West' and supporters of Israel. He closed with a lengthy benediction on the Hidden Imam and Jesus liberating humanity. Along the way, Ahmadinejad repeated his insinuation of the US government's responsibility for 9/11 to set the pretext for wars in Afghanistan and Iraq. His audience also reprised their role of 2010, some applauding but many leaving. The newspaper headlines tried to refresh the drama: 'Iran's Ahmadinejad Attacks West, Prompts Walk-Out.'[2]

But the United Nations speech was only one act in Ahmadinejad's show. For nine days before the speech, beginning in Tehran and continuing in New York, and for 48 hours afterwards, he gave interviews to US media and held press conferences. The immediate topic in the first interviews was the fate of two American nationals, Josh Fattal and Shane Bauer, detained in July 2009 while walking on the Iran–Iraq border and sentenced to eight years in prison for espionage and illegal entry. The President, beginning with NBC News and the *Washington Post,* raised the prospect of the two men's release as a 'unilateral humanitarian gesture'. That presidential declaration soon ran into trouble, however, as Iran's judiciary denied the release and then stalled on proceedings for bail. Bauer and Fattal would not leave Tehran's Evin Prison until 21 September, just before Ahmadinejad's UN appearance and after others in the regime had blunted any presidential credit. In the course of his press interviews, Ahmadinejad also castigated the US and its allies for their interventions in the Middle East and Afghanistan, and fended off queries on human rights and the disputed 2009 Presidential election: 'Who has been repressed by us? Nobody was suppressed here … I love all segments of the population.'[3]

All of this could have been expected. Indeed, most of it had been said in the President's appearances one year earlier. There was, however, one comment of significance, made initially to the *Washington Post.* Ahmadinejad declared that if the US would provide 20 per cent enriched uranium, to be used in the Tehran Research Reactor for medical isotopes and other civilian projects, Iran would halt domestic production. He stated:

> If [the US] gives us uranium grade 20 percent, we would stop production. Those negotiations took place in Vienna [in October 2009} ... I repeat: If you give us uranium grade 20 percent now, we will stop production.[4]

This was a marked departure from Tehran's stated position that it must be able to enrich at home, and Ahmadinejad reinforced it with other assertions. He brushed aside the statement of the head of Iran's atomic energy programme, Fereyoun Abbasi, that no deal was possible.[5] He said that Iran had no plans to build more enrichment plants, lying in the process – previously, he and his advisers had declared their intention to construct up to 20 plants.

Beyond the showmanship, Ahmadinejad was inviting the US and European partners to resume the talks of October 2009 – the first direct discussions including Tehran and Washington since the foundation of the Islamic Republic in 1979 – on 'third-party enrichment' of Iran's uranium. On that occasion, Ahmadinejad's promotion of the discussions initially went well, with Iran and the 5+1 Powers (US, Britain, France, Germany, China, and Russia) agreeing on technical talks to fulfil general principles, but they were suddenly halted by opposition within Iran to the President's initiative. American officials, who had been leaking details of the deal to the media, suddenly had to figure out the domestic dynamics in Iran. The possibility of discussions remained, but gradually closed, amidst posturing – such as declarations on Iran's not-so-secret 'secret' enrichment plant at Fordoo – and the internal difficulties for the regime, which was facing an escalating challenge on the streets from the Green Movement.

In September 2011, almost no one in the US media recalled the 2009 discussion. Indeed, few noticed Ahmadinejad's gesture, even though he made similar remarks on several occasions in New York. The general theme of an intransigent president, making controversial remarks about Israel and 9/11, was unaltered and remained the mainstream American view.

Institutional constraints on forming a balanced image

While recognizing the nuances and internal power struggles within the Iranian political system would seem to be essential for a proper understanding of the motives of Iran's leaders, oversimplified views tend to dominate mainstream discourse. For instance, even if the significance of Ahmadinejad's gesture had been recognized amidst his more provocative comments, it was doubtful that the official American analysis and policy response would have placed his words within the complex context of Iran's domestic politics, caught up in the infighting that had persisted and arguably escalated since the President's disputed re-election in June 2009. That analytical and policy failure can be evaluated in three areas.

The first is the straightforward demand of getting information which is adequate both in amount and substance. With no embassy in Tehran and covert methods inside Iran severely restricted by Iran's security apparatus, the US has been dependent on a system of 'Iran watchers' attached to American embassies and consulates in neighbouring countries and in Britain. Signals intelligence is limited in how much it can offer about intentions of and discussions among Iranian officials. Reliance on other foreign intelligence services or covert networks is hindered by the conditions under which they operate within Iran, as with British officials, or the political framings of the supposed information, as with Israeli or Arab contacts.

Admittedly, some of the information collected by the watchers, especially in the Iran Regional Presence Office in Dubai, has offered insight into the current system and dynamics in the Islamic Republic. Nevertheless, a great deal of this information has lacked substance and even been misleading, as in the claim that the President had been slapped in the face by the commander of his Revolutionary Guards, or the opinions of truck drivers who said in early 2010 that Ahmadinejad would fall within a year.[6] Equally important, it is not clear whether this information has been evaluated, in Washington as well as in the field, in the context of the political environment in Iran.

The second failure has to do with the highly complex nature of the Iranian government, which makes any analysis and policy prescription difficult in its own right. The bureaucracy established in the Islamic Republic over 33 years ago went far beyond a Persian version of the adjective 'Byzantine'. The Executive has layer upon layer of institutions melding religious and secular elements – the Guardian Council, the Assembly of Experts, the Expediency Council – in addition to the manoeuvres with Parliament and the judiciary. There are multiple networks of power within the Executive, with not only the President but his vice-presidents and advisers controlling funds that may be used for political ventures. That, in turn, leads to conflicts not just between Ahmadinejad and his critics, but also between a controversial figure such as the President's Chief of Staff, Esfandiar Rahim-Mashai, and his foes.

The easy bypass of this political terrain is the claim that the Supreme Leader has ultimate authority, in reality as well as in designation, under Iran's system of *velayat-e faqih*. That, however, is a simplification. In Ahmadinejad's bid to extend his power and that of the presidency since 2005, and particularly since 2009, he has often clashed with Ayatollah Khamenei. Sometimes the President has triumphed, as in his defiance of the Supreme Leader in summer 2009, when he named Rahim-Mashai to head his office, and in his take-over of foreign policy with the designation of permanent special envoys and the dismissal of Foreign Minister Manouchehr Mottaki in December 2010. His persistence for nuclear talks should also be seen as a test of wills with the Supreme Leader, given Khamenei's likely role in curbing the October 2009 discussions. At other times, Ahmadinejad has been sharply rebuffed by Khamenei, such as when he tried to take control of the Ministry of Intelligence in spring 2011. Thus, in many respects, Khamenei is less the 'immutable ruler', but instead acts as a 'balancer', taking sides in various disputes within the government and establishment, while keeping lines open to different factions.

The third analytical weakness of the official portrayal of Ahmadinejad has more to do with the complexities inherent in the political system in Washington. The starting point is the recognition that there is not a single policy towards Iran but a competition among policies promoted by different factions within the administration. That competition often starts not from an evaluation of the information at hand but from a wedging and even construction of 'information' into the preferred policy option.

Differing conceptions of Ahmadinejad were present, even as the officials of the George W. Bush Administration laid out a path of confrontation with Tehran. Initial reports from the field varied about Ahmadinejad, an unexpected winner in the 2005 presidential election. Some observers told US diplomats that Ahmadinejad was a pragmatist 'close to Ayatollah Khamenei', or that he was 'a realist who will do what is necessary to push his agenda',[7] or even that he was a politician who 'does not intend ... to "export the revolution"; instead, his preference is to focus on domestic issues'.[8] However, the hard-line exile group, the National Committee for Resistance in Iran, said that Ahmadinejad's election 'has clearly led to a militarization of Iranian politics'.[9] Others dwelled on the new president's 'belief in the imminent return of the missing Imam'.[10]

All this, however, was peripheral to the framing of an Ahmadinejad who fit a policy of confrontation with Tehran, to the point of regime change. So, for example, Seymour Hersh's April 2006 exposé of the Bush Administration's plans for covert action and, if necessary, military operations, highlighted advisers and 'experts' who put out assertions such as '[Ahmadinejad] sees the West as wimps and thinks we will eventually cave in. We have to be ready to deal with Iran if the crisis escalates' or 'You have to really show a threat in order to get Ahmadinejad to back down'.[11] On a specific level, President Bush used Ahmadinejad as reference point to claim a 'serious threat to world peace' with his hostility: 'I made it clear, I'll make it clear again, that we will use military might to protect our ally Israel.'[12]

One claim, however, deserves a sceptical eye. Citing a 'former senior intelligence officer', Hersh wrote, 'Bush and others in the White House view [Ahmadinejad] as a potential Adolf Hitler'.[13] Hersh does not identify the source, who could well have put out the statement not to condemn the

Iranian president but to exaggerate the prospect of ill-judged US action. In all the condemnations of Iran between 2005 and 2009, 'Ahmadinejad as Hitler' is *not* a motif.

'Appeasement' did make an appearance in the administration's rhetoric, albeit not with direct reference to the Iranian President. For example, in May 2008, George W. Bush addressed the Israeli Knesset. Much of the speech was about the need to deal with the Iranian threat, and the US President put in this provocative analogy:

> Some seem to believe that we should negotiate with terrorists and radicals, as if some ingenious argument will persuade them they have been wrong all along. We have heard this foolish delusion before. As Nazi tanks crossed into Poland in 1939, an American senator declared: 'Lord, if only I could have talked to Hitler, all of this might have been avoided'. We have an obligation to call this what it is – the false comfort of appeasement, which has been repeatedly discredited by history.[14]

However, by the time Bush delivered the speech, the specific possibility of basing a policy on an assessment of Ahmadinejad as 'Hitler' was long gone. Indeed, the general strategy of confrontation had receded. The call for military action, pressed by Vice-President Dick Cheney among others, had been rejected owing to a lack of support among American allies, the uncertain prospects for the operation and its aftermath, and US difficulties in other arenas like Iraq.[15]

The Obama Administration and Iran policy

The advent of the Obama Administration and the supposed approach of 'engagement' with Iran brought different possibilities for the framing of Ahmadinejad. Obama, supported by most of the State Department, sought an opening for talks. This was put out through the general language in his Inaugural Address: 'we will extend a hand if you are willing to unclench your fist.'[16] Obama also conveyed a specific message for the Iranian New Year: 'We seek ... engagement that is honest and grounded in mutual respect.'[17] In addition, Obama wrote at least two private letters to the Supreme Leader.

Others in the Administration resisted engagement, or saw negotiations only as a path to justify tougher action when Iran rejected American terms. Dennis Ross, an advocate of coercive diplomacy, was placed in the State Department in February 2009 to supervise 'the Gulf region', including Iran, the 'broader Middle East' and Southwest Asia.[18] In their book *Myths, Illusions and Peace*, Ross and David Makovsky of the Washington Institute for Near East Policy argued for negotiations over a limited period, backed by escalating sanctions and a credible threat of force, including moving military units into place around Iran. They state:

> The possibility of the use of force is a way to make diplomacy more effective. When we are saying we are not taking force off the table, that must be more than a slogan; it is essential that the Iranians continue to believe that they may be playing with fire if they persist in their pursuit of nuclear weapons.[19]

Within weeks, reports circulated from an unnamed 'senior State Department official' that Secretary of State Hillary Clinton was telling other foreign ministers that she was 'very doubtful' that diplomacy would persuade Iran to abandon its alleged quest for nuclear weapons.[20]

Ross soon moved to the National Security Council, probably because of conflict with President Obama's envoy for Israel and Palestine, George Mitchell, but the change of venue only bolstered his possible influence as he retained the portfolio for 'the Middle East, the Gulf, Afghanistan, Pakistan, and South Asia'.[21] Supported by Puneet Talwar, who held the country brief for Iraq and Iran, and working with Deputy National Security Advisor Tom Donilon, Ross tried to pursue the challenge to Tehran. Observers soon claimed that he was successful – Clinton was described as 'ancillary', as 'policy [was] being driven from the White House'.[22]

This picture, however, is overdrawn. There were others within the State Department and the executive branch who saw realism in an approach to Tehran for genuine discussions, not only over the nuclear programme but over regional concerns. Richard Holbrooke, for example, had been brought into the State Department as the special envoy for Pakistan and Afghanistan; he and his assistant, Vali Nasr, saw Iran's cooperation as a necessity in any resolution of the Afghan situation. Another proponent of engagement was John Limbert, a fluent Persian speaker and a hostage in the 1979 US Embassy crisis – when he had discussions with the future Supreme Leader, Ayatollah Khamenei. Limbert had been named the first Assistant Secretary of State with specific responsibility for Iran.

So, in a bureaucratic context where those seeking 'engagement' confronted those who wanted to establish a clear American 'primacy' over Tehran, Iran's nuclear programme was the touchstone for discussion and debate. Those seeking engagement had to establish that the Islamic Republic – and thus Ahmadinejad – were genuinely interested in discussions; those who were sceptical had to depict an Iran striving for a militarized nuclear capability, despite a 2007 National Intelligence Estimate that set out Iran's suspension of that research in mid-2003 and concluded, with 'moderate confidence', that Iran 'had not restarted its nuclear weapons program as of mid-2007'.[23]

That 'nuclear-first' approach to Tehran and Ahmadinejad was not set aside with the drama of Iran's 2009 presidential campaign. With the unexpected surge of a politically enthusiastic population, the challenge to Ahmadinejad from Mir Hossein Mousavi, the disputed outcome, and the protest of more than a million people in Tehran, it was not inconceivable to suppose that US officials would place their main focus on promoting 'democracy', and that resolving the nuclear issue would take a back seat. To the contrary, the debate over talks quickly overtook concern with the legitimacy of both the election and Ahmadinejad. An official explained, 'It is difficult to weigh all the different considerations. But given the profoundly serious consequences of an Iranian regime that acquires a nuclear-weapons capability, the judgment in the end was that it was important to follow through on the offer of direct engagement.'[24] Thus, rather curiously, as almost every other country put the Iranian President into isolation, the US was moving towards direct negotiations with Tehran, and thus a public recognition of the government.[25]

The catalyst for a move towards direct negotiations was an approach by Iran to the International Atomic Energy Agency (IAEA) in June 2009 seeking enriched uranium for the Tehran Research Reactor. Conscious of Iran's shortage and seeing an opportunity, Obama's advisers suggested a plan under which outside countries would enrich the fuel that Iran needed. Supporters of engagement saw a breakthrough that could lead to further reconciliations, for example, on Afghanistan, Iraq and other Middle Eastern issues. On the other hand, those wanting to squeeze Tehran saw a potential opportunity to exploit Iranian weaknesses. As such, both the 'realists' and the 'hawks' recognized advantages to direct negotiations. And yet, these discussions could only be sustained by downplaying the inconveniences of 'human rights' in the aftermath of the 2009 presidential election. Despite the regime's harsh crackdown on dissent, including abuse of detainees and the killings of dozens of protesters, the Obama Administration's response was muted – bringing the call from demonstrators in early September, 'Obama, are you with us?' – and made no connection between Ahmadinejad and the general issue.

Meanwhile, the Iranian President remained hostage both to the battles within the Iranian establishment and to the pressure from Washington. In late October 2009, with engagement promising to move to technical talks, figures such as Speaker of Parliament Ali Larijani declared that Iran was giving up its sovereignty. Although Khamenei never publicly declared a position, it was evident that Ahmadinejad could not gain his support. The technical meeting never took place.

There was a glimmer of hope as Japan tried to broker a new arrangement for a uranium swap. High-level Iranian officials, including Larijani, visited Tokyo. The initiative foundered when Japanese Foreign Minister Katsuya Okeda visited Washington in January 2010 and was rebuffed, being told that National Security Advisor James Jones could not meet him face-to-face. Then the US government delivered an even firmer blow to the Iranian President. The leaders of Turkey and Brazil, believing they had Obama's support, travelled to Tehran in May 2010; after three days of intense negotiations, they managed to reach agreement with the Iranians, despite the tensions within the regime, on a uranium swap similar to the American vision of autumn 2009. Washington, however, was now committed to tougher sanctions on Iran through the United Nations. Obama, in a meeting with 37 Jewish Democratic members of Congress, said he was committed to the economic pressure, while Clinton said the Turkish and Brazilian efforts had made 'the world more dangerous'. There would be no further discussions between high-level Iranian and European representatives, let alone Tehran and Washington, until January 2011.[26]

Stymied internationally, Ahmadinejad's priorities were on the domestic front throughout 2010. He finally began to implement the subsidy cuts, the centre-piece of his economic approach, in December, albeit in an economy beset by worsening unemployment and inflation, and by allegations of mismanagement and corruption among his advisers and ministers. His bid to extend presidential power spurred rivalries and led to conflicts, including with the Supreme Leader. Yet the President had not given up on his goal of *rapprochement* with Washington. In February 2011 he tried to despatch his senior aide, Rahim-Mashai, to New York for back-channel talks with American officials.[27] Once again, he was checked by others in Tehran. Rahim-Mashai never went to the US – he was accused by some conservative opponents in Iran of being an American spy, or worse, a Zionist – until he travelled with the President in the autumn to New York.

It is in that context that, when one strips away the rhetoric and takes away the framings of Ahmadinejad's September 2011 appearance in the US, there is a president who, in his manoeuvres for power, was quite willing to explore reaching an accommodation with those whom he had publicly called 'enemies' and the 'greatest scourges of the oppressed and dispossessed in world history'. Far from being apocalyptic, he was quite Earth-bound, even 'realist', in his approach to international relations as well as his domestic calculations.

But of course, it is projections that rule. And in this case, the projection of Ahmadinejad – setting aside information, if that information was available or was considered of significance in Washington, and setting aside the complexities of politics within the Iranian system – had to fit the objectives of the faction in the US Administration winning the foreign policy debate. By autumn 2011, advocates of engagement such as Limbert were gone. Officials in the NSC, buttressed by the Pentagon, had prevailed in the quest for a strategy based on backing Tehran into a corner and weakening it before any substantive talks. As such, Ahmadinejad's 'realism' in his proposal over uranium enrichment was not even acknowledged, let alone rejected. Instead, the US pursued the implementation of a plan – buttressed by allegations of a Tehran-backed plot to kill the Saudi ambassador to Washington and an IAEA report on Iran's nuclear programme – to ratchet up sanctions to bring the Islamic Republic to the point of collapse.[28]

Hard-line triumphant

On 22 November 2011, National Security Advisor Tom Donilon, a key figure in the drive for a tough stance towards Tehran, addressed an audience at the Brookings Institution: 'With the broad support of the international community, we have steadily increased the pressure on the Iranian regime and raised the cost of their intransigence.' There was not a single reference to 'engagement'; instead, Donilon set out five 'lines of actions': 'an unprecedented array of sanctions', isolation of Iran diplomatically; cooperation with partners to 'counter Iran's efforts to destabilize the region, especially during the Arab Spring'; development of defence partnerships in the region with an 'enhanced ... and enduring U.S. force presence in the region'; and the declaration that the US was 'not taking any options off the table in pursuit of our basic objective'. Donilon concluded that this approach would 'continue to ratchet up the pressure and price for Iran's intransigence'.

Donilon's speech marked the triumph of the faction that, from the start of the Administration, had sought the approach of dominate first, then negotiate. He summarized, 'Iran's leaders ... must know that they cannot evade or avoid the choice we have laid before them.' There was no reference to the Iranian position in the October 2009 talks, to its initiative with Brazil and Turkey in the Tehran Declaration of May 2010, or to Ahmadinejad's attempt only two months earlier to revive discussions. Indeed, there would be almost no reference to Ahmadinejad at all. Apart from the Iranian President's supposed admission that sanctions were 'the heaviest economic onslaught' upon the Islamic Republic in its history, he only appeared in this passage:

> The Supreme Leader and President Ahmadinejad seem increasingly headed toward a confrontation over the direction of the country. The Supreme Leader has even talked about consolidating his power further by abolishing the Office of Presidency. We see fissures developing among the ruling class.[29]

While Donilon's assertion had some basis in events, he made no attempt to explain what had caused the confrontation. There was no consideration of Ahmadinejad's position on domestic issues, his approach on foreign policy generally, and the nuclear issue specifically, or even his attempt to extend power that had crossed the red line of Ayatollah Khamenei's authority. The President only existed for Donilon as a symbol that the vaunted American pressure was working and should be redoubled.

Conclusion

Ahmadinejad, if he ever existed beyond the 'hateful' and 'offensive' denier of the Holocaust and affirmer of a US government conspiracy behind 9/11, is now an 'avatar', to be summoned but not critiqued, let alone engaged. And in that avatar is the paradox: for while it has a spectral power when its threat is invoked, it is stripped at the same time of any political significance. As Hillary Clinton framed and then dismissed the unnamed 'Ahmadinejad' on 27 October 2011:

> It's been a little confusing because we're not quite sure who makes decisions anymore inside of Iran, which, I think, is an unfortunate sign and kind of goes along with the ascendancy of greater military power, because I think Iran, unfortunately, is morphing into a military dictatorship.[30]

Of course, there is an Ahmadinejad who is far more than a cipher. As I write this in February 2012, he is the president who is fighting for authority against conservative rivals within the establishment. This week, he claimed to have in his possession two 45-minute audio-tapes of a meeting among leading politicians plotting against his government – an apparent challenge to Tehran Mayor Mohammad-Baqer Qalibaf, Speaker of Parliament Ali Larijani, and Mohsen Rezaei, the Secretary of the Expediency Council and 2009 presidential candidate. He is the president who is trying to mobilize forces so that his allies can prevail in March's parliamentary elections. He is the president who is trying to ensure a legacy through his succession by his controversial Chief of Staff, Esfandiar Rahim-Mashai.

He is even the president who has taken on the Supreme Leader. Despite his failure to take control of the Ministry of Intelligence, Ahmadinejad has pressed his claim for executive authority, not through a direct challenge to Khamenei, but through a series of administrative and political manoeuvres. In those manoeuvres, he has not given way to Clinton's 'military dictatorship' but has taken on the Islamic Revolutionary Guards Corps, once thought to be behind the President but now aligned with the Supreme Leader. He has accused them of running illegal goods into Iran, as supportive media warn the military against any move on the President's advisers.

Ahmadinejad is a more than insignificant presence in the politics of the Islamic Republic, if you take account of the internal dimension. But it is that internal dimension which is tangential in Washington's constructions, if not its perceptions. On 30 January 2012, Director of National Intelligence James Clapper, presenting the intelligence community's Worldwide Threat Assessment, avoided discussion either of Ahmadinejad or of Iran's complex internal political dynamics, as he presented poorly sourced allegations such as:

> The 2011 plot to assassinate the Saudi Ambassador to the United States shows that some Iranian officials – probably including Supreme Leader Ali Khamenei – have changed their calculus and are now more willing to conduct an attack in the United States in response to real or perceived U.S. actions that threaten the regime. Iran's willingness to sponsor future attacks in the United States or against our interests abroad probably will be shaped by Tehran's evaluation of the costs it bears for the plot against the ambassador as well as Iranian leaders' perceptions of U.S. threats against the regime.[31]

'When the legend becomes fact, print the legend.'[32] In the months after this chapter is written there may or may not be an Israeli military attack, with or without US support, against Iran. There may or may not be a significant outcome from the tightening US-led sanctions. There may or may not be a breakthrough in discussion on Tehran's nuclear programme. There may or may not be an internal political and/or economic tremor which supersedes war, sanctions and nukes. Whatever happens, however, it is near-certain that the legend of Ahmadinejad – if there is an Ahmadinejad in the narrative – will trump any realistic appraisal by Washington of the Iranian President and the system within which he operates.

Notes

1   There were a few studies and biographies in English of Ahmadinejad during his first term as President, though interestingly, little since his re-election in 2009. See e.g. Saïd Amir Arjomand, *After Khomeini: Iran Under His Successors* (Oxford: Oxford University Press, 2009); Yossi Melman and Meir Javedanfar, *The Nuclear Sphinx of Tehran* (New York: Carroll and Graf, 2007); Ali Ansari, *Iran Under Ahmadinejad: The Politics of Confrontation* (Abingdon, Oxon: Routledge, 2007); Anoushiravan Ehteshami and Mahjoob Zweiri (eds), *Iran's Foreign Policy: From Khatami to Ahmadinejad* (Reading, MA: Ithaca Press, 2008). Studies of domestic politics and US–Iranian relations, intersecting with perspectives on Ahmadinejad, include Ali Ansari, *Crisis of Authority: Iran's 2009 Presidential Election* (London: Chatham House, 2010); Hamid Dabashi, *Iran, The Green Movement and the USA: The Fox and the Paradox* (London: Zed Books, 2010); Hooman Majd, *The*

Ayatollah Begs to Differ (London: Penguin, 2009); Trita Parsi, *A Single Roll of the Dice* (New Haven, CT: Yale University Press, 2012).

2   Chris McGreal, 'Mahmoud Ahmadinejad's UN Speech Prompts Diplomatic Walkouts', *Guardian*, (22 September 2011); Alistair Lyon, 'Iran's Ahmadinejad Attacks West, Prompts Walk-out', *Reuters*, (22 September 2011); Robert Bernstein, 'Deaf Ears to Hate Speech', *Washington Post*, (28 September 2011).

3   'Iran Video: Full Ahmadinejad Interview with NBC News', *EA WorldView*, (14 September 2011). Available online at: http://www.enduringamerica.com/ home/2011/9/14/iran-video-full-ahmadinejad-interview-with-nbc-news.html.

4   'Transcript of the Ahmadinejad interview', *Washington Post*, (14 September 2011). Available online at: http://www.washingtonpost.com/ world/middle-east/transcript-of-the-ahmadinejad-interview/2011/09/13/ gIQA7cF1PK_story_4.html.

5   Nicholas Kristof, 'An Interview with Mahmoud Ahmadinejad', *New York Times*, (21 September 2011).

6   Warren Strobel, 'State Department Cables Reveal U.S. Thirst for All Things Iranian', *McClatchy News Service* 17 April 2011; 'WikiLeaks and Iran Special: Did Ahmadinejad Get Slapped by His Revolutionary Guard Commander?', EA WorldView, (3 January 2011). Available online at: http:// www.enduringamerica.com/home/2011/1/3/wikileaks-and-iran-special-did-ahmadinejad-get-slapped-by-hi.html.

7   Manama to State Department, Cable 1421, (3 October 2005), 'Crown Prince Discusses Internal, External Situations With Ambassador'. Available online at: http://www.cablegatesearch.net/cable.php?id=05MANAMA1421.

8   Dubai to State Deparment, Cable 4824, (3 October 2005), 'One Iran Expert's View of President Ahmadinejad'. Available online at: http://wikileaks.org/ cable/2005/10/05DUBAI4824.html.

9   Vienna to State Department, Cable 2684, (10 August 2005), 'Iran Exile Group Says New Regime Determined to Build Nuclear Weapons'. Available online at: http://wikileaks.org/cable/2005/08/05VIENNA2684.html.

10 Dubai to State Deparment, Cable 10, (2 January 2006). Available online at: http://leaks.hohesc.us/?view=06DUBAI10.

11 Seymour Hersh, 'The Iran Plans', *The New Yorker*, (17 April 2006).

12 'President Bush Discusses the War in Iraq', *Washington Post*, (20 March 2006).

13 Hersh (2006).

14 'Prepared Text of Bush's Knesset Speech', *Wall Street Journal*, (15 May 2008). Available online at: http://online.wsj.com/article/SB121083798995894943.html.

15 Warren P. Strobel, John Walcott and Nancy A. Youssef, 'Cheney Urging Strikes on Iran', *McClatchy News Service*, (9 August 2007); Seymour Hersh, 'Shifting Targets', *The New Yorker*, (8 October 2007).

16 'Barack Obama's Inaugural Address', *New York Times*, (20 January 2009). Available online at: http://www.nytimes.com/2009/01/20/us/politics/20text-obama.html.

17 'Videotaped Remarks by the President in Celebration of Nowruz', (20 March 2009). Available online eat: http://www.whitehouse.gov/the_press_office/ Videotaped-Remarks-by-The-President-in-Celebration-of-Nowruz/.

18 Scott Lucas, 'Treading Softly on Iran: Dennis Ross Sneaks into the Administration', *EA WorldView*, (24 February 2009). Available online at: http://www.enduringamerica.com/february-2009/2009/2/24/treading-softly-on-iran-dennis-ross-sneaks-into-the-administ.html.

19 David Makovsky and Dennis Ross, *Myths, Illusions, and Peace* (New York: Penguin, 2010); Tony Karon, 'Will Dennis Ross' Resignation Raise Pressure on Obama for a Tougher Iran Stance?', *Time*, (14 November 2011).

20 Paul Richter, 'Clinton Says U.S. Diplomacy Unlikely to End Iran Nuclear Program', *Los Angeles Times*, (3 March 2009).

21 Stephanie Condon, 'Iran Adviser Moves To National Security Council', *CBS News*, (25 June 2009).

22 Roger Cohen, 'The Making of An Iran Policy', *New York Times*, (30 July 2009).

23 National Intelligence Estimate, 'Iran: Nuclear Intentions and Capabilities', November 2007. Available online at: http://www.dni.gov/press_releases/20071203_release.pdf.

24 Cohen (2009).

25 After his showpiece appearance with Russian President Dmitri Medvedev at the Shanghai Co-operation Organisation on 16 June 2009, Ahmadinejad met few if any heads of state over the next three months.

26 Parsi (2012), pp. 127–48, 183–94.

27 Scott Lucas, 'Iran Special Analysis: US Hikers Released – Everyone, Including Ahmadinejad, is a Winner (for Now)', *EA WorldView*, (22 September 2011). Available online at: http://www.enduringamerica.com/home/2011/9/22/iran-special-analysis-us-hikers-released-everyone-including.html.

28 Charlie Savage and Scott Shane, 'Iranians Accused of a Plot to Kill Saudis' Envoy', *New York Times*, (11 October 2011).

29 White House, 'NSC Advisor Donilon at Brookings Institution on Iran Sanctions', (22 November 2011). Available online at: http://iipdigital. usembassy.gov/st/english/texttrans/2011/11/20111122144640su0.8725789. html#axzz1nyHthowa.

30 Hillary Clinton, 'Interview With Bahman Kalbasi of BBC Persia', (26 October 2011), *US Department of State*.

31 James Clapper, 'Unclassified Statement for the Record on the Worldwide Threat Assessment of the US Intelligence Community for the Senate Select Committee on Intelligence', (31 January 2012).

32 Maxwell Scott (played by Carleton Young) to Ransom Stoddard (Jimmy Stewart), *The Man Who Shot Liberty Valance* (1962).

INDEX